ARCHITECTURE
AND THE ESTHETICS
OF PLENTY

*The American dilemma of material abundance
was already pictured with unwitting irony
by the painter Thomas Cole in 1840,
in this painting titled* The Architect's Dream.

ARCHITECTURE

AND THE ESTHETICS

OF PLENTY

BY JAMES MARSTON FITCH

COLUMBIA UNIVERSITY PRESS, New York and London

Designed by Paul Grotz
Copyright © 1961 Columbia University Press
Library of Congress Catalog Card Number: 61-8510
Manufactured in the United States of America
ISBN 0-231-02311-1
9 8 7 6 5 4 3 2

ACKNOWLEDGMENTS

"The 'American' in American Architecture" was first read at the Columbia University Seminar on American Civilization. "The Impact of Technology" was read as the 1958 Spencer Trask Memorial Lecture at Princeton University. "Architects of Democracy: Jefferson and Wright" was first read at the Baltimore Museum of Art. "Horatio Greenough, Yankee Functionalist" was first published by Casabella (Milan). "Our Domesticated Utopians" has appeared, in more abbreviated form, in *American Heritage.* "The Two Men in Sullivan's Tomb" was read at the rededication ceremonies of the People's Bank in Owatonna. "Frank Lloyd Wright and the Fine Arts" has appeared in *Horizon* magazine. "Homage to a Hero" was published, in somewhat shorter form, by *Architectural Forum;* "A Lever Long Enough" appeared in the same magazine. "Miës and the Climate of Plato" was read at the Four Great Makers Convocation at Columbia University. "American Pleasure Garden" was first published, in somewhat different form, in *Treasury of American Gardens,* Harper & Bros. "Skyscraper: Skin for Its Bones" has appeared in *Scientific American* and *Stile Industria* (Milan). "Unfinished Church" was first published by *Architectural Forum.* "In Defense of the City" was prepared for delivery at the Academy of Political Science, New York. "The Engineer: Aid or Enemy?" was published in *Architectural Forum.* "The Critic's Shifting View" was read, in shorter form, at the Society of Architectural Historians. "The Esthetics of Plenty" was first published in the *Columbia University Forum.*

J. M. F.

June 19, 1961

CONTENTS

ILLUSTRATIONS

Illustrations

PART I

As the Twig Is Bent

1. THE "AMERICAN"
IN AMERICAN ARCHITECTURE

What is American about American architecture? The question is easier to ask than to answer—especially if, as is so often the case nowadays, we are really trying to isolate those aspects of our national life which are uniquely good rather than merely unique. So we had best rephrase the question: Does American architecture display qualities which we can safely describe as characteristic, irrespective of whether or not we can be proud of them? This we can answer affirmatively. There are many areas in which our architecture is easily distinguishable from that of the rest of the world. The single family house, for example, shares with its foreign contemporaries the basic elements of plan (rooms for sleeping, bathing, cooking, resting, etc.); the same general types of furnishings (tables, chairs, beds, etc.); the same utilities (gas, electricity, water). And yet the way in which these elements are organized into a whole gives our houses certain qualities which we can call "typically American." The use of large areas of unprotected glass, the window wall, is one such. The large size of garage and motor court and the degree of mechanization in the kitchen are others. Middle-class houses in São Paulo or Helsinki will also have glass, garages and mechanical equipment. But the *concentration* of these elements is far higher in our houses than in the rest of the world; and this purely quantitative factor makes for qualitative differences—though of course the differences are seldom as important and almost never as favorable as we should like to imagine.

It is even more hazardous to attempt to generalize upon the purely formal aspects of American architecture since, during the three and a half centuries of its history, it has employed so many idioms, so many various means of expression. Visually, it presents a pattern of bewil-

3

dering complexity; this complexity is, however, but a reflection of Western experience generally. Fortunately for our purposes, the basic *qualities* of a national architecture are much more permanent than the *forms* it assumes at any moment. And from this point of view, three dominant qualities seem to have been always present in our architecture. They are:

1. Acquisitiveness—its tendency to rely upon imported forms.
2. Plasticity—its lack of inertia, its ability to react to external stimuli, to adapt itself to rapid rates of change.
3. Productivity—its ability to modify the new form to some average level of mass taste, adapt it to mass production, then produce it seriatim indefinitely.

American architecture was acquisitive from its very inception. It began with borrowed means and has borrowed ever since. Architectural forms and building techniques were acquired in two ways. First, from the settlers themselves who, in wave after wave of English, French, Dutch, Swedish, German, Italian, and Middle European immigration, naturally brought with them their own familiar tools and techniques, their own esthetic standards. The second source of new forms was more generalized: from the first, American architecture showed itself extremely sensitive to world fashions, to the styles of the European centers. And then, from the beginning of the nineteenth century, the development of transportation and communication made the broadcasting of these changing fashions ever easier. They were registered on the American scene with the speed and accuracy of a seismograph. Scott had but to write a novel, Ruskin to read a paper, or Norman Shaw to build a new country house for the impulse to be at once reflected in our architecture here.

This acquisitiveness was undoubtedly characteristic. But can it be proved unique? Obviously, no other country had comparable immigration, but immigrant taste, while pervasive, was never as decisive as the international fashions of the upper class. Certainly, the stylistic gyrations of the last 150 years have been more quickly felt and widely echoed in America than in stagnant areas like Spain or southern Italy. But Paris, London, and Berlin were also swayed by these fashions: in fact, one or the other of them was the source of most vogues. Gothic

Revival churches, Italianate villas and Art Nouveau subway kiosks were forms actually invented there and only subsequently imported to America. Only recently, in forms like skyscrapers or abstract expressionist art, can America be said to have started a vogue.

The unique property of American acquisitiveness seems thus to be its scale. We undoubtedly have built more Gothic churches, Tuscan villas and Art Nouveau subway kiosks than other lands. But they have not been "better," so that our leadership is largely statistical. Of course, even here a difference in degree becomes ultimately a difference in kind. For if the building industry is intensely active, as it always has been in America, then these exotic stimuli become more quickly imbedded and more widely distributed in the whole body of its concepts and practices. Thereby they affect future as well as contemporaneous forms. And this brings us to a second quality of American architecture: its plasticity.

It began, as we have seen, with a series of imported forms, none of them particularly well suited to the climate or economic conditions of the New World. And of course it began in a landscape in which no pre-existing concepts or technologies held sway. (The only exception to this would be the Spanish in the Southwest, who found settled cultures of a relatively high order with a building technique not unlike their own.) Thus, on the one hand, there was in colonial America every incentive to radical modification of inherited building technologies and forms; and on the other, no inertia of a cultural or economic nature to resist it. Under these conditions, American architecture developed a remarkable ability to adapt itself to change. This quality becomes especially evident when the rate of change itself accelerated with the expansion of the original colonies across the Appalachian barrier at the end of the eighteenth century.

The opening of the West confronted the building industry with new demands. Changes in climate, in available building materials, in the speed of construction required, and the short length of tenure anticipated—all of these placed a premium on flexibility, adaptability, plasticity in both process and final product. Nor have these forces diminished; to the contrary, they have steadily increased, especially in the years since the Second World War. They have produced a new kind

5

of obsolescence in the field. Buildings which are still perfectly sound physically are technologically so obsolete that it is more economical to wreck than to remodel them.

This quality of plasticity, then, is characteristically American: to what extent is it unique? Here again the answer is not easy. Despite our rapid rates of both growth and change, one can always find examples of identical change as early, or even earlier, in Western Europe. We have come to think of steel and concrete as being peculiarly American materials. Yet both Bessemer steel and Portland cement are English inventions; and the discovery of reinforced concrete is French. Moreover, the application of these materials to structural problems predates ours by decades. England was building daring iron bridges before 1800, and her beautiful iron railway sheds were a commonplace by the 1830s, when our railway system was scarcely begun. The Crystal Palace was English, and the Eiffel Tower was French; these were for decades the largest and the tallest modern structures in the world. In the application of metal to more orthodox architectural problems, Labrouste's magnificent libraries in Paris—the Ste. Geneviève (1850) and the Nationale (1858–68)—appeared years before any similar use in this country.

The same thing must be said about many amenities now commonly held to be American. Steam heating was common in English greenhouses long before it appeared in the American home. All the elements of the bathroom—pump, running water and plumbing—were English before they were American. Faraday and Kelvin did the theoretical spadework for the electric refrigerator, though the refrigerator using natural ice for food preservation does seem to be indisputably an American invention. The list could be continued indefinitely. How does it happen, then, that all these characteristic features of modern architecture are so commonly regarded as American?

It seems to me that the answer must lie, not in who used these elements *first*, but in who used them *most*. In Western Europe they appeared early but remained alone, isolated phenomena which did not substantially affect subsequent practice. (It is almost as difficult to get a central heating plant or a bathroom in France or England today as it would have been in 1850.) In America, on the other hand, these features were adopted and absorbed into the very tissue of theory and practice. They became as integral a feature of the building as its floor or roof. (I do not mean to imply that there are not, even now, plenty of buildings in this country which have neither plumbing nor heating, but rather that they are generally recognized as shameful departures from the norm.)

Here, it seems to me, we come closer to a quality in American architecture which is unique: its tendency not merely to respond to change but to respond in *depth*, from top to bottom, throughout the nation's whole structure. Its genius seems to lie, not so much in invention as in application. And this brings us to a third, and to my mind most important, characteristic of our architecture and the industry which produces it: its powers of productivity. If it is acquisitive, and if these acquisitions are to be effectively put to work, then it must operate on a massive scale, be organized on an industrial basis geared to rapid change, to serve an expanding market which is never (except for periodic depressions) saturated. To accomplish this—to put into widest use the new concept, the new structural system or the new piece of equipment—it is always necessary to modify it to meet two sets of requirements: those of the industrial process itself and those imposed by the standards of taste of the American people.

This entire process has always been conditioned, in America, by a fact of immense significance: labor has always been scarce and hence expensive, while materials have always been plentiful and relatively cheap. This ratio of labor to material costs seems to have held as well in 1781 (Jefferson, in Paris, found he could get printing done for a fourth of what he had been asked in the United States) as in 1950. It is, moreover, the exact reverse of conditions in Europe and the rest of the world, where the cost of labor is low relative to the cost of materials. Finally, the relation between these two ratios has been constant throughout our history. For architecture this has important implications, since the American ratio is an incentive towards industrial production, while the other tends towards the persistence of handicraft.

Of all the areas colonized by an exploding Europe since the sixteenth century, North America alone offered no native populations which could be exploited or enslaved. Thus, unlike other colonists in

South America, India, or Africa, the Americans were confronted by a labor shortage from the start. Our deliberate destruction of the small original Indian population and our subsequent introduction of Negro slaves did little to abate it. This made it mandatory that Americans build America with their own hands and, in the very process, reconstruct their building techniques as well as their very character.

The Patent Office presents an impressive record of our response to this situation. No machine was ever too expensive to build, out of no matter what materials, if it promised to increase the productivity—i.e., reduce the unit cost—of labor. This drive towards rationalization has dominated our building activity from the very beginning and gives to our architecture certain formal qualities which may be described as distinctive, if not unique.

In structure, for example, we have always avoided the load-bearing, mass masonry which was our dominant heritage from Europe. The reason was simple: it demanded too much labor and there was no way of reducing the labor component until reinforced concrete came into common use around 1900. Thus we find no masonry tradition in the United States; I doubt if there are fifty genuine masonry vaults or domes in the whole country. (The masonry walls which we see in most buildings are not load-bearing—on the skyscraper they are mere curtains—and even where they do carry a load, they require a skeletal trussed roof or floor to complete the enclosure.)

The structural form which we did adopt, and which we have cultivated intensively ever since, is the skeleton. There were two great virtues to skeletal structures. The first was purely technical: it was more efficient than mass masonry in resisting loads and, because of its specialized curtain walls, could be made much more effective in repelling climatic attack. The second virtue was economic. The skeleton was *possible* in America, as nowhere else in the modern world, because ample supplies of the proper materials, wood and steel, were at hand. But it was *desirable* because the skeleton frame and its curtain walling are subject to a high degree of rationalization. The economies in labor were so pronounced that it has remained for three centuries our most popular structural form.

It is instructive to observe how quickly these forces began to operate in colonial building. The English settlers brought with them the concept of a skeletal structural system as expressed in late medieval wood-framed houses and barns. Its members were all hand worked, and it was fairly primitive from both a structural and an environmental point of view. Its members were heavy, crude, and inexact. Its walling, which merely filled the interstices, did not protect the skeleton itself from the great extremes of the New England climate, and it rapidly deteriorated as a result.

Radical modifications of this structural system were called for, and they were not long in appearing. The first steps were towards the lightening and simplification of the skeleton and the development of a continuous skin or sheath of either clapboards or shingles with which to protect the skeleton from the elements. Although it was possible to split shingles by hand, clapboards and floorboards had to be sawed; sawing would also speed up the production of structural timbers. Thus, though there was no tradition of sawmills in England (they had, as a matter of fact, been forbidden), we find waterpowered sawmills appearing as early as 1633 at the Falls of Piscataqua, on the line between New Hampshire and Maine. In the succeeding century and a half, a giant lumber industry was to rise, spurred on by the appearance of the steam-powered sawmill at the end of the eighteenth century. However, the development of that authentically American structure, the balloon-framed wooden house, was delayed until the 1830s by the exorbitant cost of handmade nails. Until machine-made nails appeared, the skeleton had to be put together with pegs or mortise and tenon; these connections required bulky framing members and they were often hand hewn. But with the appearance of the wire-cut nail, hand-worked members disappeared almost at once. The entire structure was immeasurably lightened, and site labor greatly reduced. By 1840, in the Midwest, the typical frame house was built completely of milled elements.

But, long before the elements were completely machine-made, the fabrication of hand-sawed and even hand-adzed wooden structures was also being rationalized. Thus, there are records of prefabricated house frames being made as early as 1578. The Louisiana French were shipping them to the West Indies as early as 1727. A prefabricated house was stolen from a Natchez, Mississippi, wharf in 1791; and the Utopian community of the Rappists at Economy, Pennsylvania, erected

9

Mid-nineteenth-century lithograph showing balloon-framed wood construction evolved from milled lumber in standard sizes and machine-made nails.

200 identical dwelling houses in the years 1824–1830, prefabricating them from a single set of shop drawings. By the time of the California Gold Rush, prefabricated houses were being manufactured in Chicago and shipped out to San Francisco by boat. Houses are not as completely fabricated even today as they obviously could be, due to the resistance of the *rentier* element in building financing: but even so, the proportion of labor done on the site has been reduced to a fraction of its former amount and could readily be reduced to almost zero if builders so desired.

In its development and exploitation of the wood frame, America is almost unique. Only the Japanese have approached us in this respect. But, though their walls are models of rationalized construction, surpassing ours in their clarity and grace, their roof framing is clumsy and inefficient. For some odd reason, they never discovered the truss, relying upon very heavy cribbing to support their roofs. Hence their wooden skeletons are, from a qualitative point of view, inferior to ours. While we cannot claim to have invented the truss (the Romans used it in their basilicas), we have certainly brought it to its highest level of development. With it, we devised a completely three-dimensional skeletal framing system.

The most significant American contribution to the field of skeletal structure, however, has been in metal rather than wood. Here again our contribution has been more in the area of exploitation than invention since, as we have seen, England pioneered in the manufacture and use of cast iron, wrought iron, and steel structural members. Our adoption of the metal-framed building was entirely logical. We had had over two centuries of experience with the wooden skeleton when the metal frame became possible. The two materials are roughly similar in their structural behavior, both having high resistance to tensile as well as compressive loading. And, as it turned out, we had enormous supplies of iron ore and of coal wherewith to smelt it. Hence our transition to metal was easy and—because of the enormous expansion of the mid-nineteenth century—very rapid.

The first substitutions of metal for wood occurred in precisely those areas where its greater strength and predictability were most appreciated: in mills, factories, and railroad bridges. We find metal columns, beams, and trusses in New England textile mills in 1835; prefabricated non-load-bearing cast iron curtain walls in New Orleans, St. Louis, and Pottsville (Pa.) at about the same time. And we find the two combined in an all-metal building in New York by 1850. There was a slight decline in the years after the Civil War, when several disastrous fires proved that though iron did not burn like wood, it melted and collapsed even faster. But fireproofing techniques were evolved and the completely articulated steel frame found its most typical—though by no means most brilliant—expression in the skyscraper. This building type, together with the elevator which made it possible, can certainly be reckoned as uniquely American.

Today, the cubical steel skeleton of the skyscraper dominates the American skyline, both literally and conceptually. Its particular form is the one which we have cultivated to the exclusion of all others, even

11

in many buildings which are not multi-story and need not be cubical. Yet it is efficient and economical only within the reference frame of American conditions. In the abstract, it is neither. The criterion of structural efficiency is that the minimum material does the maximum work. In this light, the cubical skeleton is only moderately efficient. Suspended structures like the George Washington Bridge or stressed skin structures like the molded plywood speedboat have a much more favorable ratio of material to work. Nor is the skyscraper frame economical except in relation to the high cost of labor and the plentitude of steel in this country. In most parts of the world, the steel frame is prohibitively expensive. So great is the prestige of this particular steel form that we even duplicate it in concrete, though the unique potentials of this material are best exploited in shell structures, as the steel-poor countries of Latin America and Europe are so brilliantly demonstrating.

Thus, beyond some point not easily determined, the most characteristic quality of American architecture—its power of rationalization —displays serious limitations. While, relative to the rest of the world, it always produces a statistical predominance (most skyscrapers, most bathrooms, most heating plants) and in many respects a high average level, rationalization tends to inhibit qualitative superiority of design. There seems to be a cyclical effect in rationalization, especially in these days of intensive mechanization. This permits us, at one stage, to appropriate the best of existing ideas and leap into world leadership with their concrete application. But the very process of "tooling up" introduces a rigidity into the picture which, at another point of the spiral, acts to slow down qualitative advance. This is precisely what happened to Henry Ford. He completed the first production line assembly in the world before 1920 and with it was catapulted into absolute priority in his field. Yet within a decade he had lost it to the competition with newer and more flexible production lines.

Though they have many problems, less massively industrialized countries than our own do not suffer from this liability. In a quantitative sense their systems support fewer architects than does ours, but they do at the same time offer these designers greater freedom of action. They produce fewer buildings, and many of these are low by any standard; but some of them are very high by any standard. And it is due to this paradox that Rio de Janiero and Mexico City, Milan and Stockholm often produce more stimulating modern architecture today than New York or Chicago. This fact should expose a widely held American fallacy that statistical superiority leads automatically to qualitative preeminence. Unfortunately, in design, at least, this does not follow. There is a necessary correlation between building many skyscrapers and building the best. But this proposition cannot be read backwards: to have the most skyscrapers is no automatic *guarantee* of having the best.

Moreover, it must be observed that a scarcity of materials seems often to have a benign effect on both design and workmanship, while abundance leads often to vulgarity. This is especially evident in metal-poor countries like Italy. Here steel is very expensive. It can only be used where nothing else will do, as in trains and automobiles; and here the sheer brilliance with which Italian engineers wring the last milligram of performance out of each millimeter of material is an exciting experience for the designer to witness. The Italians, like most of the rest of the world, actually have only one material out of which to build: reinforced concrete. Because of this, they are *forced* to exploit its potentials to the utmost, using 3-inch thick shells to span great voids where American practice would call for 24-inch beams and 8-inch slabs. In social life poverty has nothing to commend it; but in design its astringent discipline often stimulates the designer's imagination beyond the power of plenty.

These, in greatly capsuled form, are the qualities which make American architecture American. On close examination, it becomes apparent that only one is possibly unique, and it by no means uniquely good. There is much cause for pride in the past of American architecture and some reason for confidence in its future, but no excuse at all for being complacent about it.

2. THE IMPACT OF TECHNOLOGY

The impact of modern industrial technology upon contemporary architecture can be easily traced at every level—theory, practice, finished product. The effect is most clear and most poignant at the theoretical level. Nineteenth-century technology set in motion among architects a whole train of speculation as to its significance, its probable course of development, and the possible responses of architecture to it. This speculation spread in steadily widening circles, involving all the theoreticians of the past century and a half. Greenough, Pugin, Ruskin, Viollet-le-Duc; Sullivan, Wright and Geoffrey Scott; Le Corbusier, Gropius, and Mumford—all these men were activated by the shock waves of the impact. Nor have these speculations ceased. On the contrary, the implications of technology for architecture are in many ways more ominous and obscure than they were a hundred years ago.

These successive waves of speculation are also revealed with great clarity in the architecture of the period. Each has left its deposit, and these the historian can trace as easily as the geologist reads his core or the archaeologist his trench. It is a stratigraphy of unparalleled confusion. For though technology, by its sheer mastery of external nature, has made possible unprecedented advances in architecture, it did, by the same ironic token, make possible more bad architecture than the world had ever seen. Architecture, unlike the fine arts, is at once the prince and the prisoner of the kingdom of necessity. It can never escape the iron laws of physics: indeed its greatest examples are precisely those in which these laws have been most scrupulously observed. The majesty of such constructions as Hadrian's Villa or Chartres Cathedral springs from the most exact and elegant knowledge of the limits and potentials of masonry vaulting. Acceptance, not defiance, of the laws of statics was the basis of all preindustrial architecture. Because modern technology so extended man's power over external nature, modern architects have often acted as though these iron laws had been repealed. The result, for perhaps the first time in all history, was bad architecture—ugly to look at, unsatisfactory in use.

One of today's basic assumptions is that architecture, thanks to modern technology, has made great advances in the past century. In many respects, of course, this is true. But the implication is that these advances have been steady and continuous and that we stand now at some pinnacle of accomplishment. Unfortunately for our complacency, this is not the case. The great germinal structures of the past hundred years are not evenly distributed throughout its span; on the contrary, they fall in clusters, and rather closer to the beginning of the period than its end.

If, for the sake of brevity, we simplify the historical record, then we may take Joseph Paxton's Crystal Palace (1851) as marking the opening of our era. Here was the first structure in the western world which clearly demonstrated the arrival of a new period. It not only used the materials of the new technology—iron and glass—but it used them in an explicitly novel way, purged of all reliance on historically determined form.

We do not find this new architectural idiom immediately adopted by the West. On the contrary, four or five decades elapse before we find a statement of equal clarity and vigor in Sullivan's use of steel and glass in the multi-story Schlesinger and Meyer Building of 1899; here was a perfect understanding not only of steel cage construction but, even more important, of the asthetic expression of its essentially static non-directional quality. Four years later, in 1903, we find in Toni Garnier's *Cité Industrielle* an equally mature understanding of the structural nature and esthetic potentials of an even newer material—reinforced concrete.

But these seminal structures, in the United States, had no immediate progeny. Half a century elapses before we find the idiom picked up again in such buildings as Miës van der Rohe's Chicago apartments or the Lever House of Skidmore, Owings, and Merrill. Thus, it has taken us better than a century to stabilize, refine, and bring into general use an architectural idiom expressive of the new technology; and this despite the fact that, in a very real sense, it was perfected at the very start.

Crystal Palace, London, 1851. Joseph Paxton, architect.

Schlesinger and Meyer Department Store, Chicago, 1899. Louis Sullivan, architect.

Transportation center, *Cité Industrielle,* 1903. Toni Garnier, architect.

Lever House, New York, 1952. Skidmore, Owings, and Merrill, architects.

Why has this paradoxical state of affairs been true?

It is largely due to the fact that, while architecture has been exposed to the full blast of technology, it has been only obliquely touched by the sciences which lay behind it. With a few notable exceptions, architects have always stood outside the scientific tradition. Habitually preoccupied with problems of esthetics, they were completely unprepared *theoretically* for the emergencies with which industrialism confronted them. Their only contact with science was through technology; and advances in this field came so rapidly, and were of such earth-shaking magnitude when they came, that they occupied the architect's entire attention.

Moreover, many of the most significant advances were in the field of pure structure. And since the expression of structure is always geometry, they tended to focus architectural attention on that most formal and abstract of scientific disciplines. For this, contemporary architecture has paid a heavy price.

True, the march of science has amply confirmed that there *is* order, rhythm, law in nature. But, as a system, nature is found to be infinitely more complex than it appeared even to that contemporary of Paxton, Charles Darwin. And for this new perspective of nature, geometry is found to offer a very inadequate representation. The essential qualities of nature—life and movement, and time (the dimension in which they both occur)—are precisely the qualities which geometry cannot describe.

Now, I do not mean to suggest that actual buildings can avoid geometric form, any more than growing tissue can be organized without the cell. But for architects geometry has inherent conceptual dangers, of which they should at least be aware. The principal one, of course, is formalism—that is, interest in the form to the neglect of its content or function. Modern science teaches us the danger of formalism. A module never got an airplane off the ground. Nor did the Golden Mean ever help to discover the arrangement of the molecules of penicillin. And architecture can never fully discharge its tasks so long as the geometry of its forms is considered as an end rather than a means.

In saying that the architecture of the last hundred years has shown rather less forward movement than we often assume, I do not mean to suggest that this course of development has been "bad," still less that it

Reliance Building, Chicago, 1895. Burnham and Root, architects.

has not been historically necessary. But any honest assessment must recognize that there is little qualitative difference between Burnham and Root's Reliance Building of 1890–95 and our most "advanced" skyscrapers of today. Nor can we honestly argue that any upper-class house of the 1950s represents a qualitative advance over Frank Lloyd Wright's Coonley House of 1908. We have, in short, made far less use of our resources than did either Root seventy years ago or Wright fifty years ago. We have instead been coasting on the momentum generated by these men.

19

If this is true, two questions immediately arise: How did the situation come about? How can it be corrected in the future? I think it came about because we have been too concerned with the formal qualities of our work and too little with its behavior and performance in use. We are fond of assuring ourselves, nowadays, that we are aware of this. We are quick to criticize the formalism of Alberti and Palladio, of Charles Follen McKim and Stanford White; but we are oddly blind to exactly the same tendencies in Miës van der Rohe's campus for the Illinois Institute of Technology or Le Corbusier's *Unité d'Habitation* in Marseilles. They make just as many concessions to preconceived ideas of the façade as Palladio ever did. We will correct this weakness in our architecture only when we cease to confuse mere technology with science, when we rid our theory of gadgetry and illuminate it with truly scientific thought.

In a purely formal sense, of course, modern architecture is often extremely handsome. For example, Eero Saarinen's new General Motors Technical Center, with its clarity of line, crispness of color and sharp articulation of mass and volume, is visually very satisfactory—incomparably finer, certainly, than any of the cars which have so far come out of it. But when we try to generalize such buildings into the idiom of the future, we come a cropper. For logic and experience show us that the problems of architecture, in the tempestuous context of American life and American climate, are anything but simple, crisp, and clear. They are, on the contrary, incredibly complex. Do our current esthetic criteria of crystalline clarity and classic repose—do these really correspond to the demands of contemporary reality? Or are they accomplished only at the sacrifice of invisible but very real requirements, sacrifices which only life and not photography reveal? I am afraid, if we are to trust the evidence of our own senses, that many of these handsome structures are neither economical to build, comfortable to live in, nor simple to keep in operating order. Our obsession with pure geometry, in other words, leads us to make of much modern architecture a sort of Procrustean template which falls like a murderous cookie cutter across those living processes which do not happen to conform to its outlines.

This sort of formalism operates to limit the usefulness of many modern buildings. Look, for example, at the current use of glass. Glass is a

General Motors Technical Center, Detroit, 1955. Eero Saarinen, architect.

Crown Hall, Illinois Institute of Technology, Chicago, 1955. Ludwig Miës van der Rohe, architect.

wonderful material, and its availability in hitherto-unheard-of sizes has been one of the principal factors in the creation of our own architectural idiom. But—pictorial evidence notwithstanding—glass does *not* simplify the design process: on the contrary, it complicates it quite unbelievably, especially when glass comes to constitute the entire wall. This glass wall is very complicated, whether viewed from the angle of physics, physiology, or psychology. It requires a massive assortment of auxiliary devices, if it is to be genuinely successful at any level higher than that of the picture books. These devices are necessary to provide for ventilation, privacy, insect protection, weatherproofing, insulation, light and heat control. Moveover, because of the extreme variations of our seasons, all these devices must have a high degree of flexibility.

Here, then, is the paradox. Transparency, as an esthetic criterion, dictates certain formal qualities in architecture—simplicity, structural clarity, repose. But transparency, at the biological level, often raises exactly contrary demands—complexity, opacity, changeability. How are these two contradictory sets of values to be reconciled? By meeting the requirements of the whole man? Or by imposing a merely visual order based on *a priori* conventions drawn largely from the field of painting?

Currently, the protagonists of an architecture of pure geometry offer two sorts of apologia for it. The first is actually an old and familiar one —i.e., that beauty in architecture is, in the last analysis, more important than "mere" creature comfort. The other is that, thanks to the miracles of modern technology, the problems raised by their crystalline geometry can be solved by exclusively mechanical means.

Both of these arguments are, in the final analysis, fallacious; and a detailed analysis of the glass wall offers a good opportunity to demonstrate the fact. The first proposition, for example, sets up a false conflict between esthetic satisfaction and physical well-being, implying that the two are *always* antithetical in any architectural system. Yet modern physiology and psychology alike indicate that the two are in reality only opposite sides of the same coin. The esthetic enjoyment of an actual building (as opposed to a mere photograph of it) is not exclusively a matter of vision but of total sensory perception. Thus, to be truly satisfactory, a building must meet the demands of all the senses, not just those of vision alone. It is not the eye but the whole man who reacts to architecture. Yet, even on the purely visual plane, much of our architecture seems to me to display either contempt for, or ignorance of, optical reality. Under normal daylight conditions, most glass is as opaque as granite when viewed from the outside. The same glass under the same conditions, many prove intolerably bright and glarey when viewed from inside the building. At night, conditions are reversed: then, externally viewed, the glass is really transparent but, by the same token, it is opaque from the inside. But this nighttime opacity distorts the luminous balance of the room. These areas, conceived of as being light sources, are now actually jet black, light-absorbing areas. In real life, in short, glass behaves in a quite complex fashion.

I do not argue that these paradoxes cannot be overcome by good design. I am merely pointing out that they very seldom are. Thus, even if architecture were exclusively a matter of vision, a wide range of extremely subtle problems in optics are raised. These can be solved only by a truly functional analysis, and their solution will almost certainly dictate all sorts of eyebrows, *soleil brise*, curtains, and blinds. And these would certainly complicate the architecture of pure geometry.

The second argument—that modern technology can, single-handedly, compensate for the deficiencies of the glass wall—seems to me even more hazardous. Technology has indeed greatly extended the

Two aspects of the optical reality of glass: the same building as it appears in daytime (left, below) and at night (right).

range of our control over such various environmental phenomena as temperature, humidity, light, and sound. But the limits, even here, are real and obdurate. The amount of solar energy or chilling winds which act upon a given building is of a high order of magnitude, even in these days of atomic energy. And it is dangerous nonsense to argue that, with modern air conditioning, the architect can now ignore this fact—dangerous both technically and philosophically.

Henry Wright has recently shown that "for every 100 square feet of unshaded, unfavorably oriented glass used in a tall building in most parts of the United States, an additional ton of air conditioning must be provided." Occasionally there may be budgets in which such costs are unimportant, or certain building sites where poor orientation is unavoidable. In such cases, we can have no quarrel with the use of extra air conditioning. But the danger is that we generalize such exceptions to become the rule. For the fact is that most budgets *are* affected by such costs and that there are few planning problems which inexorably dictate poorly oriented glass.

But the problem goes beyond costs to a consideration of human comfort. Cooling the man behind such unshaded glass is nearly impossible. Anyone with a black body thermometer—or, for that matter, an ordinary house cat—can convince himself that the solar energy transmitted by a sheet of glass is primarily radiant. Such heat is not stopped by any combination of blinds or shades *inside* the glass; nor can it be directly absorbed by any conventional cooling system. Such heat can be deflected only *outside* the glass. Thus, in the final analysis, no optimum solution to this problem is possible by purely mechanical means, no matter what the budget. It can only be solved at its highest level by the proper adaptation of the building to its site, exposures and microclimate; by external shading devices, whether they be trees, vines, or *soleil brise;* in short, by architectural means. Only when all these means have been employed, can the glass and the cooling system be expected to operate at maximum efficiency.

One of our more imaginative air-conditioning engineers has recently complained that many architects "handed him raw space and expected him to make it habitable." He put his finger on a real and present danger to architecture, our tendency to use technology merely as a means of correcting basic errors of design. This tendency, carried to its logical

This elegant, glass-sheathed cube is feasible because it is shaded to the east, south, and west by neighboring skyscrapers. Manufacturers Trust Company, New York, 1954. Skidmore, Owings, and Merrill, architects.

conclusion, leads to nothing less than the architect's abdication of his historic responsibilities.

We have, fortunately, some recent buildings which demonstrate that this tendency is not universal. One of them is the handsome Fifth Avenue branch of the Manufacturers Trust Company in New York. This steel-and-crystal cage has been justifiably praised by many critics as being a very successful building. But none of them, to my knowledge, has called attention to the central factor which makes it successful—makes it, one might almost say, possible at all. That factor is its orientation. The building not only faces north and east; it is also shaded to the east, south, and west by very tall skyscrapers. Obvious and simple though it is, this single fact spells the difference between success and failure for the building. Rotate it so that it faces south and west, remove the sheltering neighbor buildings, and this crystal cage would be uninhabitable for a large part of the year, with or without air conditioning. The architects here have acted correctly. They have made fundamental decisions of an architectural nature; and these, in turn, have placed any subsequent use of mechanization in its proper reference frame. Thus, air conditioning in this building is not employed merely to make a bad building habitable but to make good architecture even better.

Plate glass and summer cooling are only two small aspects of contemporary architecture. But current use (and abuse) of them acts as a lens through which we view a central problem in our relations with technology: is it to be a useful tool in our hands or will it become our blind master?

Another hazard to which our obsession with pure geometry exposes us is its hostility towards the forms of art. Modern architecture's distrust of sculpture and painting, of ornament and enrichment, even of color itself, borders on the pathological. This prejudice, of course, has deep roots in the very history of our movement. For it was in protest against the progressive corruption of architectural art during the last century that the modern idiom arose. The esthetic stringencies of the de Stijl group in Holland, of Le Corbusier in the Paris of the 1920s, or of Gropius in the Germany of the Bauhaus, were historic necessities which are not subject to question at this late date.

But here we deal with events which are already from a quarter to half a century old. The question today is not whether these pioneers of modern architecture were correct in 1920—clearly they were—but rather what use we intend to make of their explorations. Here we stand in a kind of frozen, tasteful mimicry. If we consider at random some of our most successful American buildings—Lever House, Manufacturers Trust Company, General Motors Technical Center, the new campus of the Illinois Institute of Technology—we are confronted with compositions with which the cultivated taste cannot quarrel. But we must recognize that no artistic statement, no matter how abstract or elliptical, mars the perfect geometry of their walls. Signs, street numbers, flagpoles are suppressed, even the curtains and blinds are rigidly standardized. These buildings must constitute, short of the pyramids, the most noncommittal body of architecture in history.

This noncommittance may be a perfectly permissible line of development. Compared to the great mass of building today, it seems actually admirable. But can we—or, what is more to the point, will the American people—accept it as the prototype of the architecture of the future? I think not. All sorts of voices are being raised against this "architecture of poverty," within and without the profession. The motives are mixed and the proposals often of doubtful value, but they all demand that the forms of art be returned to their historic role in architecture. Admittedly, to move from our safe position of the past few years, where the solution was simply to banish all art forms, exposes us to the necessity of making some exceedingly hazardous decisions; but not to move is impossible.

To reestablish the forms of art in our architecture means, first of all, to reestablish connections with our own tradition. We must learn, somehow or other, to live at peace with our own past. We must not make the mistake of treating this past as our grandfathers did—that is, of regarding it merely as a vast grab of prefabricated iconographies which could be donned or dropped at will. Here in America we have a long and agonizing record of this attempt to adapt the actual forms of traditional ornament to the needs of modern structure. This record includes not only the mediocrities of the late nineteenth and early twentieth centuries but also of some authentic giants: Louis Sullivan, Claude Bragdon, and Bertram Goodhue devoted years of hard work and great talent to this task. They failed tragically at any solution. Only Wright

27

(and this at a very early age) saw the impossibility of any such reconciliation. We must, as Horatio Greenough put it at the very opening of our period, study the past for its principles, like men, and not copy its forms like monkeys.

Fortunately, contemporary architectural theory is increasingly irradiated by the objective scholarship of adjacent fields—art history, archaeology, and cultural history. This is bound to create a new attitude toward the art of the past, and will help us to avoid both eclecticism and antiquarianism. It must, of course, be observed that contemporary architecture has at its disposal all the resources of contemporary painting and sculpture. These are immense; there was never a time in American history when architects had so rich and varied a production on which to draw. It is this art, so close in spirit to our own, to which we must turn for help.

But the reestablishment of the forms of art in modern architecture must also rest on a profound understanding of the esthetic potentials of its structure. Here again it seems to me a truly scientific analysis will indicate the broad lines along which this development should advance. If, as we have seen, an analysis of the wall and the man who lives behind it reveals the complexity of its task then we have the specifications for a rich, rather than a poverty-stricken, façade. If science indicates that architecture, despite all technological advances, has not been removed from its umbilical relationship with the landscape and the natural forces which play upon it, then we have the specifications for a far more varied, colorful, and stimulating landscape than any we look upon today. If we follow the guides of modern historiography, then our handling of the monuments of the past can avoid both American extremes: the dry and mechanical copying evident in Colonial Williamsburg, on the one hand, and the ruthless destruction of historically and artistically significant buildings everywhere else.

PART II:

Giants in the Land

3. ARCHITECTS OF DEMOCRACY: JEFFERSON AND WRIGHT

It may, at first glance, seem paradoxical to link together two such men as Thomas Jefferson and Frank Lloyd Wright. They appear, superficially, so disparate, so unlike: Jefferson, the cool, objective classicist, Wright the passionate, subjective innovator. The idioms they employed, the architectural styles they worked in, the very language of their creative effort, seem as far apart as Eskimo and Egyptian.

Yet it is my feeling that these two architects have played very similar roles in the development of our country's domestic architecture. They are not even very far apart in time, incredible as it seems to say so: Wright was born only 43 years after Jefferson's death. The points of their similarity are many and important. Each, for his time, has been the inventor of new concepts of comfort, amenity, and grace. Each has sought to democratize these concepts, to make them actually available to wider circles of Americans than previously. And each has accomplished this through the widest and most imaginative use of the technical and cultural resources of his time.

There is, of course, one great difference: the forms of their architectural vocabularies. Jefferson came at the very end of the preindustrial Western world, when the fertilizing impact of science upon technique was scarcely a dream. Wright appeared at the very moment of maturation of this process. For Jefferson, therefore, the old language of classic form was entirely adequate. For Wright, on the other hand, the invention of a completely new language was mandatory. But this difference makes apparent still another similarity: they have both become world-historic figures precisely because of their timeliness. Each speaks the quintessential language of his epoch.

Jefferson's houses express a way of life which is, in some respects, more remote from us than that of the Romans. To appreciate them, therefore, it is necessary to see them in their context. All of us are familiar with the great old houses of the Middle Atlantic Seaboard—especially those which are so admirably preserved by the various antiquarian societies. These houses reflect their owners' efforts to live comfortably within the characteristic social and economic conditions of their times. But as they exist today they are only polished relics, shorn of the cumbrous and ugly system which supported them. For the salient characteristic of their society was, of course, handicraft production by slave labor.

The plantation was, to an extent almost impossible to realize today, a self-contained manufactory. And the great house was the administrative center of a whole network of shops, warehouses, and offices; for breeding and raising cattle, swine, mules, and horses; for blacksmithing and wagonmaking; for woodworking, carpentry, nail-, brick-, and lime-making. All these operations were essential to the existence of the plantation. But on them were superimposed all those directly concerned with the maintenance of the great house, with housekeeping and family care: ginning, dyeing, weaving, tailoring, and shoe making; cooking, baking, butchering, distilling, milling, washing, cleaning, sewing, and mending.

Few of these processes are beautiful, even today. And in Jefferson's time they ranged from the merely unattractive to the squalid and noisome. If to this we add the fact that, for reasonably efficient operation, they had to be located relatively close to the great house, we can begin to understand how much ingenuity it took to live well and beautifully in eighteenth-century Virginia.

This is the central contradiction which Jefferson tries to solve in all the houses which we can surely attribute to him: Barboursville, Poplar Forest, Farmington. And it naturally reaches its highest expression in his own home at Monticello. If we study this lovely complex with the attention it deserves, we will see how accurately it reflects the architect's philosophy toward life.

First, his attitude toward work. Jefferson had no fear of and no contempt for work. In 1818, at the age of seventy-four, he was following a daily schedule on the University at Charlottesville which would prostrate most of us today. But neither had Jefferson any romantic illusions about the sordid aspects of most manual labor. Least of all did he approve of forced labor. He was the first man in all human history to draft legislation for the complete abolition of slavery. Years later, writing his *Autobiography* at the age of seventy-seven, he was still opposed to slavery. "Nothing is more certainly written in the book of fate than that these [Negroes] are to be free." But then—disconcerting for the modern mind—he proposes emancipation *and* deportation to Africa "since it is no less certain that the two races, equally free, cannot live in the same government."[1] But he remained, after all, the master of a big, slave-powered plantation. And around this paradox revolve many of his most characteristic architectural devices.

Wherever he can save or eliminate labor, for either humanitarian or esthetic reasons, we find him doing so. Monticello is full of machines for this purpose: wine lifts, double-acting doors, weather vanes with inside dials, self-winding clocks. Where he cannot eliminate labor, he tries to make it as pleasant as possible for both the served and the servant. The whole basement level of Monticello is organized around all-weather communications passages, dry overhead, dry underfoot. It is hard to imagine any item of daily use which cannot be reached comfortably without having to go out into the weather. By this device, he achieves a level of comfort and convenience for the servants which none of the other great houses of the period can approach.

But notice one thing further: where he cannot eliminate hard labor or unattractive processes, he conceals them completely from the eyes, ears, and noses of his family and guests. And this is why the entire service system at Monticello, unlike those at Mount Vernon or Westover, is completely submerged below the main living floor. Here Jefferson has manipulated his contours in such a canny fashion that not a single window of the main house looks out on anything except landscaped vistas. Not a single aspect of domestic activity—drying clothes, washed dishes, burned bread, or curried horses—can be seen, smelled, or heard in the main house. And yet he has not buried the servants in clammy malodorous vaults. The passages and store rooms are dry, well-lighted, and airy. The kitchen, dairy, and servants' quarters have a southeast exposure. Even the stables and wash house along the northwest side have a handsome quota of light, air, and view.

Model (above) and plan (below) show how Jefferson submerged his service floor beneath the *piano nobile* of Monticello to win convenient service and maximum amenity for the family.

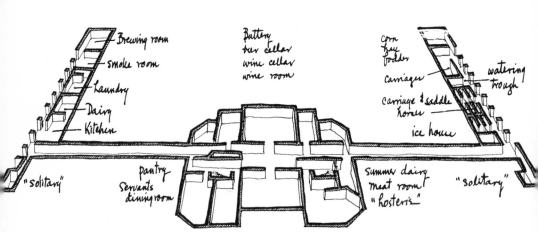

Brewing room
Smoke room
Laundry
Dairy
Kitchen

Buttery
beer cellar
wine cellar
wine room

Corn
hay
fodder
Carriages
Carriage & saddle horses
ice house

watering trough

"solitary"

pantry
Servants
dining room

summer dairy
meat room
"hostens"

"solitary"

34

The plan of Monticello has certain obvious similarities with those of Mount Vernon, Shirley, Stratford, and other great houses of the Tidewater where the service areas are symmetrically organized into low wings flanking the great house. All of these, of course, stem from the Renaissance, most specifically from Palladio. Thus Jefferson is not the inventor of the plan, any more than Wright is the inventor of radiant heating or plate glass. Jefferson is rather the innovator who takes an existing prototype and carries it to its highest possible stage of development.

In the process, he introduces many innovations of great importance. We have already seen one of them—the device of submerging the whole service level below the *piano nobile.* Another complementary device is his solution of vertical communication. It seems incredible that Jefferson should have been criticized for "forgetting" the central stairway at Monticello. As an architect he may have had his deficiencies, but forgetfulness was never one of them. We can assume, therefore, that he had very definite reasons for omitting the grand stairway. And very convincing they are.

As a frequent visitor to the palaces of Europe, Jefferson could not have missed what others less observant had commented upon: the conflict between the ceremonial and the functional use of stairways. In the evening at Versailles, for example, the stairs would display glittering cascades of elaborately dressed courtiers; the morning after, they would carry a more sordid traffic of milch goats and slop jars. Even in the great houses of Virginia, stair traffic would have been offensive to one of Jefferson's taste. Twice a day, servants would have to run up and down with fire wood, ashes, cold water for drinking, hot water for shaving, warm water for bathing; with bed warmers, night jars, candles, and lamps; with clean and soiled linen. And the standard Palladian plan with its grand stair and central halls, would direct all this traffic through the heart of the living area.

Today, most if not all of this service traffic is mechanized. It moves silently and invisibly through ducts, tubes, and wires embedded in the walls. Lacking such technical resources, Jefferson unlocked this paradox in a very direct and sensible way. He abandoned the central stair altogether and replaced it with two service cores, consisting of stairs, halls, and cupboards, which penetrate Monticello vertically from basement to attic. These cores serve every room in the house and create two quite separate circulation patterns—one for the family and its guests, one for the servants. With this scheme Jefferson comes as close to modern standards of service as his times permit.

For such crassly functional reasons alone, Jefferson would have been justified in this ingenious plan. But there were other reasons also. As a thorough-going republican he had nothing but contempt for the pomp and pretension of European palaces. ("Under the most imposing exterior," he warned his readers, the courts of royalty conceal "the weakest and worst parts of mankind.") Under such circumstances, the grand stairway had symbolic aspects distasteful to him. His way of life did not include great balls or great ladies, either, to sweep up and down stairs displaying their hoopskirts and *décolletage*. Actually, for all its elegance and refinement, Monticello is not a pretentious house. It is not very big —many a comfortable farm house even then was larger—and Jefferson went to great lengths to maintain its small scale. It is basically a single-story affair, and when the necessity for more guest rooms forced him to add bedrooms above he resorted to all sorts of ingenious devices to conceal or minimize its increased size: e.g., framing the main floor and low attic windows together on the east façade, so that they read as one and concealing those on the west behind a balustrade.

When it came to creature comforts, no house on either side of the Atlantic displayed more attention to detail. Its sanitation alone is remarkable. Monticello has rainwater for washing, well water for drinking, a special pond for storing live fish, an ice house for refrigerating other foods. In addition to outdoor privvies for fair weather use (with charming views across the valley), Monticello has indoor privvies on each floor. These are served by vertical zinc-lined shafts which lead down to a subterranean tunnel. Here, on tracks, were parked zinc-lined carts which were rolled out of the tunnel and emptied each morning. The shafts were independently vented directly through the roof to the outdoors. All in all, this was as far as domestic sanitation could be carried until the mechanical pump made running water and the water closet conceivable.

It hardly needs repeating that, both as architect and decorator, Jefferson was a thorough-going modernist. There was no antique furniture at Monticello in his day. All of it was modern, much of it his own design: adjustable reading stands, revolving tables, drawing boards, and desks. He used the recessed French bed for cold weather snugness. But in his own bed, at least, he also provided for warm weather comfort by providing through ventilation. His triple-hung sash provided for flexible ventilation. He used what was probably the first storm sash in history on the northwest exposure, as well as our earliest sun porch. His storage facilities are phenomenal for the time. The central service core on each floor is flanked with closets and cupboards—facilities completely lacking in most of the great plantation houses.

In terms of site development and landscaping, Monticello is astonishingly modern. Even his contemporaries noticed that he did not follow the usual plantation procedure of locating the great house in a valley, near the fields, highways, and waterways. Instead he chose a mountaintop whose only asset was its beauty. For this he paid a heavy price in terms of roadways and utilities, but he paid it gladly. Obviously, he wished to place his family and friends in a setting of real nobility from which every vestige of the grimy, everyday world of work had been removed.

In developing this mountaintop he is once again very like the modern American architect. The entourage of Monticello was planned as a unit with the house itself and involved literally remaking the mountain top. To achieve those lovely vistas which are an integral part of each room he moved thousands of yards of soil, built hundreds of feet of walks, drives, and walls. He had complete planting schemes for the garden, and they were begun long before the house was complete.

We have already seen how adroitly he utilized a change in grades to submerge his service areas. But it is necessary to add that in terms of orientation to sun, wind, and view, Monticello could scarcely be improved upon. Only two of the eleven ground-floor rooms face north; all the most used face south or west. The kitchen and its auxiliaries have a southeast exposure while ice house and carriage house and stables face north. All the food storage areas for roots, grain, wine, beer and the like are underground for low, even temperatures the year around.

Jefferson distrusted the aristocracy, but not so much that he could not learn from it. For it was precisely the aristocracy which had hitherto monopolized the world's beauty and comfort. It was Jefferson's lifelong determination to make available to the people of the American Republic this beauty and comfort: to sift the wheat of true culture from the chaff of feudalism, to cleanse and democratize culture. Monticello is, on the architectural plane, a clear and imposing record of this determination.

Jefferson is not popular with many younger architects today because, architecturally, he spoke the idiom of Classic antiquity. This is tantamount to criticizing Shakespeare for using Elizabethan English or Homer for writing in archaic Greek. The real problem of criticism, of course, is not what language a man speaks but what he has to say and how well he says it. The simple fact is that, in Jefferson's day, the Classic idiom was the absolutely universal language of the West. And it was still a perfectly adequate system of expression. Neither social needs nor building techniques differed substantially from those of the ancient world. The post-and-lintel, the load-bearing wall, the masonry arch and vault were as appropriate for Jefferson as for Vitruvius. Jefferson understood this perfectly; there was no more need for novelty in architectural expression than, in the drafting of the Declaration of Independence, there had been a need for literary innovation. There his task had been, he later wrote with dry but winning candor, "not to find out new principles or new arguments, never before thought of; not merely to say things which had never been said before; but to place before mankind the common sense of the subject, in terms so plain and firm as to command their assent and to justify ourselves in the independent stand we are compelled to take." And just so, in designing houses for himself and his friends, he sought merely to take the best available and put it to work for them. Political or architectural, his labors neither aimed "at originality of principle or sentiment, nor [were they] yet copied from any particular and previous writing." They were, instead, "intended to be an expression of the American mind."[2]

When we come to Frank Lloyd Wright, we cross the threshold of another world. Science, technology, and industry had by their advances thrown into solution all the old verities of Jefferson's republic. A new world was waiting to be born, and with it, a new architecture. To its creation Wright contributed as much as any man alive. He has been called the inventor of the modern American house. Certainly, during a long and fruitful life, he brought to the suburban house a level of comfort and amenity which, before him, could have been found only at Newport or Fifth Avenue and a kind of domestic beauty which was entirely new. His houses have made available to the ordinary middle-class American family an environment of spacious ease and luminous urbanity, such as only the very rich could have enjoyed before.

Like Jefferson, though in a quite different context and at a higher level, he took the burgeoning material accomplishments of his world and put them to work for the emotional enrichment of our people generally.

When Wright began his architectural practice in Chicago, in the early 1890s, a basic change had already occurred in American life. The old, self-sufficient family of Jefferson's republic which produced most of the food it ate, the clothes it wore, the furniture it lived with, the very house that sheltered it—this family and this way of life were already declining. In that family's place was appearing a new kind of family of consumers which, instead of producing what it ate and wore, bought it with earned wages from the stores.

Today, beset with contemporary problems, we may tend to regret this change. We look back to this preindustrial way of life with a rosy nostalgia not very firmly bedded in fact. Today, the words "home-made" and "hand-made" are terms of praise, trade-marks of chic. We forget that, fifty or seventy-five years ago, these same words were terms of disparagement, of reproach and contempt. Now there were doubtless real merits to home-baked bread, home-cured meats, hand-woven cloth: but the hard and often noisome labor connected with their preparation was not one of them. Here we must take the word of our own grandmothers, who had to do this work and only too gladly gave it up. For them, housework meant the stupefying heat of the kitchen on a July day, the squalid labor of the wash tub, the stench and flies from the pig pen. The fact was that most homes were little factories and most wives were slaves to a sweatshop schedule. Under such conditions, most houses were uncomfortable to live in, unbeautiful to look at.

Here again we must take the testimony of the women. Why did they labor so hard to create *front* yards, *front* doors, *front* rooms if not to conceal the ugliness of the rear? Why this effort to create little islands

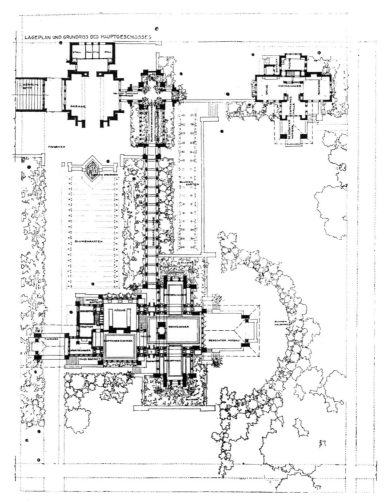

Plot plan, Martin residence, Buffalo, 1904. Frank Lloyd Wright, architect.

Block plan, typical suburban land platting, c.1880.

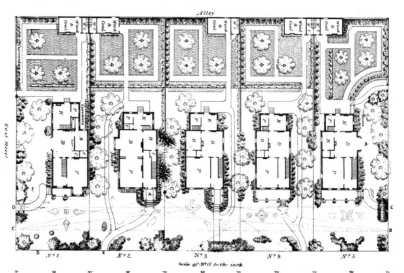

of peace and beauty if not for occasional escape from the grinding routine of preindustrial housekeeping? For those women, cleanliness meant a constant struggle: comfort they sometimes won, beauty almost never. No wonder, then, that they were turning with such enthusiasm to the labor-saving, comfort-making devices which American factories were turning out in the decade Frank Lloyd Wright began to work.

Thanks to industrialization, the never-ending drudgery of housekeeping was being lifted from the housewife's shoulders. The most degrading and stultifying processes of family sustenance were being mechanized, either in the factory or at home. The ordinary housewife was able, suddenly, to join the human race, to enjoy that comfort, leisure, and self-respect which had hitherto been the prerogative of rich, slave- or servant-attended women.

But there was another—and for architects an even more important—side to this coin. The same process which was removing from the house the causes of hard labor, inconvenience, and discomfort was also removing the causes of most of its ugliness. For the first time in history the home of the average family could be a thing of beauty. Not just the parlor or the front yard, but all of it, inside and out, could be an object of pleasure and delight.

We can say without fear of contradiction that Wright was the first American architect fully to comprehend this new fact, fully to exploit its exciting possibilities.

It would be nonsense, of course, to claim that Wright, in those early days of the new American house, was the only or even the first architect to use central heating, plumbing, electricity, and the like. His contemporaries used all these new things enthusiastically, but they forced them into the mold of old, conventional designs. They employed steam radiators but masked them behind Renaissance grilles; steel columns and beams, but sheathed them to look like wood or marble; modern plumbing fixtures, but panelled them to look like bishop's chairs.

Wright's role was of quite another order. He saw that all these developments, taken together, demanded nothing less than a totally new system of architectural expression. The old traditional forms simply could not contain the new reality; a new kind of beauty was called for. The same science and technology which had wrought such changes in the family life had also given the architect a whole new palette of building materials: structural steel, reinforced concrete, plywood, huge sheets of rolled plate glass. And Frank Lloyd Wright—almost alone it was Wright, in those early days after the retirement of his *lieber Meister*, Louis Sullivan—argued that these should be employed boldly, honestly, in new forms, and not tortured into traditional ones. As a result of this independent approach, Wright was able to make very important architectural contributions to design, many of which became standard elements in the modern house.

By 1900, everybody who could afford it demanded central heating—either hot air furnaces or steam heat. All the architects were quick to include it in their new houses, but only Wright saw its ultimate implication: that it made obsolete the old honey-comb plan of boxy, air-tight rooms strung like beads in a necklace. This had been a logical arrangement in cold climates so long as fireplaces and stoves were the only way of heating each room. But Wright was quick to see that, if all rooms could be kept equally comfortable with almost invisible heat sources, rooms could flow freely into one another. Doors and whole walls could be eliminated, rooms could dissolve into one another. The open plan was the result—the instrument which enabled Wright to create those splendid interior vistas for which his houses are justly famous.

By 1900, everyone was aware of the therapeutic value of sunshine and was demanding more of it in his house. Plate and rolled glass made possible windows of unprecedented size. But while other architects used more glass, they used it in conventional patterns, cutting up their sash into little Colonial rectangles, Elizabethan diamonds, or leaded Medieval bull's-eyes. Only Wright saw the dramatic possibilities of these huge transparent sheets. He saw that with them he could destroy the iron boundary between indoors and out. Here was another instrument of great power and beauty at his disposal; with it he could extend the living area to include not merely the enclosed area, but the terraces, porches, and gardens beyond. He thereby brought his interior space into a new and exciting proximity with nature.

By 1900, everyone was demanding electric lighting in his house. Its advantages over oil lamps and gas were obvious and immense. But electricity was not merely a substitute for kerosene or coal gas; it made possible a totally new concept of illumination. Instead of the niggardly pinpoints of earlier light sources, electricity made it possible to flood whole areas with light. Spaces could be modeled, forms dramatized, textures enhanced. Who besides Wright, in those early days, understood this? While the rest of the profession continued to mask their Mazda bulbs in fixtures of conventional form—candelabra, chandelier, and sconce— Wright went boldly ahead building the unadorned bulb into the very fabric of his house. Light itself, not just the fixture, became a source of pleasure and delight.

These are just three examples of Wright's electrifying touch, of his ability to transmute simple technological developments into new esthetic experiences. And if we turn to the more prosaic aspects of his houses, we see the same great talent at work. Take, as an instance, his kitchens. A whole series of developments had revolutionized this area, and he was by means the only man to see this. New ranges, sinks, dishwashers, refrigerators, cupboards, and counter-spaces were being used more and more.

But the same forces which had removed the ugly chores from the kitchen had also removed the servants. The cook who had formerly canned peaches in the kitchen was now canning them, at higher wages and shorter hours, in the factory. This meant that more housewives than ever would have to work in the kitchen. And this implied, in turn, that the kitchen must not only be labor-saving and convenient, it must also be as pleasant esthetically as the living room.

Moreover, if the wife was to spend a good part of her working day there she could not be isolated, exiled, from the rest of the family. Wright grasped this fact decades before his colleagues, and the steps he took to destroy the separation, psychic as well as physical, of the kitchen from the house have had a profound and benign effect upon the new American house.

In the catalogue for his 1954 Exhibition house, Wright said wryly that he would be accused of arrogance if he claimed that his early houses were "the first truly democratic expression of our democracy." Yet it is true that a distinguishing mark of his houses had, from the start, been their *modesty*. Even large and expensive ones such as the Coonley or the Kaufmann houses lack that brow-beating pretentiousness which was always the trademark of the great house, at least until the depression.

The terrace, Taliesin, Spring Green, Wisconsin. Frank Lloyd Wright, architect.

The living room, Taliesin.

Big or small, Wright's houses have always had the grace and urbanity of the mansion. Yet this is never the result of just shrinking the mansion down to cottage size, as the Amazon headhunter does his trophies. Many of his contemporaries tried that, but not Wright. Even his own house at Taliesin East, actually one of the largest country houses in America, is so demurely fitted into its terrain that its real size is never apparent—is, on the contrary, deliberately concealed. There *are* impressive, even majestic, vistas in these houses, but they are designed to delight the inhabitants, not to overawe the passerby.

All elements of a house were to Wright equally important and hence equally beautiful. It had no "front" and consequently could have no "back"—thereby dealing a mortal blow to the hypocrisy of the Victorian house with its "Queen Anne front and Mary Anne back."

Wright's houses were also, from the start, democratic in the choice of materials. The cost or rarity of a material was never, for him, an argument either for or against it. He could create interiors of magnificent warmth, of skin-stroking luxury, with the simplest materials—wood, brick, plaster—while his contemporaries were using imported marbles, cut velvets, and gold leaf with much less effect. How can one explain this? Wright says it was because they had no real feeling for the *nature* of materials; because of this they cut, carved, chiseled, clipped, painted, and stenciled. He, on the contrary, extracted from each material its peculiar properties and then expressed them clearly in the way he used them. The result was a lack of bombast and pretension which had not been seen since Jefferson's day.

Jefferson and Wright are linked, then, by this common quality—a vision of the splendid potentials of culture, a determination to employ it for the enrichment of the lives of their countrymen. They chose to do this not at the level of university or museum but at the level where they were most vitally involved—their houses. That their work was so widely accepted is the best measure of the correctness of their vision.

4. HORATIO GREENOUGH,
YANKEE FUNCTIONALIST

Had the nineteenth century followed the advice of the American sculptor, Horatio Greenough—instead of that of its favorite estheticians, Pugin, Ruskin, and Morris—its sorry record of tormented design might well have been telescoped, if not by-passed altogether. For this Yankee artist, in a series of essays published between 1843 and 1852, at the very dawn of American industrial production, foresaw both its promise and its dangers for American art and design. It was he, moreover, who first set forth for Americans the principal axioms of modern architecture. It was he, and not Louis Sullivan in the 1890s, who first formulated the notion that in architecture, as in nature, all form should derive from function. It was Greenough, and not Frank Lloyd Wright in the early 1900s, who first raised the demand that architectural ornament and embellishment should be an organic part of the structure. It was Greenough who, eighty years before Le Corbusier, pointed out that buildings should be regarded as machines, designed to produce comfort and convenience for their inhabitants. And it was he, and not the Walter Gropius of the pre-Hitler Bauhaus, who was first to declare that the men who built machines and ships were often closer to the essence of art than the professional artists themselves.

There is not the slightest reason to suppose that any of these four great figures of modern architecture ever heard of Greenough, much less that they had read his essays.[1] And the oblivion into which Greenough sank after his premature death in 1852, separating him from the very men who might have most profited from his thinking, completes the paradox of his career. For Greenough was not an architect but a sculptor—and not even, by modern standards, a very good sculptor. He was not a professional writer or critic, having taken up the pen only to defend himself when his early sculptures came under savage attack in this country for their nudity. He had no first-hand contact with modern industrial production, his whole adult life having been spent in non-industrialized Tuscany. Yet no one saw its potentials more clearly than he.[2] Harvard (where he graduated in 1825) taught him none of the anatomy, biology, and evolutionary theories which mark his adult knowledge; yet few artists have made a more deliberate effort to use science as a tool for understanding nature and mastering the problems of design.

That Greenough was an extremely well-informed man is clear from his writing. It is also clear from the comments of his contemporaries. "A man of large powers and various accomplishments," George Hilliard wrote of him, "in whom the practice of his art was but one mode of intellectual expression. . . . He has read and thought much upon art, and those laws of beauty which art interprets. His general cultivation is ripe and full. . . . No one could meet him without feeling that he was a superior man." [3] And the statesman Charles Sumner wrote in 1839 that "Greenough at Florence is a wonderful fellow, an accomplished man and a master of his art—I doubt not, the most accomplished artist alive." He was, Sumner found, "a thinker of great force and a scholar who does not trust to translations but goes to the great originals." [4] And Emerson, that cool New England sage, found "his face so handsome and his person so well formed . . . a superior man, ardent and eloquent, and all his opinions had elevation and magnanimity."[5] In fact, said Emerson, Greenough's was "quite the most magnanimous theory of art and artists I have ever chanced to hear from one of themselves." [6]

Elevated or not, however, effective theories of art do not come merely from wide reading. Theory must be checked against practice or, as Greenough put it, against "tangible, palpable, everyday truths." [7] Actually, his theories seem to have been slow in maturation, involving much pedestrian work in the studio. His speculations begin, necessarily, with the human figure in its two aspects—the general (or "ideal," as it was then called) and the particular (that is, the portrait). The latter constituted the bulk of the professional sculptor's market. And to this subject we find Greenough, like his American and Italian colleagues in Florence, paying the closest attention. Generally speaking, the criterion

47

in portraiture was a facsimile of the subject, a "speaking likeness," though the ladies commonly asked for dimples instead of pouches and the men occasionally for different types of beards or hair styles. The material was always Carrara marble—as white as paper, as anonymous as lard. It had a close, even texture without veining or flaws. It was as easily manipulated by the skilled Florentine carvers who actually did the work as was the clay or plaster in which the artist did his model. It was, in short, a three-dimensional equivalent of the daguerreotype so soon to be invented.[8]

In his marble portraiture, Greenough was strictly documentary. He was so successful that, by 1839, he felt compelled to raise his fees to one hundred napoleons per bust. "I care not if I never get any more orders of that sort. Our good folk think statues can be turned out like yards of sheeting."[9] And so they could—at least when his American clients came to his Florence studio. But, as his fame spread, he got an increasing number of commissions from good folk who did not come to sit for him but ordered by mail. The customary documentation in such cases consisted of "casts" (i.e., life masks or death masks), oil portraits, pencil sketches. These were not always adequate and this caused Greenough a conscientious concern. In a letter of August 1837, he observes "with disappointment that there is no portrait of Mrs. Emily Otis. How this happened, whether from Alexander's or Mr. Otis's unwillingness to have a good picture cross the water, I cannot decide; but this is sure, that I cannot risk a bust made from the cast alone. . . . What I have is useful but will not suffice."[10] By March of the following year, the missing portrait was in his hands. "With all its imperfections," he finds it of great use. In this same letter, he acknowledges receipt of a batch of sketches of Alexander Everett's child. But here the problem is too much data. "Had it been an old man's head, I would be sanguine; but these little milk sponges are so subtle in their forms, so difficult to copy under the most favorable circumstances, that I fear it will be labor lost."[11]

Often the art of elegant portraiture extended to the family pets. Greenough's research here is quite as careful as if it were for the portrait of a duchess. "I have begun Perkins's dog, and have had the very deuce of a time for want of a model. Madame Catalini's is dead and buried, and that of the Grand Duke dead and stuffed, and I don't know which is most entirely out of my line. I am going to send to Paris for a good lithograph which, with a St. Bernard specimen, must answer." [12]

The problem of accurate documentation always dogged him, even in his "ideal" works. Typical of the seriousness with which he approached his subject matter was his work on *The Rescue*, a monumental group ordered by President Van Buren in 1837 for the United States Capitol. Charles Sumner, who saw it half finished in the sculptor's studio, describes it thus:

The woman is on the ground, so that she does not conceal the Indian, who is naked (except for an accidental [sic!] fold about his loins); and the settler who appears above the savage, restraining his fury, is dressed in a hunter's shirt and cap. The passions are various—the child, the mother, the father, the husband, the savage, the defender, etc.; and all these various characters are blended in a group. [13]

The expression of these various passions had not come easily to Greenough; when Sumner saw the group, he had already been at work on it for a number of years. Nor did he consider it complete until 1851, when he added the family dog to the composition. [14] The figure of the Indian troubled him especially. Though he had met, admired and sketched a group of Cherokee chiefs in Washington in 1828, he did not trust his memory. He wrote repeatedly for documentation—"skulls, dresses, and drawings"—but to no avail. In 1842 he ran the risk "of being obliged to make my savage by guesswork or description, unless I get speedy relief." [15]

The Rescue differed from most "ideal" groups in that it dealt not with allegorical figures—a favorite subject of Victorian sculpture—but with actual events which had scarcely become history. His objective, therefore, was a kind of documentary realism. This interest is apparent even in his portraiture. His first studies for a group portrait of the Sears children proposed to show "the little daughter teaching her brother to read." And when the parents found this proposal "somewhat too matter-of-fact," Greenough then modeled in clay a composition "in which the daughter has a squirrel held by a string, and her brother is trying to make it play about." [16] This attempt at stop-watch action in a sculptural group reaches an apogee in Greenough's portrait of the Thompson brothers. This consisted of two life-size statues of the young lads, designed to occupy diagonally opposite corners of the

The Rescue, U.S. Capitol, Washington, 1851. Horatio Greenough, sculptor.

The Dying Abel, Pitti Palace, Florence, 1842. Giovanni Dupré, sculptor.

Thompson drawing room in Boston. One of the boys "stands with the shuttlecock ready to let drive at his brother, who is standing ready for it." The statues, he adds, seem "to please everybody highly, for the novelty and the expressive action." [17]

That such nonsculptural commitment to specific action was entirely successful esthetically, even for a contemporary audience, we may question. Today, it makes one either smile or flinch. And yet such experiments show us Greenough's attempts to free sculpture from the dead grip of neo-Classicism, preparing the way for greater freedom in both subject matter and formal composition. Whatever his accomplishments here, his ambitions extended far beyond mere technical invention. He had, in fact, contempt for those *tours de force* so common in Victorian art whose mechanical ingenuity "constitutes their sole source of interest. The achievement here has no fruit or result, it [stands] alone and naked." Technical dexterity, he says, is no guarantee of great art:

The Flemings devoted to the exact image of an oyster floating in its shell, or a wineglass twinkling in the light, more apparent delicacy of the hand and eye than the Italians had, when they dared to draw the profile of Christ. [Yet] Beato Angelico takes you to heaven with less drawing and color than those Dutchmen required to show you a butcher shop. . . . The real difficulty both in Art and Letters seems to be not to do—but to know what to do and where to stop. [18]

In his revolt against neo-Classicism, Greenough had the company of his sculptural contemporaries in Florence—the Americans, Powers and Crawford; the Italians, Bartolini and Dupré. Even the Grand Ducal *Accademia delle Belle Arte*, in fact, was the scene of a revolution. Dupré, in his memoirs, writes that when Lorenzo Bartolini was appointed Master of Sculpture in 1841 "he took possession of the school with the air of a conqueror. . . . He prohibited all study from statues, and restricted the whole system of teaching to an imitation of nature only; and he pushed this principle so far that he introduced a hunchback into the school and made the young students copy him. This daring novelty raised a shout of indignation." [19]

Giovanni Dupré was himself the center of the same controversy when his sculpture, *The Dying Abel*, was first shown at the Academy in the fall of 1842. "Its truth to nature . . . made a great impression

51

upon the public." It was so accurate a picture of the young model, in fact, that other artists claimed it was a mere cast from life—not art at all. These men, said Dupré, one night after school had closed

> obliged the model, Antonio Petrai, to undress and, laying him down in the same position as the statue, they proceeded with compasses and strips of paper to take all the measures of his body in length and breadth. Naturally, they did not agree in a single measure; for without intending to or thinking about it, I had made my statue four fingers taller and two fingers narrower across the back.[20]

Thus cleared of fraud, Dupré was further vindicated when Bartolini, returning for a forgotten umbrella, discovered the men with their tape measures. All Florence laughed at their discomfiture.

In Greenough's first important public commission, the *George Washington* ordered by the United States government for the Capitol Rotunda,[21] we begin to see the special qualities of his mind, if not his art. Here he is confronted with a tantalizing mixture of the ideal and the documentary. The statue, by definition, must be heroic, but it must also be Washington. Thus both rationalization and research are called for. "I have followed [Houdon's head of Washington] closely" he writes his brother,[22] and he has also studied closely all the painted portraits, and he is satisfied with the excellence of his authorities "since there is little difference in them but that of age." Like all the other portraitists, he ignored the smallpox scars with which Washington's face was pitted. Like them, too, he accepted the prognathous jaw produced by Dr. Greenwood's set of false teeth.[23] Some liberties were, however, necessary. He "found it necessary, while adhering to the way of dressing the hair which you observe in the portraits of Washington, to open and loosen it more about the head. A smooth head looks weak and mean," he feels, when enlarged to heroic proportions.[24]

So far, the work was largely documentary. But when it came to deciding how to clothe the figure, Greenough found himself in a quandary. Artistically, the problem of costume was two-pronged. On the one hand, *any* clothing concealed the human figure beneath it; on the other, *all* of it worked against the artist's ambition for the monumental, the timeless, the heroic. The sculptor aspired to the essential: every act of the *couturier* and the tailor was toward the specific, the topical.

Their very craft made certain that, tomorrow or the day after, the person dressed by them would be subjected to the merciless ridicule of ever-changing fashion. Greenough had anticipated this problem very early in his work on the Washington: in 1834 he had already raised the question with his friend the painter S. F. B. Morse:

If people would [only] consider the abstract nature of sculpture . . . they would cease to look to it for information on points which are better explained by other arts, in other ways. They would as soon expect to hear Washington's dress described in a Fourth of July oration as to see it sculptured in an epic statue.[25]

Thus he chose the most generalized costume available. Thanks to the Classic Revival atmosphere of the late 1830s and early 1840s, the decision to dress the President in a Roman toga was acceptable. But the decision to drop the toga from the shoulder to the waist was fraught with peril. Nudity was dangerous, as he had learned from the furor which greeted the public showing of his *Chanting Cherubs* in Boston in 1831. Yet it was nude to the waist that Greenough elected to sculpt him. He felt that he had no choice:

Had I been ordered to make a statue for a square or other similar situation in the metropolis, I should have represented Washington on horseback, and in his usual dress, and have made my work a purely historical one. I have [instead] treated the subject poetically, and I confess I should feel pain at seeing it placed in direct and flagrant contrast with every day life.[26]

As expected, the storm broke when the statue was unveiled. Though the sculptor was not present to defend it, he had stalwart friends who were. They did their best. Alexander Everett wrote: "to preserve the costume of the period, already out of fashion, would have been unsuitable. . . . The colossal size, the antique drapery, the more youthful air of the face are circumstances which, without impairing the truth to nature, increase very much the moral impression, and instead of furnishing grounds of objection, are positive merits of high importance."[27] George Calvert wrote from Newport: "If the artist clothes him with the toga of civil authority, he represents the great statesman; if with uniform and spurs, the great general. . . . He was both; but he was more than both. . . . To invest the colossal image of so towering, so everlasting a man, with the insignia of temporary office is to fail in

George Washington, Smithsonian Institution, Washington, D.C., c.1841. Horatio Greenough, sculptor.

presenting a complete image of him." [28] And Edward Everett, the orator, thundered this eulogium: "I regard Greenough's *Washington* as one of the greatest works of sculpture of modern times . . . whether we consider the purity of the taste, the loftiness of the conception, the truth of the character, or, what we must own we feel less able to judge of, the accuracy of anatomical study and mechanical skill." [29]

But these loyal friends were side-stepping the central issue. It was nudity, not anachronism, which outraged Washington society. The irate Congressmen were shocked not by the toga but by the powerful, masculine torso it exposed. Greenough understood the issue[30] and tackled it head on. He recalled that "the infantine forms" of his *Chanting Cherubs* "had roused an outcry of censure which . . . all the harlot dancers who have found an El Dorado in these Atlantic cities have failed to reawaken." Now, a decade later, history repeats itself: "The same purblind squeamishness, which gazed without alarm at the lascivious fandango, awoke with a roar at the colossal nakedness of Washington's manly breast." [31]

This purblind squeamishness, this refusal to face the facts of the body and the beauty of the naked human form, disturbed Greenough more and more. "The assertion that the human body is other than a fit exponent and symbol of the human being is a falsehood. . . . In nakedness I behold the majesty of the essential, instead of the trappings of pretension." [32] And this morbid, mincing puritanism "which has cloaked and crippled and smothered the human body" [33] is precisely what produces immorality. Even the "harlot dancer" must be understood in this light. Though Greenough shares his period's inability to distinguish between a professional prostitute and a professional dancer, he comes eloquently to the defense of both. "Feeling a void in our hearts, amid the negative requirements of the lawgiver and the priest, we ask the spectacle at least of untrammelled life, and hire the dancing girl to give [us] a vicarious grace and joy [which has been] driven from among us by a sour and one-sided dogma." There *is* sin here, Greenough tells us, grievous sin—"not in the light of the eye that flashes, not in the music of that frame that takes captive of the senses, not in the panting of that perhaps virgin bosom—but in the hireling divorce of these phenomena from their normal and organic sequences in human life. *There* lies the prostitution."[34]

Thus, by the terms of his own logic, Greenough is led directly from a defense of Washington's "manly breast" to that of the "perhaps virgin bosom" of the dancer. Here the arguments for nudity are simultaneously ethical and esthetic, but both derive, in turn, from strictly functional considerations. He attacked Victorian dress not only because it was less beautiful than the body it concealed but also because it impaired the movement, comfort, even the health, of that body. In a pungent little essay not published until after his death he asked:

Has the cravat ever been invented that would allow the wearer to turn his head left or right, and raise or depress his chin, without the body's feeling a crippled sensation? Observe the beautiful play of the shoulder blade in a naked figure, how the collarbone allows it to come forward, and how the cowl muscle and trapezoid pull it back. Can these motions be made in a coat?

The absurdity of men's clothing! "Strap your pantaloons over your shoulders to keep them up, and under your feet to keep them down; complete the work by a pair of boots that were fitted when your feet were cool." Dress yourself thus and then try to walk with the ease, grace, or comfort that the Creator intended!

Of course, as a practical matter, he was not arguing for the same nudity in people that he demanded in epic sculpture. On the contrary, climate might require clothing even where convention did not. What he sought in civilized dress was the same respect for physiological necessity and climatic fact that he found in primitive cultures like those of the Bedouin or the American Indian. There, he says,

. . . man is wise—he feels the sting of want and is in earnest. Observe how the people of the [Near] East have consulted the laws of color, that their dress might not absorb the sun's rays; how they have contrived to wear ample garments and yet allow the air a passage to their skins.

For the same common sense response to reality he admires the Indian's footgear: "Observe [his] moccasin, that shields his sole from thorns, yet is pliant enough to grip the ground." [35]

In the first decade of Victoria's reign, this kind of basic reexamination of the problems of nudity and dress is remarkable for its courage and candor, even though, as he says, "God's care upholds us with so many pounds to the square inch of pressure on every side." [36] But his exploration of human beauty was not only ethical. He was, after all, a

56

sculptor, and he explores his subject matter not merely as one who has drawn from the casts of the *Accademia*[37] but also as an anatomist who had worked in the dissecting rooms of the medical school in Florence. And he checked and rechecked his evolving theory of beauty against palpable biological fact.

Each historical period tends to formulate a set of esthetic standards which it imagines to be absolute. But the rejection of these standards by the most advanced minds of that epoch promptly becomes almost ritual. The standards of Greenough's young manhood had been precisely defined by late eighteenth-century estheticians, especially by the Englishman Edmund Burke in his monumental book, *A Philosophical Enquiry into the Origin of our Ideas of the Sublime and Beautiful.* The wide popularity of this book forced a response from Greenough; and the way in which his observation and practice illuminated his theory is wonderfully clear in his essay, *Burke on the Beautiful.* One by one he takes Burke's meager absolutes—smoothness, smallness, delicacy, etc.—and demolishes them. Smoothness, for example: there are many smoothnesses.

It is a relative quality . . . the smoothness of the eyeball is, on the one hand, a ball-and-socket smoothness like that of the head of the femur and the acetabulum, a lubricated smoothness. It is, on the other hand, a crystalline smoothness, related to the function of transmitting light and color. The smoothness of cutlery, as it comes from the hand of the artisan, is an organic smoothness. The perfection of the polish proclaims the entireness of the promise. It begins to lose that polish as soon as its action commences and at last retains mainly the beauty of form.[38]

Smallness of scale? Delicacy of color? But these describe the nauseous skin disease of impetigo quite as accurately as they do the painting of Boucher. Burke's absolutes, in short, are absolutely relative.

In comments like these, we begin to see the ground upon which Greenough stood. Both as artist and as critic, he is fighting his way through a jungle of esthetic formalism. Independent beauty does not exist: the periwig, the bound foot, the long fingernail—these are creatures of convention, "ridiculous except in the time, place, and circumstances that gave them value."[39] Nor can he find any abstract form that is universally beautiful. Hogarth's line of beauty, the S-curve, is

57

indeed beautiful on the horse's flank, "but transfer it to his metatarsal bone and you have a cripple." [40] Everything is relative.

If Greenough's passionate interest in the forms and processes of life protected him from the prudery of his Puritan ancestors, it was equally effective against the squeamish romanticism of his Transcendentalist friends. It was the very heyday of cemetery art, though nobody dared look death in the face. Nothing was considered more "elevating," more "refined," than a Sunday afternoon stroll through Mt. Auburn (if one lived in Boston) or the English Cemeteries (if one lived in Florence or Rome) or—most famous of all for its sculpture, both ideal and portrait—the fashionable Cimiterio di Staglione in Genoa. Yet, as Greenough pointed out, despite a morbid interest in *pompe funébre,* "the sight of a skull, whether of man or beast," caused "an instinctive horror" to most Victorians. But scientists had no such revulsion "because they have minutely investigated its relation to *life.* All its forms, surfaces and dimensions speak of its former contents, vestures and capacities." For such men "that pale, spheroidal dome is a model of the globe, those lackluster eyeless bones . . . echo the distant sun." [41]

His interest extends to all forms of life. All he finds equally remarkable, and all he discusses in terms of scientific precision. He shares his period's fondness for the lily but he speculates that its beauty must have a functional origin. "It is arrayed in heavenly beauty because it is organized, both in shape and color, to dose the germ of future lilies with atmospheric and solar influence." [42] "Since the tints, as well as the forms, of plants and flowers are shown to have an organic significance and value," [43] a functional necessity lies behind their beauty. This, he begins to generalize, must be true throughout nature. Even in the depths of the ocean he finds that submarine animals are furnished "with complicated glands and absorbents to nourish those dyes" which give them their beautiful colors. And he cannot delude himself into thinking that all this is done merely "to charm my idle eye as they are tossed in disorganized ruin upon the beach." [44]

Everywhere he finds the modification of the organism to meet its environment. If submarine life is often blind and eyeless, the reason is not far to seek. "The eye is the creature of the sun: for I find it made in [the sun's] own image, and I seek it in vain in such fishes, for instance, as know him not." [45] "I find the length of the vertebrae of the neck in grazing quadrupeds increased, so as to bring the incisors to the grass; I find the vertebrae shortened in beasts of prey, in order to enable the brute to bear away his victims; if I find the wading birds on stilts, the strictly aquatic birds with paddles; if, in pushing still further the investigation, I find color arrayed either for disguise or aggression, [then] I feel justified in taking the ground that organization is the primal law of structure." [46] Life, he begins to understand, is *process*. "The significance of yesterday, today and tomorrow is this, that we are in a state of development" and this "law of development . . . can only be withstood by perishing." [47] What is the direction of this development? What else but the "unflinching adaption of forms to functions"?

This concept of organic evolution, formulated so clearly and applied so fruitfully, illuminates Greenough's whole field of vision a good ten years before the publication of Charles Darwin's *Origin of Species* in 1859. Though he might have been unique among artists in thinking thus, his speculations would not have seemed so novel to the natural scientists, from which they clearly derived. There he would have been responding (in much the same way and at much the same time) as were Alfred R. Wallace and Darwin to a century of discovery and speculation about the origins of life. Though Greenough was always generous in acknowledging his indebtedness to others, he has left us little direct information here. If we are to take Sumner's estimate literally ("he does not trust to translations but goes to the great originals") then we can assume that his references to Buffon and Lamarck show first-hand familiarity with the great body of French literature on the subject of evolution. In Buffon he would have found it described as a retrograde process for all forms of life but man; in Lamarck he would have found it described as a progressive force, with the theory of environmental adaptation clearly formulated; in Saint-Hilaire he would have found the thrilling picture of the animal kingdom as a single unbroken series of structurally related organisms.

Like most of the foreign colony of Florence, Greenough belonged to the private library and reading rooms run by a leading figure of the Tuscan intelligentsia, Gian Pietro Vieussieux, in whose *Gabinetto* he would have found Samuel Coleridge, with his special brand of metaphysical functionalism in art. There, too, he may well have read

Chambers's *Vestiges of the Natural History of Creation.*[48] Emerson, with whom he checked most of his theories in this area, had "found it a good approximation to that book we have wanted so long and which so many attempts have been made to write. . . . [Chambers] has outdone all the rest in breadth and boldness."[49] To modern eyes, however, Chambers seems anything but bold in his anxiety to side-step any possible conflict with organized religion. The first edition was published anonymously, with the characteristically Victorian apologia for scientific advance that "the Divine Author of Nature could never be truly injured by any additional insight we might gain into His works and ways." The *Vestiges,* nevertheless, was a popular presentation of pre-Darwinian theory with some surprisingly up-to-date concepts of comparative anatomy such as the one that "the changes of an embryo fell little short of the advances from species to species."[50] From literature such as this, Greenough derived his functionalist theory.

If function is the source of form in nature, how could it be otherwise in art? "We [men] must make the shapes, and can only effect this by mastering the principles."[51] And we can do this only by following nature's principles: "first, by strict adaptation of forms to functions; second, by the gradual elimination of all that is irrelevant and impertinent."[52] How true this had always been of human artifacts became very clear to him, one January day in 1843, when he and Ralph Waldo Emerson went to the Patent Office in Washington to see a newly mounted exhibit of "curios" from the South Seas. They stopped to admire a ceremonial war club, and Greenough reconstructs the process by which the Polynesian warrior had arrived at its finished form. "His first thought is of its use. His first efforts pare the long shaft, and mold the convenient handle; then the heavier end gradually takes the edge that cuts, while it retains the weight that stuns. His idle hour [then] divides its surface by lines and curves, or embosses it with figures that please his eye or are linked with his superstitions."[53]

It is sufficiently notable that a Protestant American, in the very decade when his missionaries were launching a great campaign to bring civilization to "the heathen head hunter," could view his instrument with such detachment. That he could actually view it as a work of art seems, in the context, remarkable. He praises it for "its effective shape, its Etruscan-like quaintness, its graceful form and subtle outline. We admire," he says, "and yet we neglect the lesson it might teach." [54] What, for a West in the throes of the industrial revolution, was this lesson? He formulates it with electrifying precision:

If we compare the form of a newly invented machine with the perfected type of the same instrument, we observe, as we trace it through the phases of improvement, how weight is shaken off where strength is less needed, how functions are made to approach without impeding each other, how straight becomes curved, and the curve is straightened, till the straggling and cumbersome becomes the compact, effective, and beautiful engine. [55]

Today, a quarter of a century after the Bauhaus, this is a familiar thesis, subscribed to (if not always followed) by designers the world over. But where, among Greenough's contemporaries, can one find a similar point of view? Where, in the decade of Barry's Houses of Parliament, can one find another architectural critic whose theory of building is this:

. . . a scientific arrangement of spaces and forms [adapted] to functions and to site; an emphasis of features proportioned to their *gradated* importance in function; colour and ornament to be decided and arranged and varied by strictly organic laws, having a distinct reason for each decision; and the entire and immediate banishment of all make believe. [56]

In measuring the inadequacies of the new architecture around him, he adopts the objective standards of technology and engineering. In fact, for all practical purposes, buildings *"may be called machines,* (my italics, JMF) each individual of which must be formed with reference to the abstract type of its species."[57] Why not design them accordingly?

No longer could the mere tyro huddle together a crowd of ill-arranged, ill-lighted and stifled rooms and, masking the chaos behind the sneaking copy of a Greek façade,[58] usurp the name of architect. If this anatomic connection and proportion has been attained in ships, in machines and . . . in such buildings as made a departure from its fatal, as in bridges and in scaffolding, why should we fear its immediate use in all construction?[59]

If only architects would follow the design principles of the Yankee Clipper ships! Here is

the result of the manly use of plain good sense, so like that of taste, and

The graceful American sailing ships and the speedy trotting wagons were examples of the anonymous, industrialized design that Greenough hailed as pointing the way to the future.

genius too. . . . Mark the majestic form of her hull as she rushes through the water, observe the graceful transition from round to flat, the grasp of her keel, the leap of her bows, the symmetry and rich tracery of her spars and rigging and those grand wind muscles, her sails! Behold an organization second only to that of an animal. . . . What academy of design, what research of connoisseurship, what imitation of the Greeks produced this marvel of construction? Here is the result of the study of man upon the great deep, where Nature spake the laws of building, not in the feather and the flower, but in wind and wave, and he bent all his mind to hear and to obey.[60]

As he grew older, Greenough became increasingly impatient with theory—at least as it was cultivated in the academies. Himself a theoretician of the most polished sort, he was nevertheless dismayed at the kind of sterile formalism it led to in art and architecture when divorced from practice. In a wonderful argument for the experimental method, penned in the last year of his life, he likens theory to the blacksmith's hammer, practice to his anvil:

The anvil below strikes as hard as [the hammer] above and is steadier, for it stands on that which talk cannot reach. . . . Not from Pliny's page or Buffon's elaborations did man learn the mystery of tiger's tooth or fang of deadly rattlesnake. The deadly nightshade "never told her love" to the eye, twas in the writhing stomach of experience that she talked the true, catholic tongue.

And then, in a change of subject more apparent than real, he lashes out at Fourierism, that same Utopian doctrine which he had ridiculed so many years before, in Paris, when his young friend Albert Brisbane had fallen under its spell. But it is actually all dogma that he is attacking—it is "procrustean, monomaniacal." He compares it to an undertaker: "I hate thy straight lines and thy arrangements for the elbows, and the lid that fits over all, with the screws ready in thy hands."[61]

Thus, like Gropius 80 years later, Greenough realizes that the old aristocratic academies will never produce the designers of the new epoch. New institutions will be required, and they must learn from industry.

The men who have reduced locomotion to its simplest elements, in the trotting wagon and the yacht *America,* are nearer to Athens at this moment than they who would bend the Greek temple to every use. I contend for Greek principles, not Greek things. If a flat sail goes nearest wind, a bellying sail,

63

though picturesque, must be given up. The slender harness and tall gaunt wheels [of the trotting wagon] are not only effective, they are beautiful— for they respect the beauty of the horse and do not uselessly task him.[62]

From this, it followed that "the mechanics of the United States have already outstripped the artists and have, by their bold and unflinching adaptation, entered the true track and hold up the light for all who operate for American wants."[63]

Such analogies, drawn from primitive weapons and modern machines alike, are rare enough in a nineteenth-century artist and critic; but the attitude towards the craftsman behind them—Polynesian head-hunter or Newburyport shipwright—is, for a nineteenth-century gentleman, rarer still. It displays none of that endemic snobbery which vitiates so much of the century's critical opinion, and it grows directly from Greenough's socio-political perspectives. In his confidence in science and democracy he stands in direct opposition to men like Ruskin.[64] He was, like Jefferson, a thorough-going, buoyant democrat, with faith in the taste and ability of the common people. For it was they who "have decided the rank of the statesmen, the poets and the artists of the world. It is the great multitude for whom all really great things are done, and said, and suffered. The great multitude deserves the best of everything and, in the long run, is the best judge of it."[65]

5. OUR DOMESTICATED UTOPIANS

No other country on earth ever painted so many Utopias—so comprehensive in coverage, yet so domestic in scale; so tidily balancing plumbing and poetry, life on earth with life hereafter, with clean fires and fresh quilts to temper the cosmic winds. The prophets were often male—George Rapp, Robert Owen, Edward Bellamy, Frank Lloyd Wright—but their programs were generally quite as domestic and woman-oriented as this one by Catharine Esther Beecher:

Let us suppose a colony of cultivated and Christian people, having abundant wealth . . . emigrating to some of the beautiful Southern uplands . . . as picturesque as those of New England [but] where the temperature rarely reaches 90 degrees in summer, and in winter rarely sinks below the freezing point, so that outdoor labor goes on all year; where the fertile soil is easily worked; where rich tropical fruits and flowers abound; where cotton and silk can be raised by children around their home; where the produce of vineyards and orchards find steady markets by railroads ready-made. Suppose such a colony, with a central church and schoolroom, library, hall for sports, and a common laundry (taking the most trying part of domestic labor from each house)—suppose each family to train the children to labor with the hands as a healthful and honorable duty. . . . Suppose all this—which is perfectly practicable—would not the enjoyment of this life be increased and also abundant treasures laid up in heaven?[1]

The time is 1869; the place is 69 West 38th Street in Manhattan; the writer a peripatetic New England feminist; the concept is quintessentially American. This juxtaposition of tropic fruits and railroads to market; of central churches and central laundries; of silk and cotton growing in the dooryard but with docile children instead of unwilling slaves to pick it—where else but in nineteenth-century America could such a combination be found? It is a doll house Utopia, at once sagacious and saccharine, poignant and petty, progressive and ineffably *petit bourgeois*. No one but an American woman could have invented it (the Utopia of Joseph Smith, the Mormon leader, did not differ greatly from it except in a somewhat wider distribution of housework and sexual intercourse among the women). And it was just such women, with just such perspectives, who gave the modern American family and the modern American home their characteristic shapes.

It was inevitable that all these Utopias should be, without exception, of either New England or Midwestern origin, for literacy was the precondition of their development. The mistress of a Louisiana plantation had no real cause for complaint as far as household drudgery was concerned. The black slave woman or the white mountaineer wife, on the other hand, was illiterate—she could not have read the Utopian tracts even in the unlikely chance that the tracts should penetrate the sealed and airless prison house of the South. And this was in the highest degree unlikely, as Southern legislators themselves were fond of boasting. The Virginia slaveholders had "as far as possible closed every avenue by which light might enter" the mind of the slave.[2] And the South Carolinians, "by reason of an efficient police and judicious internal legislation" were able to check "the fanatic and incendiary within our limits" and arrest "the torrent of pamphlets and tracts [of] the abolition presses of the North . . . the moment it reaches our frontier."[3]

But Northern reformers saw the connection between abolitionism and women's rights. Harriet Beecher Stowe had immortalized the double enslavement of pigmentation and sex in her grim and two-dimensional *Uncle Tom's Cabin;* and sister Catharine understood it, too, though her response was oblique, as we shall see. And the slovenliness and waste of Southern life, no less than its cruelty and injustice, drew the fire of other feminists. Julia Ward Howe, that model of brisk New England sanity, has left us this acid-etched account:

The whites stand around with their hands in their breeches pockets, and the blacks are helping them do nothing. Fences are down, doors are ajar, filth is in the streets, foul odors in the air, confusion and neglect are everywhere. Go into a house late at night, they are all lounging about, too lazy to go to bed; go in the morning, they are all yawning in bed, too lazy to get up. No one has prescribed duties—the master scolds and drives, the slave dawdles and shirks; and if anything *must* be done, it takes one white longer to hunt up two Negroes and force them to do it than it would take one uncorrupted [Yankee] to finish it alone.[4]

Nevertheless, the conditions of life for most American women were extremely difficult, and feminine protest against them rose steadily throughout the nineteenth century. The militancy of the suffragist Susan Anthony stemmed precisely from her remembered childhood. Her mother, married in 1817 to a New England millowner, had boarded eleven of her husband's mill girls the summer that her third child was born. She had done all the cooking, washing, and ironing with no help except part-time help from a 13-year-old school girl. The summer that Susan was twelve, she remembered in later years, her mother boarded ten or twelve brick-burners (while brick was being burned for their new house) in addition to the mill hands. Frontier wives would have fared even worse, though there the stupefying isolation led one woman to say that she had felt "lonesome until she had half a dozen children about her. She did not begin to feel crowded in the single room until the second dozen began coming."[5]

Female dissatisfaction may have generated the pressure for change, but it was usually the men who wrote the tracts. These offered a whole spectrum of choice: Albert Brisbane with his Phalanx, Joseph Smith with his seraglio, William Miller with his Ascension Robes, George Ripley with his tragi-comic Brook Farm. Brisbane, attempting to domesticate Fourier on the American scene, had the most imposing philosophical structure for a new society, holding that

the present social mechanism is not adapted to the nature of man and his passions; that it perverts, misdirects and develops them subversively and that the selfishness, oppression, injustice and crime now prevalent are attributable to this and not to any inborn, inherent depravity in the human being himself.[6]

But his coolly logical panacea, which had once offended Greenough, now frightened the Boston reformers. To them, Brisbane's scheme "seemed to have no spiritual depth of foundation; his proposition to imprison man in a Phalanx was rejected; his omission of moral freedom in the scheme was resented; no sincerity, no keenness of criticism, no exposure of existing evils" could conceal from those skittish New Englanders the fact that Brisbane-Fourier planned to use them in a new society as if they were "piles of brick or lumps of mortar."[7] They turned instead to the Transcendentalists who, under the leadership of George

Ripley, inaugurated Brook Farm on March 29, 1841. Its Constitution attempted to steer an Emersonian middle course between the lofty idealism of the French socialists and the practicality of the Yankee blacksmith. Thus the Brook Farm Associates undertook to unite

in order more effectually to promote the general purposes of human culture; to establish the external relations of life on a basis of wisdom and purity; to apply the principles of justice and love to our social organization in accordance with the laws of Divine Providence . . . to prevent the exercise of worldly anxiety by the competent supply of our necessary wants . . . the means of physical support and of spiritual progress.[8]

But this tidy balance between the ideal and the practical did not succeed in catching Emerson (who cagily stepped aside at the last moment) or Margaret Fuller (who did not like milking cows) or Nat Hawthorne (who did not like Margaret). Ripley's efforts collapsed after six years, and this would have been no surprise to Catharine Beecher or to Mrs. Lydia Maria Child, both of whom would have known that salvation lay much nearer to hand. Mrs. Child's book had appeared in 1835, seven years before Miss Beecher's first book, *Domestic Economy*. Much less ambitious than the latter, it was correspondingly more direct. Even the title and subtitle are revealing: *The American Frugal Housewife: For those who are not ashamed of economy.* Mrs. Child's Utopia is aggressively small, thrifty, and domestic. She is writing, she says on the very first page, "for the poor . . . to teach how money can be saved, not how it can be enjoyed. . . . The true economy of housekeeping is simply the art of gathering up all the fragments, so that nothing is lost. I mean *time* as well as *material*."[9]

The American Frugal Housewife is a cook book combined with a text on household chemistry and a domestic pharmacopoeia, and it has that air of crisp infallibility which has marked women's magazines ever since. Nothing dismays Mrs. Child: how to keep the pump from freezing (wrap it in a horse blanket); how to clean kid gloves (wash in cream of tartar); how to cure "inveterate" cancer (apply potash and tar). Her section on cooking is, like the rest of the book, a very bible of improvisation and make-do. Use the cheapest cuts of meat, calf's liver at two cents a pound. Save suet for soap. Avoid green fruit pies ("dear pies," she calls them) because they take so much expensive sugar. For the same reason, she is opposed to preserved fruits. "Economical people will seldom use preserves, except for sickness. They are unhealthy, expensive, and useless to those who are well."[10]

Lydia Maria Child wrote for big families whose satisfactions came from virtuous abnegation, not satiety. She was well aware that children could be a dreadful liability unless, by putting them to work, they were converted into an asset. This had the double advantage of saving them from the temptations of idleness and of helping the family, "every member of which should be employed, either in earning or saving money."[11] When other household chores were exhausted, children could be kept out of mischief by making patchwork quilts or knitting or—where the family kept geese or turkeys—by making feather fans. It was a great deal better, she felt sure, "for boys and girls to be picking blackberries at 6¢ a quart, than to be wearing out their clothes in useless play."[12] She is remorselessly energetic. Only once does she relent from this ferocious celebration of penury, when (with, we can imagine, a glass of her own raspberry shrub and a turkey-wing fan against the flies) she exclaims: "And are not *we* becoming luxurious and idle? Look at our steamboats, stages, and taverns!"[13] Always she writes with that heartbreaking mixture of snobbish gentility and pathetically transparent bravado which is the hallmark of the nineteenth-century woman with her own living to make.

Thus Catharine Beecher, when she came to paint her own Utopia, had a wide and established tradition upon which to draw. Though she clearly belongs to the same phylum as Lydia Maria Child, her own system is unique in both its power and its narrowness. A remarkable woman—daughter of Lyman, sister of the trenchant Mrs. Stowe and the eloquent pastor Henry Ward—Catharine Esther lived until May 10, 1878. But she had been born long before, in 1800, and had been mistress of her own school in Hartford at the age of 23, at a time when teaching was almost the only occupation open to a respectable middle-class woman. She was not the first woman to teach nor the first to teach girls only; but she was the first to seize upon female education as the instrument of female liberation. The Hartford Female Seminary was but one of the three such instruments she would personally construct—the Western Female Institute in Cincinnati (1833) and the Milwaukee Female College (1853) were the others—and of the dozens upon which she would lavish funds and advice. But already in 1827 she was drawing

69

general conclusions from her experience and publishing papers on the inadequacies of female education—the trashy curricula, poorly trained and underpaid teachers, makeshift school plant and equipment. Even today, a century and a quarter later, her observations are striking for their clarity and common sense.

However, her vigorous imagination leaped much further ahead than mere educational reform. She seized upon the formal education of women as the means of raising them to the status of professional men. She defined "the woman's profession" as the practice of child-bearing, child-rearing, and housekeeping; and she would free woman from thralldom to the male by the simple expedient of training for that profession exactly as men did for medicine or law. Thus, for Miss Beecher, the whole appartus of teachers, texts, and training was merely a *means;* her ultimate goal was far more ambitious. At the same time, the curricula of her schools were masterpieces of hard-headed realism. She built up a series of courses in child-care, calisthenics, cookery, and housekeeping into the disciplines we call "domestic science" today. These theories got their first comprehensive exposition in her book, *A Treatise on Domestic Economy.* And from this work, first published in 1842, we can see how clearly her vision encompassed the terrain before her.

The liberation of woman depended in large measure upon industrialization; and industrialization was the basic fact of the opening of the Midwest. One might almost say that the plow that would break the Plains would have to be the steam-powered gang plow. To settle the prairies, it would be necessary simultaneously to industrialize them. The two processes ran parallel here, unencumbered by old towns and buildings, fixed concepts, and frozen practices. They were to have profound repercussions on the family structure, the position of the wife, the fabric of the house. And Catharine was there, at the height of her faculties, to observe and record them. She had moved to Cincinnati with her family in 1832, and much of her subsequent life was spent criss-crossing the Midwest. She was in Illinois in 1832; in Iowa in 1848; at Quincy, Illinois, in 1849; in Milwaukee the same year; back in Dubuque in 1853. Physically and socially, the Midwest was familiar terrain.

Not only did these forces operate most clearly and decisively in the Midwest. Their consequences, in both technical and architectural terms, are first visible there. It is not accidental that the economy which mechanized wheat farming and meat packing would also turn to the mass production of domestic ranges and furnaces, of washing machines and mechanical carpet cleaners, of home canning and mechanical refrigeration, of the balloon frame and the prefabricated house. Time- and labor-saving devices in the fields were closely paralleled inside the farm house; what the farmer demanded, the wife soon shared. Thus a direct line of causality connects McCormick's first reaper with Frank Lloyd Wright's first Prairie houses.

The impact of industrialism upon the house expressed itself at two different levels. It radically altered the conditions of life and work, and hence the exterior social and economic landscape, the community in which the house existed. At the same time, it remorselessly altered the internal character of the house itself, whether by adding or removing housekeeping functions or by altering the very materials out of which it was built and furnished. In her books, both the 1842 volume and again in the greatly expanded version of 1869, Catharine Beecher published plans and details of "ideal" houses which mirror this development very clearly.

The designs she gives us as the architectural expression of her 1842 Utopia are surprisingly orthodox. For all her developing theories of domestic economy, which she proposes to teach at the college level like dentistry or law, her houses show as yet very little response to such theories. In plan and elevation, they correspond very closely to the Greek Revival idiom so popular in the Western Reserve in the early 1840s. Her favorite, it is true, has a "Gothic" façade, but her reason for liking it best is not esthetic. She prefers it because it "secures the most economy of labor and expense, with the greatest amount of *convenience and comfort*" that she has ever seen.[14] Spatially, the rooms are the typically undifferentiated volumes of preindustrial houses—the uses could be switched without any serious decrease in efficiency. The one respect in which Miss Beecher's plans are distinctive is in their provision of clothes closets, pantries, and storerooms (which show that she already has well-developed concepts of specialized storage) and "bed-presses," i.e., beds that folded into closets (which forecast her interest in multiple use of space). She understands that her kind of housekeeping implies specialized rooms (her Gothic cottage has a combination study and

71

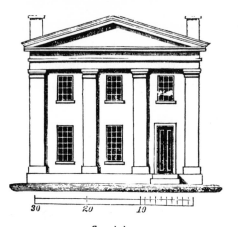

Ground-plan.

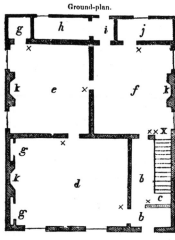

b, b, Entry.
c, Stairs.
d, Parlor, 16 by 20 feet.
e, Dining-room, 15 by 16 feet.
f, Kitchen, 15 by 16 feet.
g, g, g, Closets.
h, Store-closet.
i, Back entry.
j, Pantry.
k, k, k, Fireplaces.
x, Cellar stairs.

Second Story.

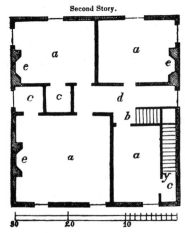

a, a, a, a, Bedrooms.
b, Stairs.
c, c, c, Closets.
d, Passage.
e, e, e, Fireplaces.
y, Garret stairs.

Elevation and plans, model house shown in Catharine Beecher's *Domestic Economy* (1842).

guest room, a nursery, a sewing room) but she is not yet able to visualize their special architectural character.

Her standards of heating and plumbing are equally modest. Every room has a wood-burning fireplace, though she does rather wistfully suggest that parlor and dining room could be thrown together with folding doors and heated by a large, coal-burning stove. Although she stresses the great convenience of running water in the house (it could be had "at half the expense of a sideboard or sofa"), she is too timid to show even a sink in the kitchen of her Gothic cottage, much less a laundry or washing room. There is no suggestion of a bathroom or of an interior toilet, though she does complain that outdoor privies are hard on the sick who "are obliged to go out of doors in all weathers. . . . A chill ensues, and fever, bowel complaints or bilious attacks are the result." [15] Her ideas of lighting are equally conservative. Though many cities were already lit by gas, she nowhere mentions the possibility. Kerosene was not yet invented: her lamps burn lard or sperm oil. She gives detailed instructions for making candles; and though it is clear that they may be bought, it is obvious that the prudent housewife will make her own with what suet, tallow, and bacon grease has not been used in making soap.

There is a great deal of household chemistry in *Domestic Economy;* it runs a tragically inept gamut from making stable dyes for fabrics, through cooking tips, to cures for sore nipples, rattlesnake bites, colic, colds, and cancer. And yet Miss Beecher's buoyant conviction that fresh air, good ventilation, and sunlight are important to health—this sounds distinctly up-to-date. She is in favor of windows to the floor, for better light and summer comfort; of insulated roofs for cool attics; of "corked" (i.e., weatherstripped) windows to reduce both drafts and fuel bills. Most of all she is in favor of cleanliness. "Every room in a house adds to the expense involved in finishing and furnishing it, and to the amount of labor spent in sweeping and dusting [it], cleaning floors, paint, and windows, and taking care of and repairing furniture. Double the size of the house," she warns us, "and you double the labor of taking care of it." [16]

Miss Beecher is really an urban person, and the audience she writes for is urban-suburban. For all the handicraft housekeeping, it is clear that the source of income for her readers is some sort of wages or salary: it is an audience of *consumers.* Yet in 1842 the overwhelming majority of families were still farm families; and the farm family of that day was an economic unit in the real sense of the word—self-sufficient to an extent hard to imagine today. Its house, for example, reflected the fact that food was not merely prepared for the table there, as it was in Miss Beecher's—it was *manufactured* there. The kitchen itself was a factory, family-run. Big as it was, it was merely the center of a whole industrial complex: ice house, spring house, well house, milk house, smoke house, root cellar, wash house, and wood pile. Further out lay vegetable garden, orchard, cow barn, pig pen, chicken run, corn crib. Beyond that, at the periphery, lay the farm itself. At the center of this food industry stood the farm kitchen, and in the center of the kitchen stood the wife.

It was not, by modern standards, a very efficient industry. Without reliable refrigeration, meat could only be preserved by smoking or salting. With only the spring house, milk could not be kept except in the form of butter or cheese. Home canning was not possible until the Mason jar (another Midwestern first!) was invented in 1858; prior to that only jams or jellies, using expensive "Havana" sugar, were possible. There was no means of extending the time of green vegetables, though cellars kept roots such as turnips and potatoes fairly well. Thus, though a prosperous farm might yield an adequate diet, it would not be very well balanced between "fat-making" and "heat-making" foods (the terms are Miss Beecher's own). Even so, it required hard, organized work on the part of the entire family to produce it.

By the 1850s, factories were supplying the farm kitchen with many labor-saving devices—from apple parers to zinc-lined boilers—to facilitate food preparation. But simultaneously another and much more profound revolution had been set in motion: the industrialized production of food itself. The process can be traced with fascinating clarity in Chicago. Cyrus McCormick established his Chicago plant in 1847. In 1849, he turned out 1000 reapers; in that year, too, the first railroad ran into Chicago. A decade later, a dense network of railroads linked Chicago to the prairies; and McCormick production was up to 5000. But mass-produced grain meant mass-produced livestock; and that in turn led to meat-packing centers in Chicago and Cincinnati. Initially a cold-weather operation, this soon had to be placed on a year-round basis.

Thus refrigeration and canning techniques came in for rapid development. Refrigerated warehouses, using harvests of natural ice, were already a commonplace by 1850, and as early as 1857 the first refrigerated railroad car appeared.[17] The technique of preserving cooked meats in hermetically sealed tins was the invention of a Napoleonic sanitary engineer, but it was Chicago that rationalized the process, and by 1870 it was a huge mass industry. Railroads and refrigeration were effecting equally radical changes elsewhere. In 1868 they brought the first out-of-season vegetables to Chicago groceries from the Gulf Coast; in 1869 they imported the first carload of bananas from the West Coast; and in 1870, the first carload of winter vegetables, grapes, and salmon from California.[18]

The implications are clear. In 1869, the year of Miss Beecher's second book, these exotic foods almost certainly would have been beyond the budget of her audience; and decades were to elapse before they would become familiar items on the farm table.[19] But the process which would shift the whole center of gravity from the home kitchen to the factory kitchen was already far advanced. She accepts this fact gladly. Her families are now wage-earning consumers. Their houses are suburban and the men commute: "Railroads, enabling men toiling in cities to rear families in the country, are on this account a special blessing." The houses sit on spacious plots and the whole family gardens, but now one feels that the motive is as much moral as economic.

The cultivation of flowers to ornament the table and house, of fruits and vegetables for food, of silk and cotton for clothing, and the care of horse, cow and dairy, can be so divided that each and all of the family, some part of the day, can take exercise in the pure air, under the magnetic and healthful rays of the sun.[20]

Elsewhere in this Utopia, she tells us that "every child should cultivate flowers and fruits to sell and give away, and thus be taught to learn the value of money and the practice of both economy and benevolence." There is no waste motion in Miss Beecher's world, no conflict between the practical deed and the morally elevated one.

But she has not modified her plans as to how this Utopia was to be won. Here the singleness of her purpose is astonishing. Between her two books on domestic science her country had been convulsed by one of the bloodiest wars in history. During this period the issues of the

Detail of kitchen cabinets shown in Catharine Beecher's *American Woman's Home* (1869).

Fugitive Slave laws, of Women's Rights and Temperance had rocked the country; but her they seem to have left untouched. She wrote on "Physiology and Calisthenics," "The Little Black Dogs of the Berkshires," "The American People Starved and Poisoned," and "An Appeal to the People in Behalf of Their Rights as Authorized Interpreters of the Bible."[21] But, aside from her polemical attack on the Abolitionists in 1837 (and her subsequent rout by the Quakeress Angelina Grimké) she had steadily avoided any involvement with all such movements. How much this was due to Yankee dislike of untidy public demonstrations and how much to a jealous fear that they would siphon off support from her own cherished cause is hard to say. But this self-imposed separation from causes she might have been expected to embrace led her into some absurd positions. Thus, while the feminists were fighting the adoption of the 14th and 15th Amendments because "the word male [was] being thereby three times branded on the Constitution,"[22] she— the defender of the enslaved sex—was insisting that "woman, in all her relations [with men] is bound to honor and obey them on whom she depends for her protection and support; nor does the truly feminine mind desire to exceed this limitation of Heaven."[23]

Nevertheless, when it came to liberating woman from the squalor, danger, and hardship of her "profession," Catharine Beecher stuck as close to reality as a squirrel to a nut. The new book gives a detailed picture of another model home—"of what may be properly called a Christian house: that is, a house contrived for the express purpose of enabling every member of the family to labor with the hands for the common good, and [that] by modes at once healthful, economical and tasteful."[24] It is clear that she has not been idle, for the house itself— while still nominally "Gothic" in style—is now firmly visualized as a true machine for living. No longer are there generalized or anonymous spaces: from top to bottom, every cubic inch has been carefully analyzed and organized for a specific purpose. Classified storage of all household objects is now fully realized as the first step in efficient housekeeping. In the kitchen it produces cabinet work of astonishing modernity, with shelving, cupboards, drawers, and countertops which anticipate current practice. In the downstairs family room it produces a full-fledged storage wall on rollers: together with a couch-bed of her own design, this makes possible the rapid conversion of the room into a bedroom. Much of the furniture is of her own design, aimed at economy, convenience, easy maintenance. Her advice on decoration is detailed and masterly; everywhere, culture is firmly wedded to convenience— as, for example, the two niches which flank the front door. They have hooks for overcoats, boxes for overshoes, a stand for wet umbrellas; topping this eminently practical arrangement is that favorite Victorian proof of culture, the white marble (or plaster) "bust or statuette."

Her services are now quite complex and highly developed. She links a basement furnace, Franklin stoves, and kitchen range into a central heating and ventilating system of some sophistication. She has eliminated all fireplaces as dirty and inefficient. Her house is now served with an essentially modern plumbing system: laundry tubs in the basement, a sink in the kitchen, a complete bathroom on the top floor, and

View of entrance (above) and plans of Miss Beecher's model "Christian" house. *American Woman's Home* (1869). Basement (right); first floor (facing page); second floor (extreme right).

an extra water closet in the basement. The water supply has two sources in the basement—a well for drinking water and a cistern for the soft rainwater so desirable for wash day. There is a hot water boiler attached to the range in the kitchen and a separate stove in the basement, where she has installed a complete laundry. Here the family linen can be washed, boiled, blued, starched, dried, and ironed and returned upstairs by a handy dumb-waiter.

The house is now fully lit by gas: it is available in most towns "or ought to be," she says. It is cheaper and cleaner than kerosene lamps, though those relatively new inventions give an excellent light. All reference to candle-making has been edited out of this edition, as has any but the most casual about soap-making. She does not yet have a refrigerator, which seems a little odd, though she does provide for an "ice closet" in the basement. However, judging from her section on cooking, refrigeration seems still to play a minor role—it sounds as though her housewives buy their fresh meats from the butcher only as they need them. In the basement there are neat cupboards for storing canned foods and perhaps root vegetables, though Miss Beecher, like many spinsters, never fully convinces one that she is much of a cook or has any interest in food beyond a purely necessary level.

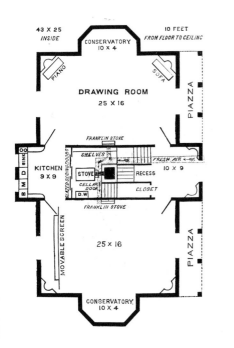
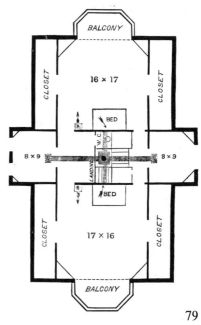

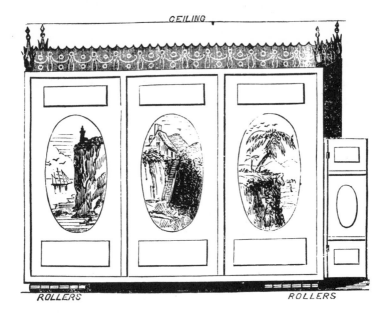

Front (above) and rear (below) views of Miss Beecher's movable "storage wall" designed for downstairs family room of her 1869 house.

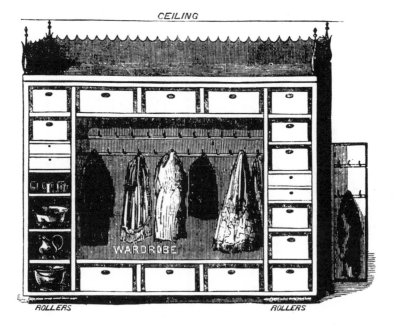

In this long and encyclopedic book she has covered every aspect of woman's profession—the management of a middle-class American family. This family is essentially modern, and so is the house she evolves to shelter it. From a functional point of view, she is decades ahead of common architectural practice. In fact, she has here set down the specifications for that free-standing, middle-class suburban house which Frank Lloyd Wright was to bring to esthetic perfection, thirty or forty years later. Catharine Beecher, dying in 1878 in Elmira, New York, when he was a nine-year-old boy on his grandfather's Wisconsin farm, had no direct contact with Wright. And a critically important period of social and industrial transition lay between the end of her work and the beginning of his. None the less, the Oak Park matrons for whom Wright did some of his finest houses typified the new woman Catharine Beecher had fought so long and so hard to create.

The dawning comprehension of both the potentials and the problems of this new phase of industrialism found expression in the theories of two Americans, Edward Bellamy and Thorstein Veblen. Miss Beecher would almost surely have disapproved of both: Bellamy for his concepts of social discipline, Veblen for his sardonic pessimism. Yet both dealt with the larger issues which she stubbornly refused to face. Bellamy's Utopia is especially impressive: the society he depicts in *Looking Backward* shows him as one of our most sophisticated and comprehensive social philosophers. For the Boston of A.D. 2000 which he constructs in this Utopian novel is designed from a truly urban point of view. Unlike Beecher before or Wright after him, he celebrates the impact of industrialization and mechanization upon the whole of society, not merely the family and the home. And yet, in his way, he is as much a feminist as Miss Beecher or Miss Anthony. His Boston is very much a woman's world. His heroine regularly spends a pleasant morning in

a vast hall full of light, received not alone from windows on all sides but from the dome, the point of which was a hundred feet above. Beneath it . . . a magnificent fountain played, cooling the atmosphere to a delicious freshness . . . walls and ceilings were frescoed in mellow tints to soften without absorbing the light. . . . Around the fountain was a space occupied with chairs and sofas.[25]

Is it perhaps a temple of some new religion? An art museum or governmental center? Not at all—it is the neighborhood shopping center, and the lady is selecting her household supplies. Her purchases, like those of all Boston housewives, will later be delivered to her home by pneumatic tube from a huge central warehouse which Bellamy describes in some detail. It is "a giant hopper into which goods are being constantly poured by trainload and shipload, to issue at the other end in packages of pounds and ounces, yards and inches, pints and gallons."[26] Yet this mechanized horn of plenty, so astonishingly forecasting the surfeited present, was only one aspect of his vision. Basically, Bellamy visualized the application of socialized industry to the perfection of urban life. For him, as for Lenin forty years later, socialism plus electricity meant the final liberation of woman, not merely from the prison of housework but from every shackle which kept her a second-class citizen. The Boston matron of A.D. 2000 is the full-fledged mate of the Boston man because all that dangerous, dirty, demeaning labor which so provoked poor Miss Beecher has been removed from the home. And it has been eliminated, not by Catharine's cheese-paring economies of saved steps or dutifully helpful children, but by the broadest application of science and technology to the entire field of family maintenance and care. Where she, almost breathless at her temerity, visualized a community gynmasium here or a common laundry there, he boldly envisioned an entire city completely rebuilt with all its services communalized, including the preparation and serving of food, the education of the young, the care of the old and the sick, the intellectual and physical exercise of the adult. His Utopia thus avoids both the suburban autarchy of Beecher and the agrarian bias of Wright, both of whom dream of middle-class suburbs, failing to see that these are actually mere appendages of the metropolis they refuse to accept.

There are, of course, all sorts of regimented activities, social obligations, dictatorial powers in Bellamy's Utopia—elements so alien to our tradition of individualistic *laissez-faire* as to make him seem surprising in 1888 and little short of subversive now. Wright, had he ever read Bellamy, must certainly have rejected him out of hand for just such reasons. Yet the fact remains that Wright's houses are a direct development, in advanced architectural terms, of the general concepts of domestic well-being, beauty, and urbanity so clearly formulated by Bellamy. Wright's houses could not appear until Bellamy's process of urban mechanization was largely completed. For though he forecast many technological developments with astonishing accuracy—electric lighting, district heating, air conditioning, broadcast music, underground transport of goods and services—it would still require decades for American industry actually to accomplish them. Thus the thirty years between Bellamy's dream city and Wright's real house for the Coonleys saw the American home, even the farm home, converted from a center of production to a center of consumption. One by one, the factory was to absorb the traditional tasks of kitchen, laundry, and sewing room; and one by one these areas began to shrink.

But it did not happen over night. "How would it simplify the burdens of the American housewife to have washing and ironing day expunged from her calendar!" the Beecher sisters had cried in 1869. "If all the money that each family spends on the outfit and accommodations for washing and ironing, on fuel, soap, starch and the other requirements" were only concentrated on central laundries.[27] By the end of the century the worst horrors of wash day had been removed. Municipal water systems brought pure water to the door: cistern well and pump disappeared. Modern plumbing carried hot and cold water all over the house: gone was the squalid drudgery of backyard washpots, tubs, and fires. Washing machines replaced the zinc-washboard, and commercial laundries banished washday from many houses altogether.

Central heating became standard: stoves and fireplaces, with their daily clutter of ashes, kindling, fuel, and paper squills disappeared forever. The untidy woodpile gave way to buried oil tank, hidden gas pipe, or basement coal bin. Electric lighting eliminated the last sooty lamp chimney or faulty gas mantle.

The continuous refrigeration of perishables (in the home, the grocery, the dairy, or abattoir) was a commonplace by Wright's day but it had taken better than two centuries for Americans to accomplish it. Generations of housewives had struggled against putrescence. A certain Mrs. Gardiner, writing a cookbook in the Boston of the 1690s, had urged housewives: "If you live in the country, where you cannot always command meat, seize the opportunity when you happen to have Beef, Mutton, and Veal in the house" and put it up for future use. The technique she advocated was a kind of primitive bouillon cube: "Take two legs of beef about fifty pounds . . ." the recipe began.[28] The New York *Daily Mirror* might smugly observe on Bastille Day in 1838 that the refrigerator had become as much an article of necessity as the dining room table. But this was poetic license, for refrigerators were still not a commonplace thirty years later when the Beecher sisters published their book. Here again a thorough-going technological revolution had to occur. Then, and only then, could milk man and butcher boy appear alongside the household refrigerator; gone forever was the heavy and noisome labor of milking and churning, butchering and lard-rendering, and soap-making. With the vanishing cow, pig, and poultry went some of the least attractive aspects of the domestic landscape—cow barn, pig pen, and chicken run, with their flies and odors.

The food industry removed the processing of fruits and vegetables from the kitchen, and another constellation of domestic facilities dropped out of sight: root cellar, ice house, vegetable garden, grape arbor. Municipal garbage collection was introduced, and trash pile and garbage pit disappeared. Municipal sewers arrived: cesspool and privy were abandoned. Finally, the trolley car or interurban, then the automobile, replaced the horse and buggy. Gone along with Dobbin were his stall, haybarn, pasture, and manure pile.

Frank Lloyd Wright was the first American architect to understand the full esthetic implications of this domestic revolution. Out of his understanding he conceived such beautiful houses as those for the Martins, the Coonleys, the McCormicks, and for himself at Spring Green. Yet he was never able to build a city out of such units, even in his imagination. Though they were the products of urban life he could never visualize the urban reality from which they sprang. The Great Depression drove Wright into his only attempt to build a Utopia. Yet his "Broadacre City" is misnamed; it was not really the central city at all that he dealt with but rather one of its satellites—a hybrid mixture of garden suburb and subsistence farm. Thus, Wright's social theories are much closer to Catharine Beecher or William Morris than they are to Bellamy. For, whatever the stringencies of his military socialism or the

84

Spartan obligations of his "national service," Bellamy at least understood that the city stood at the center of civilization, as the very etymology of the words suggest. Bellamy saw, as Wright—blinded by the confusion and squalor of the city—never could see, that it was not merely an evil necessity, a producer of luxuries to be consumed elsewhere but was instead the actual generator of culture. Bellamy, like Beecher and Wright, was a Utopianist: but, unlike them, he somehow avoided that endemic American fantasy, the passion for a happy ending which has everybody smiling, nobody hurt, and nobody a penny out of pocket.

6. THE TWO MEN
IN SULLIVAN'S TOMB

We Americans did not handle Louis Henri Sullivan very kindly when he was alive; only since his death in 1924 have we begun to get a better perspective of the man and the problems he faced. It is not an easy task, for Sullivan presents us with an almost classic example of the symbiotic relationship between a great artist and his culture. This relationship is always characterized by conflict: the artist "can't live with his contemporaries and yet can't live without them." In retrospect we can see that he was ahead of his times—that is, that he saw more clearly than the audience around him the future they both faced. In this way an artist is like a prophet. He is the scout whom society sends ahead to spy out the land. The more profound his vision, the more penetrating the reports he brings back, the less likely is his advice to be the sort the audience wants, and the more difficult, therefore, the relationship. For the future is always disturbing, studded with change and difficult choice; and the truly great artist always demands the morally necessary rather than the merely pleasant decision. It is not an easy process for either the artist or his audience. It places them, in a very real sense, at war with one another, locked in an embrace that neither can escape. And though the artist may in the end create the vision of his time, he is very often destroyed in the process.

Such was the case with Louis Sullivan.

The great conundrum of his life remains: Why in 1900, at the height of his powers and very near the zenith of his influence and prestige, did he suddenly withdraw from the great stage of life? The answer can lie only partially in the society around him, brutal as it was: for the rest, we must look to the very structure of his personality and his intellect. He was a *generalist* in a culture which, already in his day, belonged largely to the *specialist*. The task he set for himself was nothing less than the creation of a new American architecture, one which would be both worthy and expressive of the new conditions of American life. He tried to resolve singlehandedly the contradictions between the poetic and the practical in a field where industrialism had made them particularly acute. He sought, as he himself put it, "that rule which admits of no exception";[1] that law which applies with equal force to every problem, at every level. It was a noble ambition and one which might conceivably have been accomplished in the narrower medium of poetry or painting. Unfortunately, he made his attempt in that most complex, eclectic, and expensive of all mediums, architecture, and at the time when architecture was just emerging from its lowest level in all history. And he was working in a Midwest that subscribed much more readily to the philosophies of Phillip Armour, George Pullman, and Judge Gary than to those of Governor Altgeld, Jane Addams, or Carl Sandburg.

In 1876, when Sullivan buoyantly began to practice in Chicago, it was still possible for an idealist to believe that the poetic might somehow win out over the expedient. By 1900, such illusions were no longer possible. As a matter of fact, according to Sullivan's account, his own had been destroyed in February, 1891, when his colleagues on the Committee on Buildings and Grounds of the Columbian Exposition had voted overwhelmingly that the official architectural style was to be Roman Classic. Nevertheless, however brutal its power or philistine its standards, the Midwest permitted Sullivan some of his best work in the decade which followed; and in 1900 he completed his *chef-d'œuvre*, the Schlesinger and Meyer department store in Chicago. Personal, internal weaknesses must therefore have intervened to force his virtual retirement from life at this time. What these weaknesses were can only be guessed at, on the face of available evidence. Sullivan was notoriously reserved about his private affairs. He even wrote the story of his life in the third person and named it the autobiography not of a man but of an *Idea*. The late George Elmslie, who remained with him longer and knew him better than any other professional associate, said that Sullivan was always an enigma to him. It is known that, in these later years, Sullivan drank very heavily, but that would be diagnosed now as effect, not cause. The problem remains: what was the internal conflict he so proudly concealed but so sadly succumbed to?

In both his writing and his buildings we can trace the conflict. There are two Sullivans at work here, not one. One of them is the virile rationalist, brilliant, analytical: the man who could master the technical, esthetic, and social problems of the skyscraper; the designer who, like Greenough before him, saw that the origin of form lies in function; the critic who analyzed his culture in terms so accurate, witty, and fearless. The other Sullivan is also powerful but by no means so diamond-clear: a deist, a mystic, a poet who combines a certain grandeur with plain mush; a lyrical, almost feminine ornamentalist; a lover of nature closer to Thoreau than to Darwin. We can see these two halves in conflict but we seldom find them in perfect equipoise. And it must have been to this unresolved conflict, as much as to the conflict between himself and his Chicago audience, that Sullivan owed his final defeat.

He had set for himself the task of creating a new architecture. How was this to be accomplished? By the continued manipulation of the forms of Imperial Rome, Gothic London, or Renaissance Florence? But "this fradulent and surreptitious use of historical documents" was just what had brought nineteenth-century architecture to disaster. "However suavely presented, however cleverly plagiarized, however neatly re-packed, however shrewdly intrigued,"[2] he thundered, this prostitution of the past was a betrayal of the needs and aspirations of the American people. It could never be made to work.

The new architecture could only be derived from a fundamental re-examination of the problem. Its development must follow the scientific method, basing itself upon laws which admitted of no exception. Thus, fifty years after Greenough's death we find Sullivan declaring (apparently not realizing Greenough had said it first) that good form can derive only from the correct solution of functional problems and that bad form will inevitably result from their neglect or abuse. Of course, as Sullivan well knew, architectural function was itself complex, with aspects at once subjective and objective, cultural and structural, spiritual and physiological. It was not enough to plan socially, to build honestly and economically. This might be indispensable to great architecture, but alone it was by no means its guarantee. At the higher level of artistic expression it was necessary "to animate buildings with a subjective significance and value, to make them visible parts of the social fabric, to infuse into them the true life of the people, to impart to them the best that is in the people, just as the eye of the poet, looking below the surface of life, sees the very best that is in the people."[3] The very breadth of his definition is a measure of the difficulty of his task.

Sullivan's work on the skyscraper, both theoretical and architectural, is a concrete illustration of how he set about doing what he advocated; as such it must rank as one of the outstanding creative accomplishments of American history. He played no part in the technical developments which made it possible. Other men developed the steel, the elevators, the electric motors; and his contemporary, the Chicago engineer William Le Baron Jenney, actually perfected the continuous steel cage which is the skeleton of all true skyscrapers. Sullivan took these constituent elements as found and "created" the skyscraper as a modern architectural form in much the same way as Wright, two decades later, was to "create" the modern American house. The progressive way in which he met and mastered problems is clearly charted in seven multi-story buildings: the Auditorium Hotel and Theater (1886–89), the Wainwright (1890–91), the Schiller (1892), the Guaranty Trust (1893–94), the Meyer (1893), the Fraternity Temple (1895), and the Schlesinger and Meyer department store (1899). And in this progression we can see the strongest and most attractive aspects of Sullivan's personality.

His first contact with the problem of the multi-story building came when the firm of which he was the junior member received the commission to design the Auditorium. This complex project of luxury hotel, opera house, and office tower represented a challenge in plan, construction, and expression. While there were many interesting technical innovations—the special foundations, the steel trusswork for theater and rooftop ballroom, the very up-to-date kitchens, and the pneumatic ramps for the theater stage—these seem to have been solved largely by the senior partner, Dankmar Adler. There was little evidence, then or later, that Sullivan ever interested himself very deeply in the technical details of building. His main concern was always their adequate expression at the esthetic level.

Though the hotel wing was 10 stories high and the office tower 17, neither was really a skyscraper. There was no continuous steel frame;

Louis Sullivan's first study of the Auditorium Hotel and Theater, 1884.

H. H. Richardson's Marshall Field Wholesale Store, Chicago, 1886 (above), and The Auditorium as completed, 1889 (below).

the outside walls were of load-bearing masonry; and this was the way in which Sullivan sought to express them. In his earliest designs, the floors were stacked one on top of the other, in a layer cake of various prevalent styles—Eastlake, Second Empire, and Swiss Chalet. Thus far the building offered no more promise esthetically than the average work of the period. But, just at this juncture, Henry Hobson Richardson published the design for his new Marshall Field Wholesale Store a few blocks up Michigan Avenue. The design had an electrifying effect on the 30-year-old Sullivan—an effect he was always to acknowledge with winning candor. For the Field building taught him a lesson he never forgot—that of modelling a building plastically so that it could be immediately perceived as a whole, as a total sculptural entity, irrespective of the detailed treatment of its component parts. With this in mind, he quickly recast the entire exterior of the Auditorium in a frankly Richardsonian mold, thereby converting a mediocrity into a work of distinction.

Actually, as we shall see, Sullivan was to explore the subtleties of the multi-story building much more profoundly than Richardson, who died prematurely in the spring of 1886. In the Field building Richardson had been at no great pains to have the exterior render a literal expression of its internal organization. In actuality there were seven almost identical floors. Yet Richardson manipulated his fenestration to create the effect of four—a street-level basement, a *piano nobile* (actually three floors), a "second story" (two floors) and an attic. Although Sullivan was to employ the same device in several of his skyscrapers, his own analogy was more valid, since he came to regard these towers as free-standing classic columns with a base (the lobby and street-level shops) a shaft (the stacked, identical offices), and a capital (the attic). Ultimately he abandoned the analogy altogether.

Designing a skyscraper, as Sullivan quickly came to realize, posed many esthetic problems beyond having it "read" as a single, integral whole. There was the sheer verticality of the form itself. Should this fact be dramatized? In the Wainwright and Guaranty buildings he bent everything to this end, including the insertion of a false pier between each pair of real ones and the moving of these vertical lines well forward of the plane of the windows and horizontal spandrels. This device undoubtedly accented the verticality of the mass; but was it a form

91

Sullivan's triumphant expression of the structural facts of the multi-story steel skeleton, the Schlesinger and Meyer Department Store (above, Chicago, 1899), came only after years of experiment with a preponderantly vertical motif, as shown in the Guaranty Trust, 1893–94 (below).

which derived honestly from function? Aside from the redundant columns, it gave the impression that the verticals were much more important than the floor slabs they carried. This was not an accurate reflection of either structural or functional fact, and Sullivan must have realized it. He turned to the other extreme in the Meyer Building. Here the horizontal spandrels were brought forward in continuous bands, and the vertical lines of the columns were minimized. But this, too, was scarcely an "honest" expression. What to express—the support or the load? The skeleton or the volumes it defines and encloses?

The Schlesinger store presents us with Sullivan's brilliant resolution of these contradictions. Structurally the steel cage of the skyscraper is static, inert: horizontal and vertical members have identical importance. And functionally the walls are certainly no more important than the floors. The esthetic expression of these facts would be a non-directional design. Moreover, since the wall of the skyscraper is a mere membrane, stretched around the skeleton like a skin, it would be expressed most clearly as one taut, unbroken vertical plane. And this property would be further emphasized if the windows are mere perforations in the wall. All these subtleties are subsumed in the Schlesinger. Now the volumetric fact of the interior is made explicit—a honeycomb of identical bays slipped like shoe boxes into a cellular skeleton. Thus the whole story is told with diamond-sharp clarity, without the least deviation from either structural or functional fact.

Still another set of forces played upon the skyscraper. These, too, Sullivan analyzed and mastered. From the start, he was attracted to it because of "the force and power of its altitude." His own designs were always for free-standing, soaring shafts. They were, however, shafts which covered the entire plot they stood upon, and their visual impact was due largely to the fact that they stood alone. But did they? Not for long, not at least in Chicago, where skyscrapers were rising by the dozens, cheek by jowl, face to face, converting the streets into blind, traffic-choked canyons. Under such conditions, no matter how well designed, they represented "aspects of social menace and danger. . . . [The skyscraper] loses its validity when the surroundings are uncongenial to its nature; and when such buildings are crowded together upon narrow streets or lanes, they become mutually destructive."[4]

93

Sullivan's free-standing, stepped-back tower; Fraternity Temple, the proposed home office of the Independent Order of Odd Fellows, Chicago, 1895.

Who beside Sullivan saw this danger so clearly and so early? Seventy years later it is still not fully understood; yet as early as 1891 he developed the concept of the "set-back" tower, where the shaft occupies only a portion of its plot. This profile, so prophetic of the ziggurat-producing zoning laws of the mid-twentieth century, appears first in embryonic form in the Schiller Building, then, fully flowered, in the proposed Fraternity Temple Tower of 1895—a structure which, had it been built, might have altered the whole direction of zoning and city planning.

Concurrently with the systematic conquest of one set of problems, Sullivan was hard at work on another task he had set himself: the development of a new, American grammar of architectural ornament. Here the record of accomplishment is far less decisive. Despite his determination to invent new motifs, his own ornament remained derivative, eclectic. He aspired to an expressiveness peculiarly American; what he produced was actually international, with strong overtones of Aubrey Beardsley and Art Nouveau. He aimed at a new ornament congruent with the new means of building. What he evolved was a lush and yet somehow shallow calligraphy. This ornament, so closely linked to the florid metaphysics of much of his writing, was basically antistructural, hostile to most of the walls on which it was permitted to effloresce. In fact, the antagonism between Sullivan's expressionism and his ornamentalism is so acute that some of his buildings look like the work of two strangers. It is not a petty struggle, but it is not always heroic either: in most of his buildings it is merely sad. In only four or five of them is the issue fully resolved—the Getty and Wainright tombs, the Schlesinger and Meyer department store, the banks at Owatonna, Minnesota, and Columbus, Ohio.

The tombs, of course, are works of pure poetry in which no practical requirements complicate the design. They are solid sculptural masses of limestone on which Sullivan's designs can be incised with great delicacy and restraint with no violence to material or form. In the Schlesinger building, on the other hand, his ornamentalism is confined to a delicate bronze screen, prefabricated in sections, which frames the street-level show windows. The design is one of almost orgiastic splendor. Where it swells to enclose the circular entrance lobby, or erupts like a fountain in

95

Entrance detail, Schlesinger and Meyer building.

Getty Tomb, Graceland Cemetery, Chicago, 1890.

the marquee over the carriage entrance, it is an architectural sculpture much closer to Hindu fertility rites than to State Street drygoods. Here Sullivan has accomplished the theoretically impossible—the combination of ornament of barbaric richness with a structure of Puritanical simplicity. The success of this startling juxtaposition of opposites rests upon the careful way in which he has isolated the two elements, both structurally and esthetically, so that they complement rather than destroy each other.

But these masterpieces had been erected upon territory which Sullivan singlehandedly had to clear of esthetic underbrush. It had not been an easy job, either for him or his audience. His anger had fallen like a broadsword on the Pharisees, colleagues and clients alike. The eclectic architects were like clerks at the notion counter, offering "Tudor for colleges and residences; Roman for banks and railway stations and libraries—or Greek, if you like: some customers prefer the Ionic to the Doric. [They] have French, English and Italian Gothic; and Renaissance for churches. Residences [they] offer in Italian or Louis Quinze."[5] Nor did his polemics win him the affection of those big city capitalists who were wrapping Roman façades around their counting houses. "I do not relish Roman-temple banks; and the common sense Roman-temple bank particularly disagrees with me," he said in his widely read *Kindergarten Chats*. "I am going to insist that the banker wear a toga and sandals and conduct his business in the venerated Latin tongue." His imaginary student, at whom these essays are aimed, protests: "I really don't see why, as a matter of common privilege, a man shouldn't make an imitation Roman temple if he wishes to do so." And Sullivan snaps back: "I don't either, if he will make it in his own back yard . . . for his own private use, gratification or amusement. But when he puts it on the people's highway and labels it modern architecture, there are those who will cry humbug and, what is worse, prove it."[6]

It was not that Sullivan disliked the Romans, of course. He detested the ghoulish grave robbing of their tombs by a society too timid to create its own artistic language. He told the student that "the deepest reach of our scholarship will reveal only this: that the Roman temple was part of Roman life— not American life; that it beat with the Roman pulse, was in touch with Roman activities; and that it waned with Roman glory—it died a Roman death."[7]

These mordant polemics, exacerbated by his growing isolation, did not sit well with the bankers, and they reacted as might be expected: they cut him off without a dime. But his battle against Philistine standards of art brought him into headlong collision with many people besides bankers. Indeed, by the time he had finished the Schlesinger store, fashionable taste, the whole of that polite society he had so ravished a decade before with the opening of the Auditorium, seemed to have turned solidly against him. His practice declined, he was forced to give up his famous suite in the Auditorium Tower, and, as he sank into a shabby gentility, he was more estranged than ever from his Chicago audience. He was shortly to lose contact with it forever.

It was nine years before he won another important client; and when that client came, it was the hinterland and not the great metropolis which now embraced his *avant-garde* theories. Not Mrs. Potter Palmer nor Mr. Marshall Field but a small-town banker from Owatonna, Minnesota, Mr. L. L. Bennett, looked him up and engaged him to design a new building. A piece by Bennett in *The Craftsman* (significantly entitled "A Bank Built for Farmers: Louis Sullivan designs a building which marks a new epoch in American architecture") describes the way in which the Bennetts selected their architect. The piece is a model of sober common sense.[8] Mr. Bennett says that "the classical style of architecture so much used for bank buildings was at first considered but finally rejected as being not necessarily expressive of a bank . . . and defective when it comes to practical use." They consulted several architects but because they all "preferred to follow precedent or to take their inspiration from the books, it was determined to make a search for an architect whose aim it was *to express the thought or use underlying a building,* without fear or precedent." They made a search of art and architectural magazines, came upon published accounts of Sullivan's work, and promptly hired him.

Bennett praises the main features of the building. One thing of which he was very proud was the new Women's Room, designed for farm wives in town with their children. They could wait here, he says, while their husbands transacted their business in the Farmer's Exchange. For their comfort, he writes, it had "a warmer and richer color scheme [than the rest of the bank] and is provided with high-back settles, low rocking chairs, and small tables and writing desks."

People's Bank, Owatonna, Minn., 1908. Louis H. Sullivan, architect.

The Owatonna bank was skillfully restored in 1958 by the architect Harwell H. Harris. The main banking room as it is today (above) and as it appeared in 1908, shortly after completion (below).

Mr. Bennett does not tell us, in this article of fifty years ago, whether Sullivan's radical design ever caused any misgivings on the part of the customers of the bank or the citizens of Owatonna. But J. R. Wheeler, president of the Farmers and Merchants Union Bank of Columbus, Wisconsin, for whom Sullivan designed a building in 1919, confesses that "he was scared to death by those first drawings. . . . I was sure that the bank would terrify the natives. I was almost ready to call the whole thing off and run for cover. It was Mrs. Wheeler who . . . talked me into going ahead."[9] And Mrs. Wheeler, who was she? Where did her convictions come from? She tells us that she had seen and admired some buildings of Frank Lloyd Wright and had seen a postcard of an earlier Sullivan bank. Moreover, she had studied the Froebel system at the Chicago Kindergarten Training School—the same Froebel, incidentally, who had made such an impression on Wright's mother when his theories were first presented to Americans at the Philadelphia Exposition of 1876. Froebel had taught the motto "Do nothing unrelatedly," and that is what Mrs. Wheeler urged upon her husband. The bank went ahead, and "from my original timidity," Mr. Wheeler tells us, "I eventually advanced to the point where I began to worry that somebody else might copy the bank."[10]

There is something most heart-warming about this sort of principled discussion of architectural problems—Bennett's concern about the comfort of a farm wife, in town on some bitter winter Saturday, the shopping done and no place to wait while her husband finishes his trading; Mr. Wheeler's worry about whether progressive farmers practicing experimental farm techniques would accept architecture of the same progressive sort; and Mrs. Wheeler's straightforward insistence upon applying to general life the standards of behavior she was taught in school. No wonder Sullivan found these clients to his liking. In them he was confronting the rank-and-file of Midwestern democracy, the very people in whose innate good sense and ultimate worth he placed his trust. It was in behalf of these people that he had asked architects "not to betray, but to express the life of your own day and generation." And it was in their behalf that he himself did two of his most successful buildings. It was because of them that he had asked his colleagues "to infuse into [their buildings] the true life of the people, to impart to them

101

the best that is in the people, as the eye of the poet, looking below the surface of life, sees the best that is in the people."[11]

Today, half a century later, we may well have personal reservations about the decorative ornament which Sullivan employed in these banks. That is not surprising. We have all become so acutely self-conscious in these matters, so unsure of our own taste, so unwilling to commit ourselves publicly to one or another of the various schools of art available to us, that we take the easy way out: we simply use no art or ornament at all. Yet no one can look at this exuberant polychromatic ornament without feeling, at base, a little ashamed of his own timidity, a little envious of Sullivan in his confidence and courage. The place of art in modern architecture confronts us with a dichotomy which he was the first to observe and the first to attempt to solve. He said—and he was desperately serious when he said it—that architectural form should flow out of architectural function. But he never made the vulgar error of thinking that mere mechanical or structural function were the only values to be expressed in architecture. Above and beyond them stood social and cultural functions; these too had to be given expression in symbolic form. The architect, no less than the poet, had to extract and celebrate these functions. To this end, he spent a large part of his life trying to develop a vocabulary of architectural ornament in the same way that Walt Whitman evolved a whole new vocabulary of poetic imagery based upon the experience of the people.

That he did not succeed is owing to a number of factors. The first is obviously time—his place in it and the amount he had at his disposal. He stood at the Great Divide of American architecture; he was anticipating esthetic problems which, for the great majority of his audience, simply did not yet exist. No one lifetime would be long enough to solve them. As he put it, "Such a system [i.e., a complete vocabulary of architectural ornament] could scarcely be expected to reach its fullness of development short of maturity."[12] Then, there was the problem of his audience. Socially, it was very complex: exactly *whose* values were to be celebrated—those of Mrs. Potter Palmer, the great North Shore society leader? Or those of Mrs. Wheeler, the small-town kindergarten teacher? Or perhaps some sort of average between the two? Sullivan could not answer that problem singlehandedly in one lifetime.

There was, finally, the technical problem of his medium. Symbols are elusive and constantly changing phenomena. They can be expressed more quickly, more cheaply in written word or painted canvas than in the architect's immensely more obdurate materials of brick and steel. For these reasons, Sullivan's ornament seems more dated than his structure. But this does not minimize the heroism of his effort or the correctness of his vision; he has posed for us a problem which we have yet to solve.

Louis Sullivan confronts us still with one ironic question: How do we propose to handle future Sullivans, future pioneers, future generalists when they appear? Will we exile them to the Mississippi backwoods when they challenge the conformism which is smothering our country today? We generously subsidize the specialists to design rockets to get us to the moon and overpay "practical men" to build them for us. But what will happen to the peaceful, "impractical" generalist who calls attention to all the work still needed here on earth? Sullivan was not popular with many of his contemporaries because he saw the general implications of current developments and insisted on pointing them out. But whom has history vindicated—Sullivan or the practical men who brushed him off as an idle dreamer? America needs more Sullivans, not fewer; and Americans should pay more heed to their advice when they appear.

7. FRANK LLOYD WRIGHT
AND THE FINE ARTS

His last completed work, the Solomon R. Guggenheim Museum in New York City, represents a double victory for Wright: the conquest of his life-long adversary, the metropolitan East, and a final triumphant demonstration of his concept of the status of painting and sculpture in the hierarchy of art. He died just before its opening; but even in death Wright remains the focus of controversy. Everyone has been forced to comment on the museum, and no one has found it possible to be neutral. Only on one point does there seem to be agreement—that however handsome it is an architectural fact, it is not successful as a museum. Seen from the outside, the great exploding spiral is a powerful landmark; within, it is a magnificent vessel for containing the crowds, displaying them to far greater advantage than the dress circle at La Scala or the grand stairs of the Paris Opera. But it does not display painting or sculpture to equal advantage. On the contrary, with perverse if not malicious skill, Wright's museum dwarfs the art it might have been expected to magnify. He has set the individual pieces afloat in a vortex, a whirlpool, an interior volume of absolutely overpowering movement. He has taken unfair advantage of the artists: of poor, dead Kandinsky, with his intersecting circles and delicate pastels; of elegant, modest Brancusi; of gay Miró. He has reduced them all to the level of lonely little shepherd boys, piping away in competition with *Lohengrin*. Michelangelo himself would be unsafe in Wright's museum.

The realization of his "failure" must come as a disappointment to the admirers of Frank Lloyd Wright, but it should not come as a surprise. For the museum is merely a statement, in reinforced concrete, of his life-long conception of the relative importance of architecture and the fine arts. For him, architecture was always literally "the mother of the arts," absolute in her supremacy over all the others. In the last decades of his life she became more and more the *only* art. No other architect of comparable stature has minimized art as consistently as he. Little mural or sculpture appears as an integral part of his later work. In those buildings over whose interior design he exercised control there is not only little contemporary Western art, there is not even a place for it, physically or esthetically. Nor did he ever, in these later decades, give any evidence that he could collaborate with independent artists, as did the elder Saarinen with Carl Milles or Niemeyer with the muralist Portinari.

And yet Wright was not always able or willing to exclude art from his life or his buildings. On the contrary, there was a time in his early manhood when the problem of the fine arts and their relation to architecture occupied much of his attention. During the first two decades of his practice he worked closely with a number of artists and craftsmen.[1] Many of his houses employed sculpture and painting in a wide range of media—fresco, teserae, stained glass, cast concrete, wrought iron. He wrote and spoke extensively on the subject. And he began, during just this period, that collection of Oriental prints which was to make him ultimately one of the greatest collectors in the nation. What, then, is the origin of this later attitude toward art—especially modern Western art —this mixture of hostility to, contempt for, and bland ignorance of the work of his contemporaries in the fields of painting and sculpture?

In 1887, when Wright arrived in Chicago as a fastidious, arrogant, but very perceptive young man, he looked at the Midwestern art world and found it worthy of nothing but hostility and contempt. It is unfortunate, both for Wright and for art, that this initial exposure led to prejudices which were never to change. But if we follow him closely, during the critical years 1887–1913, we can only be impressed by the acuteness of his observations and the sagacity of his decisions. For they led him safely—indeed, triumphantly—through a period which was disastrous for most American architects and artists.

Wright's initial reactions were completely pragmatic. Escape from the eclecticism of the period was not merely an exercise in esthetics, it was for him a matter of urgent, practical necessity. The young architect discovered that to build he had to have materials. And in 1887 these materials—marble, brick, wood, bronze, velvet, glass—were all so tightly locked in corrupted design-forms that their real, independent properties—color, texture, luster—were inaccessible. They had, indeed, become invisible. People could literally no longer see the marble for the column, the bronze for the vase, the wood for the jig saw and lathe. Wright described the situation quite clearly: "Simple things . . . were nowhere at hand. A piece of wood without a moulding was an anomaly; a plain wooden slat instead of a turned baluster a joke; the omission of the merchantable 'grille' a crime; plain fabrics for hangings or floor coverings were nowhere to be found in stock."[2] Ornament had destroyed material; content was lost in bankrupt form.

The perception of this ugly fact and the recognition of what must be done to escape its ugly consequences distinguished Wright from his contemporaries. Even Louis Sullivan, engaged in the same struggle, did not see the issue so clearly. In his attempt to replace bad ornament with good, Sullivan became obsessed with the problem—an obsession which led him ultimately into a dismal swamp of metaphysical speculation. Wright never made this error. At first merely distrusting traditional ornament, he came ultimately to despise it. The change, of course, did not occur overnight. In these early years we see his tentative efforts to adapt other men's styles to his own ends or to evolve equivalents of his own. We can easily trace this groping for a satisfactory system of expression and, in the process, his experimenting with all the dominant architectural idioms of the day.[3] Thus the first house he designed for himself (1889) is shingled Richardsonian; the Blossom house (1892), Colonial; the Harlan house (1892), Sullivanesque; the Bagley house (1894), Queen Anne; the Roloson row houses (1894) and the Moore house (1895), Tudor.

He tries each of these styles in turn; and the results, though derivative, are characterized by their organizational firmness and clarity. But he does not repeat the experiment, clearly finding each inadequate to his needs. We can trace a parallel experimentation with the then current styles in art, furniture, and interior decoration generally. In the stair hall of his own house he uses a plaster frieze of Classic figures. Over the fireplace of the playroom (added in 1895) there is a flat mural of the Arabian Nights in a style reminiscent of Puvis de Chavannes. For the cornice of the Heller house (1897) he commissioned Richard Bock

Frank Lloyd Wright's own house, Oak Park, Ill., 1889.

Blossom house, Chicago, 1892. Frank Lloyd Wright, architect.

Bagley house, Hinsdale, Ill., 1894. Frank Lloyd Wright, architect.

Moore house, Oak Park, Ill., 1895. Frank Lloyd Wright, architect.

to do a terra cotta frieze—a line of Beaux Arts maidens embowered in Beardsley-Sullivan foliage. Throughout his interiors of this period we catch glimpses of Tiffany glass, tooled leather, stencil and applique, cattails and dried grasses—the echoes, in short, of William Morris.

But these borrowed and eclectic elements are always minor in his compositions, always handled with a restraint bordering on coolness. As the century closes, his architecture grows steadily more unified in expression; and such ornament and art as survives becomes less eclectic and more integral to the structure. His control over these art forms is increasingly apparent. And though he employed a number of artists and craftsmen in the decade between 1900 and 1910, his increasing editorship of their work is readily traceable. In both subject matter and handling, it moves toward simplification, abstraction. Stained glass, mosaic, fresco, and wrought iron all show the influence of the Orient, especially the Japanese print. Moreover, even big elements like the white wisteria mural in the Martin house (1904) or the lovely birch and sumac panels in the Coonley living room (1907) are not independent statements on the part of free artists but are carefully subordinated to the requirements of the rooms. By the same token, free-standing sculpture and framed easel painting have now disappeared altogether. In the final great project of the period, the Midway Gardens of 1913, there is a last great burst of sculpture, mural and ornament; but now it is art *designed* by the architect himself ("my own trusty T-square and triangle," as he put it) and the sculptor is in fact merely the executor of the designs.

Fortunately for us, this developing attitude toward art and ornament is not only easily inferred from his successive buildings, it is also explicitly developed in his essays and speeches of the period. Indeed, these reveal the surprising extent to which he rationalized the design process. They reveal a well-read intellectual (a role he was contemptuously to reject in later years) well aware of the artistic currents in his surroundings.

"The true value of a work of art," he told the Evanston University Guild in 1894, is that it be "perfectly adjusted in relation to the whole, in absolute poise, leaving nothing but a feeling of quiet satisfaction."[4] Evidently he found little art which met this criterion: for, two years later, he told this same organization that he permitted "no prints or pictures [to] intrude upon attention" in his houses. They were not to imagine, however, that "pictorial art is banished." He would provide a cupboard to hold "a portfolio of print or etching, paint or water color." He would also provide somewhere a simple, dark-framed surface on which to display one "or perhaps two" of the best.[5]

But the more he studied the art being offered to Chicagoans, the keener became his dissatisfaction. "A picture should be more than an imitation of a real object . . . more than a pretended hole in the wall, through which you see a story about something."[6] Exasperation drove him still further in 1908: "Pictures deface walls oftener than they decorate them."[7] Finally, two years later, he reached the logical conclusion to this line of thinking. "The easel picture," he says flatly, "has no place on the walls. Great pictures should have their gallery. Oratorio is not performed in a drawing room."[8]

This sort of generalized criticism of painting might, by itself, be dismissed as either parochial or misanthropic. But Wright did not stop with the general; he knew very well the art that was available to him, and his objections to it were concrete and specific. They dealt with both its form *and* its content. The forms "lacked repose"; they were strident, histrionic; they needed simplification, "conventionalizing." In short, they lacked that abstraction of reality which marked all great art. As for their subject matter! "The arts," he exclaims with wicked accuracy, "are today cursed by literature. Artists attempt to make literature of music, usually of painting and sculpture and . . . of architecture also."[9] The galleries and museums of Chicago were prison houses of gesture and anecdote, all of it cast in forms of photographic artificiality. "Nature is never right for a picture," he tells one audience, "that is, not ready made."[10] "If you see a picture in which perhaps a cow is looking out at you [so] real, so lifelike," he tells another group sardonically, don't buy the picture, "rather buy the cow."[11]

He had still deeper and more personal reservations. His revolt against the anecdotal in such contemporaries as the preposterous Frederick MacMonnies or vacuous Kenyon Cox is quick and sure. But it is obvious that his distrust of the fine arts extended far beyond these pallid American expressions. In fact, as time goes on, his distrust extends to

Two paintings from the International Show at Chicago in 1893: *Landscape with Cattle* by
F. De Vuillefroy (above) and *The Spoils of War* by G. Rochegrosse (below).

the whole tradition of Western art. Long before he saw Renaissance art at first hand he was almost prudishly reacting against its "sensuality and extravagance." In 1908 he urged "reticence in the matter of ornament. We crave ornament for the sake of ornament; cover up our faults with ornamental sensualties that were, a long time ago, sensuous ornament. We will do well to distrust this unwholesome and unholy craving."[12] The warning is more ethical than esthetic.

Two years later, as a forty-year-old husband and father living in Florence with a woman not his wife, Frank Lloyd Wright stood face to face with the great artists of the Renaissance. He was stunned by their sensualism. "That splendid group of Florentine sculptors and painters and architects and sculptor-painters and painter-sculptors who were architects" had erased all the decent lines of distinction between the arts. He was forced to admit that "some of the sculpture is good painting; most of the painting is good sculpture; and in both lie the patterns of architecture." Nevertheless, he found it "as amazing as it is unfortunate." For despite its magnificent power and virtuosity, it was a "corrupt" art, "confusing the curious with the beautiful." Even worse, it was corrupting, leading to "the sensuality and extravagance of later periods." Out of the Renaissance had come the "debased" styles— Baroque, Rococo, Louis XIV; out of it ultimately had come the eclecticism which had submerged his own Chicago. Whatever its original intentions, however great its potentials, the Renaissance for Wright was a "soulless blight, a warning, a veritable damnation."[13]

Strong words, these, with more than an echo of Cotton Mather. They reveal a very important aspect of Wright's personality. Despite a private life which already was feeding many a lurid newspaper story and despite a succession of designs which must rank among the most sensuously powerful in America, he remained at heart a Puritan. Here, in Florence, he was face to face with the fountainhead of the neo-Classic current which, four centuries after its inception, had overwhelmed Louis Sullivan and even now threatened Wright. His rage is understandable. It must have seemed to him (and not without reason) that he alone among American architects was fighting to establish an idiom of his own and was not, like them, a "parasite, feeding on past greatness."[14]

If, then, neither the past nor the present of Western art was usable,

112

what *was* an American architect in 1908 to do? A prophylactic measure would be to abjure ornament and decoration altogether: it was "dangerous. . . . You are usually better off without it."[15] "Look to the simple line, the clean though living form, quiet color."[16] He himself had been forced to follow this policy, he explained to a European audience in 1910; that was why his own work lacked a "complete, highly developed" system of ornament. "Self-imposed limitations are in part responsible for this lack of intricate enrichment, and partly the imperfect resources of our industrial system."[17] Then he makes this extremely significant statement: "Tenderness has often to be sacrificed to integrity." Thus, he says, he has forced himself to design buildings of a severely restrained nature "whose chief office is [to act as] a background or frame for the life within and about them." They are expressions of his conviction that "the ornamental forms of one's environment should be designed to wear well. [This] means that they must have absolute repose and make no especial claim upon attention; to be as far from realistic tendencies as a sense of reality can take them."[18] His own houses, he says, must be understood in this light. They are "a serious attempt to formulate some industrial and esthetic ideals that, in a quiet, rational way, will help to make a lovely thing of an American's home environment, produced without abuse by his own tools and dedicated in letter and spirit to him."[19]

Was this not sound advice to American artists and craftsmen in the first decade of the twentieth century? Wright is demanding no more of them than he rigorously demands of himself. His control of the birch and sumac mural in the Coonley house is no more severe than his control of the architecture of the room itself. Time is the acid test of such positions: what other living room of 1907 has worn as well as this? It must also be noted that he thought of this as a temporary policy, a sort of cooling-off period, until artist and public alike would have been purged of corrupted taste: "Ornament in the old sense is not for us yet."[20] At the same time he understood quite well that the process of developing a whole new system of art forms, dedicated in letter and spirit to the modern American, could not be artificially speeded up. "All architecture worthy of the name is a growth, in accord with natural feeling and industrial means, to serve actual needs. It cannot be put on from without."[21] It could only grow from within, "organically."

Breaking Home Ties
by Thomas Hovenden
(above) and *Christmas Bells* by Edwin
Howland Blashfield
(left).

Writing of the early 1890s, Wright recalls in his autobiography that he could not endure the "realism" of American art as represented by such immensely popular works as the Rogers sculptural groups or such widely reproduced genre paintings as Hovenden's *Breaking Home Ties.* We can only praise his judgment here. But was his knowledge of *fin-de-siècle* American art really confined to such vernacular works as these? Had he never heard of Eakins, Ryder, Homer? Had no news of Whistler, Sargent, or Cassatt reached him on the shores of Lake Michigan? The same question must be asked concerning French painting: Was he the only person in Chicago who had never heard of Degas, Monet, Renoir? Was he alone ignorant of Cézanne, Van Gogh, Gauguin? Was this, in short, a personal provincialism or one he shared with his entire culture?

The facts indicate that he was at least as well informed as the art experts who organized the great painting shows at the Columbian Exposition of 1893. One of these shows, "126 Foreign Masterpieces Owned by Americans," clearly indicated the limited knowledge and parochial taste of American collectors. They seemed wholly ignorant of Impressionist and post-Impressionist painting, showing no French painters later than Millet and Corot. As for the international section, it must have been an exercise in stupefying banality.[22] Blashfield was there with a canvas called *Christmas Bells;* J. G. Brown showed *The Card Trick;* other paintings by foreign artists were called variously *A Skating Party, Her First Born, Blind at Church.* It is true that Homer, Eakins, Sargent, and Whistler were also there, obscurely hung and awarded minor prizes, and that Cassatt had been commissioned to paint the north tympanum of the Women's Building. But the total impact of this art upon a young and perceptive sensibility could not have been less than traumatic; it alone would be explanation enough of Wright's lifelong distrust of Western painting.

Nor was the taste and knowledge of the local authorities any more advanced. In 1896, the Chicago Art Institute could not boast of a single Impressionist painter, though it did possess a Bouguereau and a Rosa Bonheur.[23] By 1901, the catalog listed forty-odd Japanese prints and a single Whistler but nothing more advanced;[24] and even as late as 1906, the Institute did not possess a single School of Paris painting.[25] It is true that some of the great Chicago collections had already begun. Martin

Ryerson would shortly begin buying Impressionists: and the lordly Mrs. Potter Palmer, who was chairman of the Board of Lady Managers of the Exposition, already owned four Renoirs, several Degas, a Pissarro, and a Sisley.[26] But these arbiters of fashionable Chicago were the exception and, in any event, were far above Wright's personal milieu. Despite a growing professional stature, his circle of friends and clients was still composed of middle-class professionals like himself—lawyers, doctors, newspaper editors. One of his few contacts with the great world of wealth and fashion came in 1907 when Harold McCormick commissioned him to design a house for a magnificent lake shore site at Lake Forest. Had it been built, the project Wright evolved for them would have been one of the greatest country houses of all times, but it was apparently far too advanced for Mrs. McCormick, who slipped off to New York one day and gave the commission to that impeccable eclectic, Charles Adams Platt.[27] Exchanging Wright for Platt was an eloquent indication of upper-class Chicago taste, which, as Sullivan had pointed out, was increasingly and grossly subservient to an Eastern taste it fancied to be more polished and secure.

Thus Wright appears no more limited in his knowledge of art, and incomparably more advanced in his tastes in it, than the people around him. Except for a handful of artists, no one in America was aware of the world-shaking events in France; and not until the great Armory Show of 1913 was the direction of American taste to be radically altered. What use Wright would have made of this art, had it been available to him then, is a matter of speculation. Certainly the artistic criteria of Gauguin, Van Gogh, and Matisse seem to us very similar to Wright's at the turn of the century; and it is pleasant to imagine an artistic union between them. Speculation aside, it is easy enough to understand why he rejected the painters and sculptors who *were* available to him. To whom, actually, could he have turned? Surely not to Kenyon Cox or Blashfield? To the Puvis de Chavannes of Mrs. Potter Palmer's *Sacred Grove?* The La Farge of the Church of the Ascension or the Frank Millet of the New York Pavilion at the Chicago Fair? In sculpture, the choice would have been no wider: MacMonnies of the plaster fountains at the Fair? Lorado Taft, whose *Great Lakes* (1913) and *Fountain of Time* (1922) were to grace Chicago? The Saint-Gau-

The painter Frank Millet (with model) at work on his mural for the New York Building, Columbian Exposition, Chicago, 1893.

French and English sculpture in the Fine Arts building, Columbian Exposition, Chicago, 1893.

dens of the *Grief;* the Daniel French of *The Angel of Death and the Young Sculptor?* We must remember that all these men and dozens more like them were on display at the Exposition in 1893. Wright probably saw them all, and we have only to look at their work to understand why he had to reject them as possible collaborators.

In effect, Wright was refusing to have any commerce with either the past or the present of Western art. This was a purely negative position and one which he could not, either as designer or as ideologue, long endure. Some alternative had to be found, and he found it in 1893 in the Japanese exhibits at the Columbian Exposition. There is some confusion about the exact sequence of events, much of it due to Wright himself, who could not endure the suggestion that his work was influenced by other men, since "influence" was for him synonymous with "plagiarism."[28] But we know that as Louis Sullivan's chief designer Wright often visited Sullivan's Transportation Building when it was under construction; he must have seen the Japanese "Hoo-o-Den" Palace and Nippon Tea House then as well as later when they were open. And he certainly saw the great show of Japanese prints, architecture, and sculpture in the Fine Arts Palace.

Whatever the details, the impact of the Japanese print upon Wright (as upon many other Western artists of his generation) was catalytic, electrifying. It opened up before him a whole new system of esthetics which illumined not only the formal problems of painting (composition, color, delineation, etc.) but introduced him to an organically unified tradition of architecture, landscape and furniture design as well. He was attracted to the Japanese for much the same reasons as had been those other American artists, James McNeil Whistler and Lafcadio Hearn. And, considering that architecture is a much more obdurate medium than painting or poetry, his response is quite prompt. A full decade would pass before the lessons from the Japanese were fully digested, as announced by the stunning houses for the Willittses (1902) and the Martins (1903–04). But already in the same year as the Fair, the Winslow house shows us that the change in Wright has begun; and succeeding years show us how his whole artistic life is being irradiated by Hokusai and Hiroshige.

Here, as elsewhere, his actual work in architecture is fully paced by essays explaining his thinking. From them we can see how profoundly

Japanese "Hoo-o-den" Palace, Columbian Exposition.

Willitts house, Highland Park, Ill., 1902.

he was moved by the principles of Japanese art and how little danger, consequently, there ever was of his merely copying their forms. At the personal level, he tells us, the Japanese print taught him the "gospel of simplification . . . that organic integrity within the work of art itself is fundamentally a law of beauty. Without it, you may make your work a meretricious mask with literal suggestions or effects but . . . the quality in the work which is real, escapes; and the would-be artist remains where he belongs, outside." The astringent simplicity of the Japanese deflates the mock heroics of Western art, showing that "a sand bank and the sea . . . may yield a higher message . . . than Angelo's magnificent pictorial sculpture. [The print] has taught that sentiment has nothing in common with sentimentality or sensuous feeling with sensuality."[29]

What dazzled Wright in Japanese art was its power of abstraction, its capacity for extracting from complex and turgid reality the artistic essence of each problem. This enabled Wright to cut his last ties with eclectic architectural idioms and with art forms full of raw gesture and anecdote. It taught him what had to be done and how to do it; the fertilizing effect is apparent in his work and generously admitted in his essays.

He drew another conclusion, more generalized and even more significant, from his experience with Japanese art. It was completely foreign to our own artistic tradition; precisely because of this "ethnic eccentricity," as he puts it, "this art is a particularly safe means of cultivation for us, because the individual initiative of the artist is not paralyzed with forms he can use ready-made."[30] This is an observation which deserves our attention, for it reveals a very clear understanding on Wright's part of the cultural dynamics of the period. The world of American art in 1900 was drowned, submerged, saturated with forms from the Western past. These forms were umbilically tied, by history and literature, to set responses and attitudes. It was therefore impossible for a young American to study them clinically: the forms of the Western past obscured the principles on which it was originally built.

Wright does not claim for Oriental art any unique mastery of the simplified, the distilled essential, the truly abstracted. He is quite aware that these properties reside in all great art, West and East alike. He does believe that they can be studied with more clarity and detachment by the young artist and designer in Oriental than in Western examples. Just because it is so eccentric to the orbit of the artist's own prejudices, he can study it without crippling entanglements, with an objectivity which he simply could not bring to bear on his own artistic tradition.

It is a matter of record that few architects or artists in 1906 were willing or able to follow Wright's advice. But he did. As if to prove to the world that these principles *would* work, in sculpture and mural as well as in architecture, he produced the Midway Gardens in 1913. Here, in this most festive of all his projects, he made a wider and bolder use of independent art forms than he ever had before or ever did again. He was determined to solve the problem, even if it meant doing sculpture and mural with his own bare hands. "I clearly saw my trusty T-square and aspiring triangle as a means to the end I had in mind."[31] As a matter of fact, there was a young sculptor named Ianelli on the Midway job. About his exact contributions Wright is vague, if amiable. But the great interior mural so oddly reminiscent of Kandinsky; the smaller geometric bas reliefs in cast concrete; the lovely caryatids around the garden wall, half geisha and half Gibson Girl, warm and tender for all their cubist modeling—all these bear the indelible mark of Wright's own genius.

It was not, perhaps, great art—Wright certainly never claimed that it was—but it was peculiarly appropriate for its purpose. Viewed in its

Midway Gardens, Chicago, 1913. Alfonso Ianelli, sculptor; Frank Lloyd Wright, architect.

Cottage Grove Avenue façade, Midway Gardens.

Robie house, Chicago, 1909. Frank Lloyd Wright, architect.

context, it stands up very well indeed. It was apparently Wright's last effort to establish a working relationship with the other arts. It was certainly the last building in which the explicit statement of art was to occupy a position of such importance. From then on, art, ornament, decoration become increasingly subdued, abstracted, oblique in statement or meaning—i.e., "organic to the structure.".

There was a time when Wright was so conscious of the need to integrate the plastic arts with architecture that he deliberately sought those forms which would harmonize with his own. He did not find them; and, though he might have been as strong willed and arrogant then as he was half a century later when he designed the Guggenheim Museum, it cannot be said that the fault was wholly his. For history has proved his standards to have been correct, those of his contemporary artists—at least those whose talents were actually accessible to him in *fin-de-siècle* America—to have been abysmally, pathetically in error.

This failure to establish contact with the fine arts was to congeal, in later years, into a contemptuous disregard of them. Architecture, always the most important art, was destined to become the only art. Similarly, the mistaken painters and sculptors of his youth were, imperceptibly with the passing years, to become to his mind typical of *all* artists. This was a tragedy—for us as much as for Wright. He proceeded to hew out for himself a beautiful, strong, and marvelously complete esthetic. Yet it was, at the same time, a uniquely private system in which, just as there was little room for collaboration with other artists when he was alive, just so there is little chance of direct progeny now that he is dead.

The new museum expresses this tragic fact. Yet that Wright's policy was a wise one, during that hazardous quarter century 1887–1913, there can be no question. It enabled him to produce a great constellation of beautiful buildings: from the Larkin (1904), Unity Temple (1906), the Coonley, Gilmore, and Robie houses (1908–1909) to Taliesin East (1911) and the Midway Gardens. No other architect in America, no other architect in the whole world, could have matched his creativity during these golden years.

8. HOMAGE TO A HERO

With the passing of Frank Lloyd Wright in April 1959, American architecture lost its one authentic giant. In sheer magnitude of accomplishment, no other American approaches him. With a courage rare among mortals, he fought for over seventy years, first to establish, and then to defend, an original body of architectural principles. On these grounds alone, he would have deserved a brave man's funeral. But the matter goes deeper than that. Time was to prove that Wright was not merely courageous; he was also, within broad limits, entirely correct. Contemporary architecture stands very largely upon foundations he supplied. And it was this much larger fact that entitled him to a hero's rites.

Wright's work, like his personality, was never neutral. It may well have made as many enemies as it did friends. But surely no one, now that his tempestuous presence has left us, can deny him his splendid scale. His successful works are majestic in themselves, earth-shakers in their impact upon architectural development; even his failures have a kind of Wagnerian splendor. To measure this scale, this impact, he will inevitably be compared with those three other great figures of modern international architecture with whom he so long and so unwillingly shared the spotlight. But the comparisons, unless we are very careful, are apt to be meaningless, for although he was only fifteen or twenty years older than Le Corbusier, Miës, and Gropius, he was not really their contemporary. A relatively small span of years marked a difference in epochs, not mere generations. These younger men stood not beside him but upon his shoulders: for, by the time they were ready to begin their first buildings, Wright's earlier work had already done much to prepare the world to receive them.

Age alone could have made him into a monument: to have lived and worked so long would have endowed him, like Shaw or Berenson, with a special dimension. Not one but several generations of architects matured within the shadow of his work and—for the younger men, at least—he was both a historic force and a living presence. The whole great corpus of Wright's work lay in the twentieth century, yet in all his basic attitudes he remained a nineteenth-century man, much closer to Jefferson than to Eisenhower. It is this fact—that he spanned the watershed of two epochs—and not merely his long life which makes it difficult to take a just measure of the man.

Much that might have seemed willful, arbitrary, or obscure in Wright will cease to seem so if we remember how different were his standards from those of present-day America. Actually many of those eccentricities for which he was so famous stemmed from a sturdy nineteenth-century consistency. He was an anarchist like Thoreau, a moralist like Emerson, a humanist like Whitman, an iconoclast like Twain. He detested regimentation, whether Moscow's or Madison Avenue's, and fought it off whenever it touched him. He believed in personal freedom *and* personal responsibility and was always willing to take the consequences of his private decisions. He believed in democracy but, as he saw it sink into modern mediocrity, he denounced it, no matter how powerful its organs of power and opinion. He had an honest contempt for social pretension and liked nothing better than puncturing the Babbitts and Plushbottoms. He challenged ugliness, no matter how profitable an ugly building might be. He hated war, *all war,* and said so no matter what the climate of opinion. These were the old-fashioned virtues on which he based his conduct. Internally, they were completely consistent; but they often gave his actions a prickly continuity which led him into collision, decade after decade, with that whole apparatus of government, law, church, and army which the English so pungently have dubbed "The Establishment."

His nineteenth-century origins also explain other attitudes in the man. The farm background of his Wisconsin boyhood gave him his love and understanding of nature, his uncanny sense of site and landscape. It probably also explains his distrust of the city, of the standards of urban life in general; it certainly explains the romantic agrarianism of his *Broadacre City.* He admired the deep and wordless knowledge of farmer and craftsman, the skills which come from work rather than study; but this led him to a distrust of formal education

125

and of scholarship itself—a distrust which, in later years, was to become simply parochial. Whatever the University of Wisconsin may have denied him, its Engineering School certainly gave him the theoretical and mathematical basis for his brilliant structural design. His proud individualism as a designer was also geared to the leisurely, small-scaled office of the 1890s. He could never bring himself to admit that it was inadequate to mid-twentieth-century demands, that the much larger size and complexity of modern building required the collaboration of specialists. He steadfastly refused to see the need for bureaucratic architecture or, as he called it, "design by committee." (A camel, he loved to say, was merely a horse designed by a committee.)

Wright always insisted upon his absolute independence from the esthetic forces of his times. He seemed to consider it an affront to his integrity as an artist to suggest that he might be influenced by his contemporaries. "Influence" was for him synonymous with "plagiarism." He had spent so many arduous years fashioning his own idiom of expression (years in which his contemporaries were the most shameless eclectics) that he could not tolerate the suggestion of a connection, no matter how remote or indirect, with the men around him. He denied all such connections, and this led him into absurd semantic difficulties, as when he called Sullivan *lieber meister* and simultaneously asserted that he owed nothing to the older man!

The fact is that Wright, like all truly great artists, was extremely sensitive to all the world around him. Verbally, he might deny the influence of Sullivan, of the Japanese and Art Nouveau, of Cubism and de Stijl, of North American Indian and pre-Columbian art. Artistically, his buildings contradict him; they show beyond a shadow of a doubt how responsive he was. Like a seismograph, his work registers every significant tremor in the world of art. But, unlike a seismograph, his great creative talent always transformed these external stimuli into forms inescapably his own. It is sad to think that he ever felt it necessary to assert his originality. His work itself proves him to be, like Picasso and Le Corbusier, among the greatest artistic inventors of all time.

Nor was the miracle of Wright's response to these stimuli exclusively a matter of esthetics. Knotty technical problems always underlay them, and Wright's mastery of them is evidence of the uniqueness of his contribution. This process is very clear, for example, in the lovely Millard and Ennis houses in California, which belong to his so-called Mayan period of the early 1920s. Though clearly influenced by pre-Columbian architecture, whose acquaintance he had first made long ago at the Columbian Exposition, they are not copies. The shining gravity of the Mayan temples sprang from their sculpture-encrusted limestone masonry; Wright could not have "copied" these, even if he had wanted to. The budget would not have permitted either carved sculpture or limestone, and the building codes of a California often shaken by earthquakes would have frowned on rubble masonry walls. We can see, instead, the Wrightian process of transmutation, the special alchemy by which he extracted beauty from his cheapest building material (concrete) fabricated in its commonest form (cast block). Some of these blocks are plain; some are cast in geometric patterns which, for all their basic simplicity, create a rich and intricate fabric when woven into a wall. And this wall is simultaneously made as strong as it is handsome by an earthquake-resistant system of integral reinforcing bars.

The apparently effortless way in which Wright solved such problems lent an air of deceptive simplicity to his solutions. One needs almost to be an expert to understand the complexity beneath them. Actually, as we have seen, he demonstrated this uncanny capacity to absorb technological advance and to convert it into new esthetic discoveries very early in his career. When all his colleagues were going to great lengths to conceal their electric lighting, steam heat, and steel frames in traditional forms, Wright was using them as a means of escape from the prison house of eclecticism. Central heating was the instrument whereby he destroyed the hermetic room-as-a-box and created instead the free-flowing space of his open plan. Modern plate glass made possible not merely larger windows but whole walls open to the garden, so that indoor and outdoor space flowed together into a single whole. Electricity meant not chandeliers converted from oil or gas but whole new concepts of dramatic lighting. And steel meant not a cheap way of building fake Corinthian columns but of creating daring new forms such as the hovering cantilevers of the Robie house. Out of technical progress Wright made esthetic invention. He is in this sense the real inventor of the modern American house.

This artistic prescience won him a small circle of friends and clients and a steadily expanding prestige internationally. It is not true, as he sometimes liked to pretend in later years, that he was recognized abroad before he was at home. As early as 1907 *The Ladies' Home Journal* had published his houses as models to be followed. But it is true that his uncompromising artistic position brought him into headlong and chronic collision with the most powerful strata of his own society. In him the keepers of official art detected a dangerous iconoclast, and they managed to ostracize him for decades on end. He was ostentatiously ignored by governmental bodies at every level—municipal, county, and state; and though he was decorated by the Emperor of Japan and made an honorary citizen of Florence, he, like Dante, was never recognized by his own national government. In the face of this ostracism, unwilling and indeed incapable of surrendering his artistic and philosophical arms, Wright was often isolated and alone.

There is, of course, nothing especially novel about a great artist's being ignored by his period. He is usually canonized only when very old or (better yet) safely dead. What was unusual in Wright was his response to ostracism. He seemed actually to thrive on it. He became a guerrilla fighter in the artistic underground. He established his headquarters in the esthetic *maquis* of rural Wisconsin and the Arizona desert; from these strong points he would sally forth to raid the fortress of official art, to attack with the *brio* and zest of an Indian horseman those keepers of culture, the clubs and museums and universities of the metropolitan East. There is no denying he was good at it. He had a sort of genius at publicity, as many big organizations—including the tax department of his own state of Wisconsin—learned at their expense. He was not always polite in these skirmishes, and sometimes he was wrong. But there was certainly justification for his anger. He lived to see great commissions—embassies and air academies, state capitols and world fairs—awarded to men who, whatever else they were, were certainly not his peers. Since the orbit of his private life seldom carried him into those clubs, committee rooms, and golf courses where such commissions are ordinarily decided upon, Wright was dogged throughout by the *fait accompli.* Survive it he did, but he could not and would not let it go undenounced. And if good manners did not always mark these denunciations, neither did justice mark the way in which he was repeatedly passed over for commissions to which, by every professional measure, he was clearly entitled.

He seldom surrendered a position, no matter what it cost him. He wrote and spoke fluently, and he loved the limelight like the lonely man he was. On the lecture platform he came face to face with that audience whose affection and support he so deeply needed, though he was too proud to admit it. These circumstances often involved him in controversies where he had no business being, led into polemics he might subsequently regret. And yet, if we plot the whole course of Wright's long campaign for organic architecture, we will not be able to deny its remarkable consistency. Few men have ever fought with more unflinching, unyielding commitment to principle: marriage, children, bank account, reputation—none of these outweighed his commitment to his art. What these principles were he tried his best to make clear to his fellow Americans. That is why he wrote so many books. That is why in later years he stood before so many microphones and television cameras. Unfortunately, a verbal exposition of architectural principles can never be fully satisfactory, even in the hands of a disciplined verbalist— and this Wright never was. Unlike his architecture, his later writing was lush, unpruned, a thunderous mixture of Whitman and Carlyle. Sometimes his writing is very perceptive, as in the wonderful essay on the Japanese print. Sometimes his prose is laced with wit; but more often it is humorless and obscure. He himself did not edit his writing, and he allowed no one else to do so.

Hence it is to his buildings, rather than his writings, to which we must turn for the clearest exposition of his principles. Here there is little possibility of misunderstanding. Already, in that first great constellation of buildings which is described between the Larkin (1904) and the Midway Gardens (1914), his principles are set forth with electrifying clarity. They announce a new vocabulary of form, a new palette of texture and color, a new attitude toward nature and man which parallels the contemporary experiments of Cézanne, Matisse, and Picasso. And the fact that these buildings, like these paintings, have still the power to move us so, is the best possible proof of the prescience with which they solved the esthetic problems of our epoch. They have, in a very real sense, created the modern vision.

It is strange indeed that men who should have known better could have misunderstood Wright's principles, could have attacked them as un-American (as the American Legion did in the United States Air Force Academy case), for a more typical American never lived. His strengths and his weaknesses are ours. His artistic declaration of independence was, at the esthetic level, the precise equivalent of our noblest social and cultural perspectives. Both envision the fullest development of the individual in a new kind of society—free of the fetters of the past, of the hierarchies of king and clergy, of hereditary power and privilege. Just as the Bill of Rights denies them existence, so Wright's architecture rejects all their iconography of caste, power, and privilege. His houses—even the largest and most expensive of them—are democratic in spirit, just as Monticello, for all its elegance, is also democratic in spirit.

The analogy is not accidental. Wright greatly admired Jefferson, and like him, he was persuaded that democracy is the best forcing bed of ability, talent, and genius. Its function is to produce for each generation a cadre of true leaders—an aristocracy of intelligence and ability, not of inherited wealth and title. Wright's youth had been spent in threadbare parsonage parlors whose genteel but coruscating poverty had provoked an allergic response of pride and arrogance from a thin-skinned and sensitive young man. Most of his adult life, on the other hand, was spent against a background of beauty and physical ease. But this never led to snobbery in the man. He was entirely unlike the typical self-made man, that parvenue American who uses democracy merely to climb to the seats of power and who then, denying his origins, dons the traditional accouterments of power. It was precisely this kind of American whom Wright detested as a climber who, in a desperate bid for a prefabricated background, bought genealogies, coats of arms, period furniture, and Georgian or Jacobean houses.

As the terrifying organs of concentration and monopoly closed down on mid-twentieth-century America, Wright's concept of social process seemed increasingly Utopian. The boss's son, the boy with good connections, the organization man—these seemed destined to run the country and form the new aristocracy. But however anachronistic his philosophy might have been politically, it was certainly successful esthetically. It produced some of America's most beautiful houses—a beauty which the world could recognize as uniquely American even if Americans themselves could not.

The personal lives of all great figures are subjected to a greater scrutiny than those of lesser men. Frank Lloyd Wright had his full share of such attention and it often led to clamorous headlines. Yet, if we examine the circumstances, we usually find that they merely involve his trying to lead a private life in the only way he thought it could be lived. We might not always accept his standards, but we can only respect the candor and courage with which he acted upon them. He is often accused of having been selfish and unkind—to his first wife, to his children, to the aging Sullivan. And indeed, at a personal level, his actions often do seem harsh and procrustean. Yet we might ask, with Wright, who was kind and considerate to him? We must understand that he saw himself in all seriousness as engaged in a great crusade, all-consuming in its importance and with little quarter asked or given. Challenged about his own activities during the battle, he might well have answered that he was always too busy keeping the cannons loaded to have had time to carry calf's foot jelly to the sick.

Because society so often placed fetters upon actions which he felt to be both necessary and moral, Wright was compelled to hew out for himself a private kingdom of behavior. By any objective measure, this kingdom had its irrational dimensions. It had, for instance, some oddly feudal relationships—with his students, with his workmen, and with his admirers and the merely curious who came in increasing numbers to gaze at him at work. If toward these latter he sometimes seemed both arrogant and belligerent, his dilemma must be understood. Like all artists, Wright needed an audience, yet this same audience could only partially understand him while it devoured his time, his energies, his patience. So, on occasion, he lashed out at it in what was actually a kind of incredulous exasperation, on the part of a brave man who dared to be himself, at men who allowed themselves to be intimidated into accepting less than their heritage.

He loved young people and was generous of his time with them. But he was not a great teacher and knew it. (He once described his disappointment thus: he had hoped to be the source, the fountainhead, of a great river of design. But, instead, people merely copied him—"they drove two-inch galvanized pipe into me and siphoned off what they needed.") The very circumstances of his life had forced his work into a very special form, a form not easily shared or communicated in a teacher-pupil relationship. Though his general effect upon the field as a whole was immense and benign, Wright's own presence was too overwhelming for most students.

The architectural expression of Wright's private kingdom took form in two of the loveliest houses in the world. To his two Taliesins, in Arizona and Wisconsin, he brought real splendor: the excitement of a presence larger than life, a touch both passionate and gentle, a composition at once lyrical and strong. No one who ever had the privilege of visiting the Taliesins when Wright was in residence there could have failed to feel himself ensconced in a special kind of oasis, in which the raw and hostile forces of surrounding life had somehow been reorganized into a landscape of blessed peace and plenty. In these two wonderful houses, of all the wonderful buildings he designed, we can most clearly see the sort of world his genius would have built for us Americans, had we but fully used it.

Frank Lloyd Wright in leaving us has bequeathed us an architecture as much enriched and deepened as was the English language upon the death of William Shakespeare. Whether we know it or not, we are all his debtors.

9. A LEVER LONG ENOUGH: HOW GROPIUS MOVED THE WORLD

The shakers and makers of the modern world—such figures as Einstein, Shaw, Matisse, and Wright—all spent their lives under a very special set of historical conditions. They lived to be very old men in a period of fantastically accelerated social change. Unlike the great prophets of past times, they survived not merely to see their predictions come true: they lived on into a world in which their works had become commonplace, the very warp and woof of everyday life. The prophet had overrun his prophecy.

This situation, so novel in human affairs, creates a dilemma both for them and for us, who have so hugely profited from their efforts. It means that they exist for us at two distinctly different levels: they have simultaneously the scale of legendary heroes and the normal dimensions of colleagues and contemporaries. And this complicates enormously the necessary task of weighing their contributions to contemporary life.

Walter Gropius, at the age of 77, confronts us with just such a dilemma. One of the few actual inventors of modern architecture, the creator of the world famous Bauhaus, and the most influential architectural teacher alive, Gropius is, at the same time, a successful practicing architect with the greatest volume of work in his entire career. He is an active and vocal member of a profession which has been powerfully shaped by standards which he himself helped establish, many years ago, in another land. The profession itself has hundreds of his pupils, hundreds of admirers, and thousands of others who, whether they know it or not, have been affected by his example. Gropius thus moves in a world which is doubly of his making: made by him then and made again today.

133

Throughout a long and active life in international architecture he has played three interconnected yet separate roles: educator, designer, and critic. His contributions in all three areas have been impressive, though they have fluctuated in relative importance from decade to decade. The disasters of modern history have played a large role in this fluctuation, sharply dividing his life into several distinct phases. But Gropius has never ceased to be active at every level of his chosen field. He has always been an outspoken critic and consistent theoretician of the social aspects of architecture, housing, and city planning. This criticism was perhaps most trenchant (as it was probably most comprehensive) during the German years (1919–34); but his recent statements show that there has been no diminution in his social convictions. He has been a continuously influential architect. It was as the designer of two sensational buildings that he began his career; his middle years were marked by immensely significant projects, including those for the Bauhaus itself; and it is as the architect of the great new University of Bagdad that his career is now being capped. But these two aspects of his career, important as they have been, are not the center of his fame and influence. The lever with which Gropius moved the world was a design of another order: a great educational invention, the school of the Bauhaus.

The revolution which he began that April day in 1919 when he created the Bauhaus was to set off a widening circle of repercussions which would utimately leave not a corner of the globe untouched. Who would have guessed, when he signed the contract with "the Court Chamberlain's Office, acting with the consent of the Provisional Republican Government of Saxe-Weimar"[1] (the very ambiguity of the phrasing reflects the political revolution which was rocking Germany)—who would have guessed that theories were being evolved which would one day shape buildings and artifacts, fabrics and furniture, in the islands of Japan, the coasts of Brazil, the steaming valley of the Tigris? And how could that young German architect have guessed that these same theories would guide him, decades later, in the design of buildings in (of all improbable places!) Athens and Baghdad for (of all unlikely clients!) the United States Government and the King of Iraq.[2] How elliptical is history!

Young American architects who have reached maturity since the Second World War are often no more aware of the historic significance of the Bauhaus than a young jet pilot would be of the Wright Brothers' work at Kittyhawk. It is possible, in such circles, either to hear this significance denied or to have the Bauhaus blamed for all sorts of disasters which have subsequently overtaken design. Yet Gropius himself said in 1960 that, had he his life as an educator to live over, he would feel it necessary to change his theories "only in detail."[3] There is no arrogance here: this is the sober conviction of a modest man. Whose estimate, then, is correct? Whose judgment corresponds most closely to objective reality?

If we analyze the ideological positions which Gropius staked out for the Bauhaus at its very inception, and if we study the body of work which grew out of it in the following decade, then we can only conclude that these principles were neither mistaken in 1919 nor obsolete in 1960. For a central aspect of his work in education has been his understanding of the dangers to design which are inherent in the separation of head and hand, theory and practice, intellectual and manual worker, artist and craftsman. He has tried always to bridge the arbitrary divisions between the two, to reunite them for the common enrichment of both. The Staatliche Bauhaus in Weimar offered the first and most comprehensive opportunity he had to put his theories into practice. Even the two existing schools which he merged to form the new institution symbolize this ambition: the Grand Ducal School of Applied Arts and the Grand Ducal Academy of Arts. The curriculum which he devised for this combination was a rational effort to merge the best of craft training with all that was valid in the academy. He was opposed to "art for art's sake," believing that every artist was first of all a craftsman: "only in rare blessed moments of inspiration, moments beyond the control of his will, his work may blossom into art."[4] Thus every Bauhaus student—no matter what his ambitions or abilities—went through the same workshop training. At the same time, Gropius was careful never to vulgarize the distinction between competence and creativity:

Art, in fact, is not a branch of science which can be learned step by step, from a book. Innate artistic ability can [not be taught but] only intensified by influencing the whole being . . . the ability to draw is all too frequently confused with the ability to produce creative design. Like dexterity in handicrafts, it is, however, no more than a skill . . . virtuosity . . . is not art.[5]

135

He aimed at avoiding both the boorish illiteracy of the modern crafts-man and the irresponsible precocity of the academically trained artist. Thus he hoped to recreate in the world of modern industrial society the same sort of healthy, organic unity in all phases of design which had characterized all preindustrial societies.

It is a measure of his maturity (as well as that of his circle generally) that Gropius was able to steer an even course between those extremes on which so many theories foundered. The specific principles upon which the Bauhaus was founded are not easily encapsulated. Gropius himself found it necessary to amplify and develop them repeatedly after the publication of the first manifesto.[6] In essence they were these:

1. "The Bauhaus believes the machine to be our modern medium of design and seeks to come to terms with it."[7]
2. All design must recognize this fact of life and distill a new set of esthetic criteria from it. Such a process would, for architecture, lead to "clear, organic [form] whose inner logic will be radiant and naked, unencumbered by lying façades and trickeries."[8]
3. The Bauhaus teaches "the common citizenship of all forms of creative work and their logical interdependence upon one another."[9]
4. The scale and complexity of modern problems necessitates collaborative design. "Any industrially produced object is the result of countless experiments, of long systematic research."[10] The design school must recognize this and equip the student with "the common basis on which many individuals are able to create together a superior unit of work.[11]
5. The education of the designer "must include a thorough, practical manual training in workshops actively engaged in production, coupled with sound theoretical instruction in the laws of design.[12]

This was the program which catapulted the Bauhaus into international prominence, making it the most important single force in the design world in the period between the wars. Every field of design registered its influence: architecture, product design, furniture; fabrics, silverware and pottery; graphics, typography, painting, advertising; photography, movies, stagecraft, ballet. And everywhere its influence was benign. As a program, its capacity to regenerate design derived from its essentially correct analysis of the relation between design and production in an industrialized world.

In its short and crisis-ridden life, the Bauhaus trained over 500 men and women in various fields. Its publications, exhibitions, and lectures so precisely filled a vacuum that its influence was out of all proportion to its size. It irradiated all of Western Europe and (after Gropius's arrival at Harvard in 1937) America. Though the Bauhaus curriculum could not be applied at the Graduate School of Design, the Gropius philosophy of design could.[13] It made Harvard a leading world center of architectural studies and produced a whole generation of designers who have now emerged as leaders of the profession. The durability of the Bauhaus concept is proved by the fact that designers have been coasting for decades upon the momentum generated by those first historic years at Weimar and Dessau. Yet education for design has not followed the precedent set by the Bauhaus; it seems instead to have taken the opposite path. Art schools and trade schools have proliferated; but where in the world today is there an institution which faces the problem as squarely, as profoundly, as did the Bauhaus in its time?

Or is this program obsolete, as many contemporary critics today maintain? Does an analysis of objective conditions reveal any fundamental change which would make it less valuable? The fact is that the conditions against which Gropius reacted in 1919 have grown steadily more acute in the Western world and most acute of all in America. Industrial production grows continuously more complex, dominating every aspect of life. The designer is more and more removed from any control over, or any real understanding of, science and technology. And the process of design deteriorates into mere cosmetics: robbed of any firm base in function, it has become the prisoner of fad and fashion. In such a context it should be clear that, far from having "outgrown" the need for a Bauhaus type of education, we need it more than ever.

Two charges, both of them esthetic, are brought against the Bauhaus by its critics today. The first is that it established a *style:* the second is that that style is "bad." These charges, though related, are not at all the same thing. Gropius has always denied that he had any ambition to establish a *style;* he has always maintained that, on the contrary, it was a basic *methodology* of design which he sought. In his very first statement on arriving in this country in 1937 he said:

It is not my intention to introduce a . . . cut and dried "Modern Style" from Europe, but rather to introduce a method of approach which allows one to tackle a problem according to its peculiar conditions . . . an attitude toward the problems of our generation which is unbiased, original and elastic.[14]

A democrat at heart and a tireless advocate of collaborative work, he has repeatedly rejected what seemed to him to be the dictatorial implications in the issue of style. When a sapling was planted in Chicago in honor of his 70th birthday, he said he hoped it would grow into "a tree in which birds of many colors and shapes [could] sit and feel sustained. . . . I realize that I am a figure covered with many labels . . . 'Bauhaus Style,' 'International Style,' 'Functional Style'—these have almost succeeded in hiding the human core behind it all." He was eager, he went on, to escape this caricature of his real position.[15] There is something at once comic and sad in the repeated efforts of this great man to disentangle himself from a semantic snare which was of no real consequence. For whenever any group of men agree upon a common method of accomplishing common tasks, a common system of expression (i.e., a style) will ultimately appear. Ours is the first period in history to be embarrassed by this cultural certainty.

Gropius has become the victim of industralism's fantastic capacity for mimicry and multiplication. A powerful designer, committed to a "suprapersonal" style of expression, he has always attracted students and disciples; and as his fame and influence spread, he was paid the compliment of piracy and parody of what he designed. The same thing happened to the Bauhaus. It furnished the world with a new set of prototypes; too often the world merely made them into stereotypes. A third of a century later these prototypes may very well be inadequate for today's tastes and sensibilities. But this does not alter the fact that the Bauhaus, in its day, was not the jailor but the liberator of the Western designer, giving him the first stylistic freedom he had enjoyed since the end of the Medieval period.

The other charge against the Bauhaus runs thus: it created a style which was "bad" because it was "cold," "inhuman," "narrowly functional," "mechanistic," etc. These are the judgments of a generation which took no part in the great esthetic battles of the 1920s and which is consequently in no position to understand the terms of that revolutionary struggle. The only way that modern form could evolve from the *fin-de-siècle* morass was to disavow *all* the past: here the artistic revolution paralleled the political. Evaluations must take account of this historic fact. The fight was very bitter, with no quarter asked or given and opinion polarized around extreme positions. After all, for "purely" esthetic reasons, the Bauhaus was twice driven out of its home (by reactionaries in Weimar in 1925; by the Nazis in Dessau in 1932.) It was denounced as "artbolshevism which must be wiped out": storm troopers called on the "national German Spirit" to "rescue" German art from the modernists[16]—a task which Hitler was shortly to accomplish with gruesome thoroughness.

There was no shortage of wit, passion, or courage among the partisans of the new architecture; here Gropius was neither first nor alone. Already before the First World War, the Viennese architect Adolph Loos had penned a wickedly effective attack on historic ornament (and, by extension, on eclecticism in general). In his famous essay, *Ornament and Crime,* he wrote: "The artist used to stand for health and strength, at the pinnacle of humanity; but the modern ornamentalist is either a cultural laggard or a pathological case." Loos argued that no ornament at all was permissible to civilized man: the Papuans, since they were aborigines, might be forgiven if they "tattoo their skins, decorate their boats, their oars—everything they can get their hands on. But a modern man who tattoos himself . . . [is] either a latent criminal or a degenerate aristocrat . . . The true greatness of our age [is] that it can no longer bring forth ornament. We have vanquished ornament," Loos boasted, "and broken through into an ornamentless world. . . . Freedom from ornament is a sign of mental strength."[17]

Gropius himself, in the first spring of peace, had written a fiery call for that new "radiant and naked" architecture:

Is not [architecture] the crystallized expression of the noblest thoughts of man, his ardor, his humanity, his faith, his religion? All this it used to be— once. But who, in our period of accursed expediency, lets himself still be enraptured by its all-embracing message? We should cry out in shame against these wastes of ugliness when walking through our streets and cities! Let us face it! These drab, hollow and meaningless fakeries in which we live and work will leave behind a mortifying testimony to the spiritual fall from grace of our generation.[18]

It was in terms such as these that the battle was fought. The furnace of controversy burned up the sweet, the pretty, the soft, with all their connotations of decadence. The new forms were to be pure, cool, and abstract—ventilated by justice, lighted by reason. How far the blazing passions of the First World War had driven the generation which fought it is dramatized in the first show of the young (and wounded) veteran from the Eastern front, Laszlo Moholy-Nagy. In 1922, in a gallery called *The Storm,* he exhibited a number of Constructivist canvases, including three which had been painted by telephone! "He dictated the paintings to the foreman in a sign factory," his widow wrote, "using a color chart and an order blank of graph paper to specify the location of form elements and their exact hue."[19] Here was the ultimate effort to purify art of all human passion, to lift it above the personal, the subjective, the fallible and to establish the objective independence of visual form, divorced from all narrative.

Much of this work aspired to be "functional"—i.e., to extract its formal properties directly from the task to be performed: surely that ambition needs no apology or defense. It is also true that, simultaneously, much of this new form drew its inspiration directly from the machine. Science and technology appeared to that generation as much safer paragons than human passion. Here again Moholy-Nagy defines its attitude, this time verbally, in one of those incandescent manifestoes which were so usual at the time: "The reality of our century is technology: the invention, construction and maintenance of the machine. To be a user of the machine is to be of the spirit of this century. It has replaced the transcendental spiritualism of past eras. . . ." And from this he draws what seemed to the period the necessary conclusions: "This is the root of Socialism, the final liquidation of feudalism. . . . Make your peace with it."[20] Most of the great figures of the period shared this general perspective. Poems, paintings, sculptures; ballet, sonata, and cinema all celebrated the forms, movements, and promises of the machine. Thus, when Le Corbusier's famous dictum ("the house a machine for living") echoed Gropius's ("we want an architecture adapted to our world of machines") both were speaking the very language of Western humanism in the early 1920s.

Yet, even in those enthusiastic years, Gropius was no blindly uncritical worshiper of technology. "Mechanized work is lifeless, proper only to the lifeless machine," he warned. "So long as the machine-economy remains an end in itself, rather than a means of freeing the intellect from the burden of mechanized labor, the individual will remain enslaved and society will remain disordered."[21] He aspired to the mastery of the machine by the designer in order to create a serene and anonymous architecture, capable of flexible response to the demands of life upon it. And this conscious effort at purification is precisely what has given the idiom of Gropius and his colleagues at the Bauhaus its amazing durability. Time has its own special method of isolating the meretricious and ephemeral in art and of exposing it to the merciless ridicule of simple distance. In this context, the Bauhaus record is admirable: few objects from that period have survived as well as Gropius's Tribune Tower of 1922 or the Adler automobile of 1931. And Paul Klee's paintings, Marcel Breuer's chairs, Anni Albers's textiles continue to display that stylistic durability which is internal evidence of continuing validity.

The diffidence of modern artists and architects before the very word *style* is understandable. It has its origins precisely in the Bauhaus period and is the result of their traumatic experience—Hitchcock once called it the dark night of eclecticism—in being forced to employ dead styles to express living artistic concepts. (We would have a roughly comparable situation today if we compelled the nuclear physicist to express his concepts of the universe in the English of Beowulf or the French of Abbé Suger.) Yet, if the revolt against the historic styles became by extension the rejection of style itself, the results would be visually anarchic as well as intellectually absurd. Gropius has always been aware of this paradox. On the one hand, he has correctly argued that "the creation of standard types for everyday use is a social necessity." And for him the search for that standard "implies the seeking out of the best, the separation of the essential and supra-personal from the personal and accidental." The standard thus becomes "a cultural title

141

Competition drawing, Tribune Tower, Chicago, 1922. **Walter Gropius**, architect.

Interior, Adler automobile, 1931. Walter Gropius, designer.

of honor."[22] At the same time, as he elsewhere recognizes, the "successive repetition of an expression which has become settled already as a common denominator for a whole period" is just what constitutes a style! Nevertheless, great danger lies in "the attempt to classify and thereby to freeze living art and architecture, while it is still in the formative stage, into a "style" or "ism." [This] is more likely to stifle than to stimulate creative activity."[23] This distinction, while it may seem subtle, has always appeared to him extremely important and he has returned to it again only recently:

Neither I nor my collaborators at the Bauhaus had the idea of reaching a "style." My notion was to avoid the usual teachings in art schools where the director or teacher produces small editions of himself. We sought to find a method of approach for giving the student objective findings related to our way of seeing and experiencing physical and psychological facts. This is very different from consciously working toward a "style." Of course, it is clear that the historian, in looking backwards, will perceive a certain style expression of the Bauhaus.[24]

His distrust of premature verbalization leads him to a characteristic position:

Styles in my opinion should be named and outlined by the historian only for past periods. In the present we lack the dispassionate attitude necessary for impersonal judgment of what is going on. As humans, we are vain and jealous and that distorts objective vision. Why don't we leave it, then, to the future historian to settle the history of today's growth in architecture—and get to work and let grow?[25]

We can accept his advice, provided that we realize that everything we do, by the very manner of our doing it, will enable future historians to identify us by our stylistic characteristics as easily as by our fingerprints.

One might almost say of the whole corpus of his work that, over half a century, it shows very little development: but this is merely an oblique way of saying that half a century's perspective shows it to have been almost completely developed and mature at its very birth. Stylistically, Gropius leapt into maturity at an early age and with scarcely any fumbling. Simple truth, therefore, entitles him to say "I had already found my ground in architecture before the First World War, as is evidenced in the Fagus Building and the Cologne Werkbund Exhibition in 1914."[26]

Fagus factory, Alfeld-am-der-Leine, 1911 (above), and stair tower, Werkbund Exhibition Building, Cologne, 1914. Walter Gropius, architect.

The Fagus factory is an unmistakably original building, with nothing derivative about it. Looking back at this factory across half a century, we are apt to miss its significance for the simple reason that it seems so familiar. That separation of building tissue into skeleton and skin which it celebrated so dramatically is a commonplace nowadays; the world is full of glass and metal curtain walls hung outside a steel or concrete frame. Yet the Fagus building is the first to extract the full esthetically revolutionary impact from this structural development. Gropius, of course, was not the first to use it; there were dozens of American skyscrapers which already employed it. His Fagus structure was actually a hybrid construction of brick columns, steel beams, and concrete floor-slabs and stairways; yet artistically the Fagus plant is a much clearer statement than many structurally "pure" skyscrapers. By reducing his wall to a transparent screen of glass and metal and then hanging it *outside* the columns, he made its non-structural function brilliantly explicit. Then, by moving the corner column back from its historic location, cantilevering out the unsupported floor slab and enclosing this open corner with a glass screen, he was able to dramatize the skeletal lightness and grace of the whole system.

The difference between Gropius and the older men under whose influence and tutelage he had matured is even clearer three years later in the great Werkbund Exhibition at Cologne. Here were Behrens with his Exhibition Hall; van de Velde with his Theater; Hoffman with his Austrian Pavilion. One has only to contrast these buildings with Gropius's model factory to see how far the younger man had progressed beyond the great pioneers. The building is notable on several counts. It displays his absolute freedom from any dependence upon historic form (a dependence embarassingly evident in the skim-milk classicism of Hoffman's pavilion). And it shows how he had freed himself of any tinge of ornamentalism (a tendency all too apparent in the sickly-sweet curves which van de Velde imposed on his Theater). Indeed, Gropius's forms have a pristine newness and contemporaneity that might almost be laid to a blessed ignorance of the past. Since we know that he was not ignorant of the beguiling alternatives of eclecticism, we can only conclude that he had completely freed himself of their grasp. Gropius, in other words, is not a transitional figure: his work lies wholly on this side of the great divide of the modern movement.

Gropius, with his Protestant background and Prussian schooling, was never idle. Believing in "the common citizenship of all forms of creative work," he could design a door handle or a line of mass-produced furniture with as much concentration and zest as he would expend upon a great theater or a city plan. His imagination and versatility as an industrial designer had already been established before the war, when he had designed a self-propelled Diesel railway car, the upholstery fabric for a sleeping car, steel furniture for a battleship, and luxury furniture for a villa. His theoretical grasp of the problems of designing for industry is clear from articles which he wrote for the yearbooks of the *Werkbund,* of which he was an active member. In 1913 he was hailing the "monumental power" and "unacknowledged majesty" of the American grain silos: the anonymous works of practical men, they could nevertheless "stand comparison with the constructions of ancient Egypt." The following year he contributed an article on the design of "automobile and railroad car, steamship and sailing vessel, airship and airplane."[27] After 1919, at the Bauhaus, there was literally no area of industrial design, from silver table spoons to automobile bodies, in which Gropius was not active, both as head of the school and as a professional designer.

The range and mastery of his architecture during this period is demonstrated in three designs, only one of which was ever realized: the project for the Chicago Tribune tower (1922); the building and staff housing for the Bauhaus at Dessau (1925–26); and the design for the Total Theater in Berlin (1927). Each of these is a classic prototype of its kind. The Tribune tower design, by its lucid rationality, exposes as sheer madness almost all the other eclectic entries in the competition, including the incredible Doric column of Loos and the Gothic prize-winner of Raymond Hood. Even today this design of Gropius's is head and shoulders above the current standard.

But it was the design of an entire new plant for the Bauhaus, when it moved from Weimar to Dessau, which challenged him to the greatest response of his entire career. This is perhaps to be expected since, of all his buildings, it was done for the client whose needs he knew most intimately. Like Jefferson at Charlottesville, he was the architect of the entire *institution,* its philosophy and curriculum no less than its physical envelope. And the Bauhaus complex is a beautiful demon-

Rear façade, Bauhaus, Dessau, 1925–26. Walter Gropius, architect.

Model apartment house lobby, Paris, 1930. Walter Gropius, architect.

stration of his conviction that "architects should conceive of buildings not as monuments but as receptacles for the flow of life which they have to serve."[28] The flow of Bauhaus life he knew most intimately; if we marvel today at the effortless poise with which the five elements fit together—classrooms, administrative offices, workshops, social areas, and dormitories—it is because the forms derived so surely from their functions. This is indeed a composition in which nothing can be added or subtracted. It is a classic precisely because Gropius has so completely abjured any personal indulgence, making himself, one might almost say, the pure vehicle or medium of the design process.

This same ability illuminates the third great project of this epoch— the Total Theater which he designed for Erwin Piscator. Here again, Gropius's knowledge of the problem was anything but superficial. Himself a devotee of all theatrical forms, he had many contacts in the field; his good friends Bertolt Brecht and Kurt Weill had played and sung for him the savagely witty score of the *Three Penny Opera* before it opened in a Berlin theater. Theater and ballet played an important role in the Bauhaus; as early as 1923 Oskar Schlemmer taught a full range of theater subjects and was able to produce his avant-garde *Triadic Ballet*, with music, dancing sets, and costumes by Bauhaus students. Gropius and Adolph Meyer had remodeled the municipal theater of Jena, in that same year; and—though he was never to build any of them—Gropius had designed outstanding theaters for Halle (1927), Kharkov (1930), and the Palace of the Soviets in Moscow (1931). He was thus peculiarly well equipped to respond to Piscator's unorthodox requirements. Basically, Piscator sought to destroy the artificial barrier which the proscenium interposes between actors and audience. He also sought convertibility, flexibility, anonymity in the actual enclosure which would permit him the greatest freedom in staging productions. Gropius accepted these criteria whole-heartedly: in the Total Theater he designed an auditorium with many movable elements which permitted either an orthodox deep stage, a proscenium, a central arena-type stage, or all three simultaneously. In addition, he eliminated all conventional walls, replacing them with provisions for movable panels which could completely envelop the audience, including transparent screens on which movies could be projected from the rear.

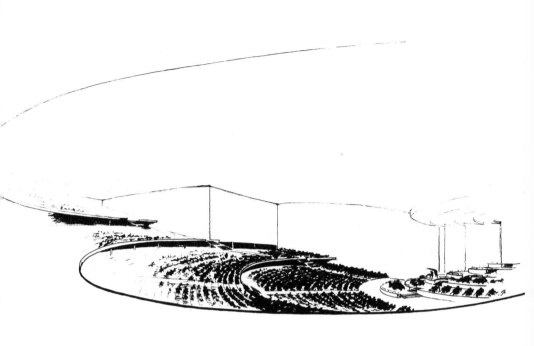

Total Theater, Berlin, 1927. Walter Gropius, architect. The sketches of the never-to-be-built Berlin project demonstrate Gropius's ambition for an architecture that, in the hands of an impresario, would be as flexibly responsive as a violin in the hands of a soloist.

The Black Friday of 1927, which brought the fantastic German inflation to a halt, also killed the Total Theater. This must be reckoned as a permanent loss, for it would have brought to full professional maturity a theater which, even thirty years later, is still unrealized. But it was a great *succès d'estime* in Europe and, seven years later, afforded Gropius both the pretext and the means of escape from Hitler's Germany. He and his second wife, the former Ise Frank, were permitted to go to Rome to attend an international theater conference; from there they went into exile in London. At that conference, Gropius read a paper which not only showed his knowledge of the theater but also his special concept of the architect's responsibility:

The task of the theater architect today, as I see it, is to create a great and flexible instrument which can respond in terms of light and space to every requirement of the theater producer: an instrument so impersonal that it never restrains (the producer) from giving his vision and imagination full play.[29]

Here he is demanding a quite extraordinary sublimation of the architect's own identity as a creative artist—a demand which all his great contemporaries would have found quite inacceptable. Indeed, it runs so counter to theater design from Palladio's *Teatro Olimpico* to Charles Garnier's Paris Opera, that most architects would have found it incomprehensible. And yet, impossibly detached or insensitive as this demand might seem, it turns out that his "impersonal instrument" is aimed precisely at audience participation in the drama. His theater is to be an instrument as amenable and flexible as a great violin in the hands of an artist. "Its ingenious devices are merely means to attain the supreme goal—*to draw the spectator into the drama.*" It will abolish "the separation between the 'fictious world' of the stage and the 'real world' of the audience . . . by erasing the distinction between 'this side' and 'that side' of the footlights."[30] Thus Gropius's theater is "a mobilization of all spatial means to rouse the spectator from his intellectual apathy, to assault and overwhelm him, to coerce him into participation in the play."[31] So it is the grave and self-effacing Gropius, and not the opulent Garnier, who emerges as the real protagonist of passionate involvement in the theater, the *Katharsis* of the Greeks.

The quality which has distinguished his career from that of Wright or Miës has been its explicit social responsibility. This has had important consequences for his architecture, since he has always interpreted it to mean not merely the solution of socially urgent problems in architecture (e.g., housing and town planning) but also their expression in "a teachable, supra-individual language of form."[32] The pull of social reality, like the tropism which turns flowers toward the sun, has thus oriented Gropius away from the intimate, the personal, the subjective. This has necessarily restricted the color and passion with which, as an artist, he might otherwise have infused his works. But it is obvious that temperament also plays a part here: sheer rationality would have prevented his committing such acts of subjectivism as Taliesin or Ronchamp.

In such a philosophical attitude, of course, he occupies a position exactly opposite to that of Wright, Miës, or Le Corbusier. These men are, above everything else, *polemical* architects. Their buildings must be understood as they themselves understand them—that is, as the most powerful and persuasive statements they can formulate of a given artistic conviction. Not one of them could accept Gropius's "impersonal instrument" theory of architecture: The Guggenheim Museum, the Seagram Building, the chapel at Ronchamp—these are highly charged artistic acts, in which we may be sure that any conflict between container and contained is resolved in favor of the container. Not one of these men could have worked with collaborators, as Gropius does, because their very concept of creativity is so private. It is not that they are wrong and Gropius right; the world needs both kinds of architects desperately. But Gropius, drawing his analogies from the world of science and technology, has tried to cross a new frontier in architecture into areas where design by the individual genius is simply no longer possible. For this reason, throughout his professional life, he has always had collaborators: Adolph Meyer in Germany from 1911 to 1924; Maxwell Fry in England (1934–37); Marcel Breuer in America (1937–41); and since 1946 The Architects Collaborative. That he made these associations always from a sense of duty rather than from any fear of his own powers is proved by the fact that the finest buildings he ever did—the purest, most consistent and flawless—were precisely those done in the only period when he was alone, after Meyer's tragic drowning in 1924. But we must remember that perfection of stylistic expression, while important, has never been for him decisive; and when it be-

151

Library compound, Baghdad University, Iraq, 1957–. Walter Gropius and The Architects Collaborative, architects.

comes simply a means of personal expression it is, for Gropius, an "arrogant misapprehension" of the architect's task. That task is discharged only when he brings "inert materials to life by relating them to the human being. Thus conceived, his creation is an act of love."[33]

The very structure of his mind has always propelled Gropius into social speculation. Unlike Wright or Miës, he was never able to focus his whole attention upon the design of the individual building to the exclusion of its social setting. Like Le Corbusier, he was always compelled to examine the larger organism of which the individual building was but a cell. As he put it,

My idea of the architect as the coordinator—whose business is to unify the various formal, technical, social, and economic problems that arise in connection with building—inevitably led me on, step by step, from study of the function of the house to that of the street; from the street to the town; and finally to the still vaster implications of regional and national planning.[34]

Not only was he led on, step by step, to examine the fabric of modern society, he was forced to comment on it. Though this often led him into exposed positions, it is to his credit that he always chose the principled (rather than the merely expedient) course of action. Rather than submit to the reactionary demands of the Weimar government in 1925, he moved the Bauhaus to Dessau. When fundamental differences between himself and the state government appeared in 1928, it was he who resigned rather than wreck the Bauhaus. And in 1934, rather than face life in a Hitler-dominated Germany, he left his homeland forever.

The ferocity of the attacks which had been leveled against him in the Bauhaus, even in the pre-Hitler days in Weimar, seems hard to explain in rational terms. For Gropius was never other than what he appeared to be—a consistent and principled democrat. Certainly, the socio-political perspectives implicit in his early manifestoes seem modest enough. The individual might be "enslaved" and his society "disordered"; yet he felt that any solution depended upon "a change in the individual's attitude toward his work, not on the betterment of his outward circumstances. . . . Only work which is the product of inner compulsion can have spititual meaning." At a distance of four decades this sounds like an almost Tolstoyan doctrine of personal regeneration; it is not even a call to simple trade unionism, much less to radical political action. Some of his defenders tried to point this out, in the days when the Bauhaus was under the most savage attacks. One of them said that the Bauhaus manifesto "clearly stated that harmonious creation is an ethical problem to be solved by the individual. . . . A blunter rejection of Marxism and kindred Utopias is inconceivable."[35]

Non-Marxist it might have been, but Utopian it certainly was—and this alone was enough to bring down upon it the blind and bloody wrath of the Hitlerites. Yet the plans of those early days are suffused with a youthful idealism which seems, in retrospect, like Eden before the Fall. We read in one prospectus:

A vegetable and fruit farm, leased from the state, was worked by the Bauhaus and [this] made the kitchen independent of price fluctuations in the markets. A plan was being evolved for single houses and apartments. . . . The construction of these community buildings was to be directed by the Bauhaus and was to provide contracts for its workshops.[36]

It all sounds more like the Brook Farm of Transcendentalist New England than the Germany of the Dawes Plan.

In an effort to protect (or at least to isolate) the school from the political convulsions around it, Gropius forbade any political activity on the part of staff or student body. Finally, since so much of the Rightist wrath seemed focused on him personally, Gropius tried to deflect it from the Bauhaus by resigning as director. But none of this saved them from the Nazis. Though the political program of the Bauhaus might extend no further left than a kind of mild cooperativism, its esthetic program was uncompromisingly radical. This the Fascist madmen understood. The Bauhaus stood for the complete liberation of the creative personality from the servile eclecticism of the past. It called for the fullest and freest examination of the fundamentals of design and for the reconstruction of the world of visual form. In this capacity, it had consistently and courageously attracted some of the most advanced artists in Europe. From a practical point of view it was, as Giedion has pointed out,

. . . sheer madness to jeopardize one's reputation and position by the appointment of artists such as Klee, Kandinsky, Feininger, Schlemmer and Moholy-Nagy as government servants in a state institution: artists whose significance was appreciated only by a very small circle and whose work and outlook excited the strongest expressions of outrage, abuse and detestation throughout Germany. . . .[37]

Moreover, in its publications it espoused movements like Cubism and Nonobjectivism, foreign artists like Mondrian, van Doesburg and Malevitch. This uncompromising policy drew to its defense all that was healthiest in German culture: the architects Behrens, Miës van der Rohe, Poelzig; the novelists Werfel, Sudermann, Hauptmann; the painter Kokoschka; the composer Schönberg; the producer Reinhardt; the scientist Einstein. In short, Gropius stood—then, as always—on the side of life; this the Nazis understood and could not forgive.

10. MIËS AND THE CLIMATE
OF PLATO

As disastrous as it was for Germany and the world, Hitlerism did America a great service when it gave us men like Einstein, Gropius, and Miës van der Rohe. Each of these men brought great talents, which our country was able to employ directly and immediately, with scarcely a dropped stitch in the changeover. There is a special kind of poetic justice in the spectacularly successful transplantation of Miës to Chicago. Who better than this poet of glass and steel could carry on the skyscraper tradition of Chicago? Chicago, although she did not invent glass and the steel skeleton, had certainly done her full share to make them famous. And Miës, in the years since he migrated to the Midwest, has raised the skyscraper to its highest level of elegance and refinement. The most talented and conscientious architect to work on this building type since Louis Sullivan finished the Schlesinger Building in 1899, Miës has brought to it a combination of monumentality and meticulous detailing, which the bluff and pragmatic city had been in too much hurry to accomplish by herself, and too insensitive to miss.

When he came to this country in 1938, Ludwig Miës van der Rohe had to his credit a total of 27 building projects, 11 of which had actually been executed.[1] Even today, his immense prestige is based upon a far smaller corpus of work than that of Gropius or Le Corbusier, and of course only a fraction of Wright's. Yet 30 years ago the fame of this man was already international. He had several honors to his credit, including directorship of the Bauhaus (1930–1933) after his friend Gropius had resigned. But Miës's fame was really grounded on two buildings, both of them comparatively small, one of them so evanescent that it had come and gone before anyone had a chance to grasp fully its significance. These two buildings—the German Pavilion at the Barcelona International Exposition of 1929 and the Tugendhat residence of 1930 in Brno, Czechoslovakia—proved to be two shots that would indeed be heard around the world.

Although both buildings played important roles in the battle for world-wide acceptance of the modern style, the Pavilion was perhaps the more influential. This elegant little building lasted only a few months, and few people who saw it in the flesh, so to speak, appreciated its significance. Fortunately it was photographed before it was dismantled, and through this medium it survived to engrave its dazzling image on the modern retina. No other single building of the twentieth century was to do more in shaping the taste of the era. It was one of those statements, so rare in the world of art, which establish the artist at one stroke, imperishably. Miës could have died that summer, at the age of 43, and his position as a world-historic figure in design would have been secure.

How was this possible?

The building's success was certainly not due to its size or cost or complexity; in these terms, it scarcely existed. It was not due to any single innovation in plan; both Wright and Le Corbusier had already employed the hovering roof, the nonstructural screen wall, the floor-to-ceiling glass. Nor was the building especially advanced technically; though it used chrome-sheathed columns, its marbles would have been familiar to the Romans. No, the greatness of the Pavilion lay in something more subtle: the fact that it managed to express, in the most exquisitely polished and exact terms, the highest aspirations of a Europe wracked by war and inflation. Here was the clarity, order, peace, it longed for; here were the noble spaces, unpolluted by any connotation of a discredited feudal past; here were fine materials, freed of decadent motifs and moldy symbols, glowing with their own intrinsic beauties. Here was a catalytic image which was to clarify problems of design for whole generations of men.

In this building Miës was able to dissolve the ordinary elements of enclosure (floors, walls, ceilings) and magically reconstitute them as abstract planes divorced from structural function. Then—on a floor plan which might well have been a composition by his friend the painter von Doesburg—he has reassembled these planes, not to form box-like

German Pavilion, International Exposition, Barcelona, 1929. Ludwig Miës van der Rohe, architect.

Exterior pool with sculpture.

Exterior detail (above) and interior (below). Floors are Roman travertine; screen is green Tinian marble; walls are grey and green glass; ceiling is white plaster. Bronze and pigskin furniture is also designed by Miës.

rooms, but to modulate a continuously flowing space. The elements are few and simple: an unbroken floor plane of creamy Roman travertine; a floating roof slab of immaculate plaster; and between these two horizontals, a series of vertical planes in green Tinian marble and grey and green translucent glass which intersect or slide by one another. Aside from his own throne-like chairs of chrome and blonde pigskin, two pools, one with a sculpture (with his usual consummate taste, Miës had wanted a sculpture by his friend Lehmbruck, recently dead, but he could not get it) there was nothing else in the building. Nothing else! A statement of such shattering power and purity could have been possible only under the circumstances which surrounded its erection. A last-minute government decision to build a pavilion, a limited budget, no exhibit material, and no time to collect any. "It is very curious how buildings come to pass," Miës said many years later, recalling this incident. "I was told: 'We need a pavilion. Design it—and not too much class!' I must say it was the most difficult work which ever confronted me, because I was my own client. I could do what I liked. But I did not know what a pavilion should be."[2] In retrospect, it is easy to see that the greatness of the Pavilion stems precisely from this lack of program. It gave free rein to his authentically Platonic ideal of architectural perfection, without so much as a travel poster or a receptionist to complicate the design.

In the Tugendhat house of the following year we can see another aspect of Miës's great talent. This is perhaps the least abstract, the most functionally satisfactory building of his entire career. Here he is faced with a concrete and complicated program, as well as a challenging site. The design is a model of domestic felicity. The way he exploits topography and exposure to win sunlight, view, and privacy for every room in the house; the beautiful fashion in which areas are zoned for efficient service and pleasant family life—these make the house a mechanism which must have functioned beautifully. Nowhere does a formal preconception obtrude to mar the plan, even though the interiors have much the same splendor as the Pavilion—the same pure forms, uncluttered flowing spaces, severely restrained furnishings. It is, for Miës, an unusually humane and considerate design, giving all the appearances of having been carefully tailored to fit a family ke knew and liked. And

Garden façade (above) and dining room (below) with furnishings by architect. Tugendhat house, Brno, Czechoslovakia, 1930. Ludwig Miës van der Rohe, architect.

Living room in daytime (above) and at night (below). Tugendhat house.

yet, if we are to take at face value an account he gave in later years, the Tugendhats got a distinguished house in spite of themselves. With a sardonic mixture of wit and genial contempt, he tells the story:

Mr. Tugendhat came to me. . . . He was a very careful man. . . . He did not believe in one doctor only; he had three. . . . He picked me out for a curious reason. He saw a house I built when I was very young. . . . It was very well built. . . . He expected something similar. . . . I went there and saw the situation. I designed the house. I remember it was Christmas Eve when he saw the design. . . . He nearly died. But his wife was interested in art; she had some of Van Gogh's pictures. She said: 'Let us think it over.' . . . On New Year's Eve he came to me and told me . . . I should go ahead. . . . He said he did not like the open space; it would be too disturbing; people would be there when he was in the library with his great thoughts. He was a business man, I think. . . . Later on he said: 'Now I give in on everything but not about the furniture.' I said: 'This is too bad.' I decided to send furniture to Brno from Berlin. I said to my superintendent: 'You keep the furniture and shortly before lunch call him out and say you are at his house with the furniture. He will be furious but you must expect that.' [Tugendhat] said 'Take it out' before he saw it. However, after lunch, he liked it. I think we should treat our clients as children.[3]

In over half a century of architectural practice (he entered the Behrens office in 1908) Miës van der Rohe has displayed an imperturbable, an almost glacial, continuity in his work. The absolute consistency of his style is astonishing. So, for that matter, is the constancy of his subject matter. In all his life, he has been content to work in two forms only—the single-story pavilion and the multi-story skeletal tower. This unchanging and unchangeable path appears in retrospect both heroic and endearing. By his life Miës has established the fact that he is incorruptible, absolutely impervious to the dictates of fad and fashion, to the club-and-carrot techniques that society employs to bring the balky artist to heel. Though his standards of craftsmanship are merciless, he is a kind and gentle man. He is not conceited, merely secure. Not taciturn, merely reserved. It has literally never much mattered to Miës what the world thought of him, though it is apparent from his work that he has thought long and hard about the world. His unchanging style of expression is not the mark of an insensitive or isolated man. The Barcelona Pavilion by itself establishes him as one of the most sensitive designers of the century; his life has been spent in close contact with many of the greatest artists and intellectuals on both sides of the Atlantic. The fact seems simply to be that Miës is an extremely self-sufficient individual. Unlike Wright or Le Corbusier, he seems never to have felt it necessary to convince people that they should follow him. Hence the scarcity of Miësian polemics: where those two wrote dozens of books and manifestoes, he has a total of fourteen short articles to his credit.[4]

His attitude toward work is Germanic. He describes one of his job superintendents as "terrible. He wrote letters. He should have worked instead of writing letters."[5] This is the essence of Miës van der Rohe: deeds, not words. All of his buildings have a kind of glowing perfection of craftsmanship which comes from flawless detailing in the office, relentless supervision on the job. This passion for fine workmanship is undoubtedly the legacy of his youthful apprenticeship as a stone mason before he entered Behrens's office. Two slogans are widely attributed to Miës: *Less is More* and *God is in the Details.* Characteristically scrupulous, he disclaims inventing either; the first, he says, came from Peter Behrens; the second, he thinks, comes from the art historian, Erwin Panofsky.[6] Whether or not he coined these dicta, it is perfectly apparent that he lives by them. He expresses himself in short, declarative sentences that often have the pungency of the early Hemingway. For example:

One little building . . . was painted blue on one side, red on one side, yellow on one side and black on the other side. . . . I said: "Paint it white." . . . I said: For heaven's sake, can you not do better than that?" He said: "You are afraid of color." I said: "No. You are color blind."[7]

Or again:

I was once asked by an expert: "Why should everything be straight?" I asked him: "Why should it be curved?"[8]

Or finally, when asked if he was influenced by the Japanese:

I have never seen any Japanese architecture. I was never in Japan. We [in our office] do it by reason. Maybe the Japanese do it that way too.[9]

The surprising fact is that Miës seems to design in exactly this pellucid, pragmatic, and disarmingly unpretentious fashion. He says, for example, that the module (and hence the whole scale) of the Barcelona Pavilion was established by nothing more abstruse than a block of magnificent marble he was given for it. He had it sawed into as many thin slabs of veneer as possible: stacking two of these, one atop the other, gave him his ceiling height; all other proportions derived from this.[10]

Another anecdote of the same sort concerns the design of the Metals Building at the Illinois Institute of Technology, whose end façade has been widely compared to a Mondrian painting. While observing that he had been an old friend and admirer of the Dutch painter, Miës says the origin of the design was much simpler. The lot for the building, between a railroad and a parallel street, was so wide. Some company had donated a travelling crane; it was so wide and so high and required an outside door of a given size. The remaining space along the street was the only area left for classroom, and they had to be stacked three high to get the required number. These volumes were all marked diagrammatically by the exposed steel skeleton, painted black; the grey brick panel infillings were standard for the campus. The only arbitrary act in the whole design process, Miës insists, was the selection of paint for the crane door![11] Of course, the real mystery of the creative process escapes from these anecdotes like water from a wicker basket. But they serve at least to demonstrate the directness and simplicity, at the *conscious* level, of Miës's approach to his art.

Nevertheless, behind this apparently casual method of design there operates a philosophy of design that is absolutely Cartesian in its rigor and inflexibility. When Miës took command of the architectural department of the Illinois Institute of Technology in 1938, he said he had "a single goal: to create order out of the desperate confusion of our time. We must have order, allocating to each thing its proper place and giving to each thing its due, according to its nature."[12] No one, from amidst the squalid anarchy in which we live today, can quarrel with this ambition. But every serious architect must ask what *kind* of order Miës has in mind. The answer is, of course, visual order. However, this raises as many questions as it answers because the creation of visible order in architecture is not—as it is in the other visual arts—a separate, self-contained act, an end in itself. Architecture differs from painting and sculpture precisely in the fact that its more intricate sensory impact upon the spectator involves him in a more complex sensuous response. No one, least of all the architect, will deny that the visual response is important in architecture. It may well be the primary one but it never, in real buildings, occurs in isolation. The entire spectator, not just the spectator's eye, responds to the impact of architecture upon his body. True order in architecture can therefore never be based upon solely visual phenomena; it can only be derived from the resolution of a whole nexus of forces which play upon man, forces which though equally important are disparate, even contradictory, and very often not visible at all. To organize these forces rationally is to produce, inevitably, a visual order; but it is apt to yield forms less balanced and serene than those that Miës demands. Miës, therefore, imposes upon reality a metaphysical order of his own.

Even this dilemma might be soluble if only the ideal world for which Miës designs his buildings corresponded more closely to the real one. Unhappily it does not. He has created an architectural order, "imperturbable" and "implacable" (the adjectives are those of his admirers), for an ideal landscape. Nothing ever happens here. It is airless, timeless, filled with light—though not sunlight, since it has no heat, no direction, no fluctuation of color or intensity. No gales howl here, no dust blows, no insects fly. There are no excesses of summer humidity or drifting winter snows. And there are no preferred orientations or exposures since there is no weather in his compass-less world. In sum, Miës designs for the golden climate of Plato's *Republic,* though he builds in Mayor Kelly's Chicago.

The consequences of Miës's metaphysics may be discovered in both the skyscraper and the pavilion, though they will vary in scale depending upon the program given, the budget at his disposal, the climate in which he builds. An analysis of the theoretical and practical limitations of his approach in skyscraper design appears in Chapters 2 and 12. These are equally apparent in his pavilion. This is what has been called his "universal space": into this classic envelope he has been able to fit, with only minor adjustments in scale or structure, such varied operations as a museum, a bank, a rum manufacturer, a national theater, an architectural school; these in such diverse climates as Houston, Des Moines, Santiago de Cuba, Western Germany, and Chicago. As visual phenomena, they are without exception handsome; but this does not tell us how, in multi-dimensional reality, they will actually perform.

In Barcelona, the pavilion worked magnificently. Specific functional requirements were all but nonexistent, the building had only to meet the demands of one genial summer on the Costa Brava. But when, twenty years later, Miës repeated this design in an Illinois river bottom, as a house for a single woman, the contradiction between the real and the ideal could not long be suppressed. This house achieved worldwide acclaim for its beauty. And in purely visual terms (especially in terms of the photographs on which most critical judgment seems to have been based) it is a little building of ravishing grace and elegance. No one has ever denied that, including the owner. She merely claimed (in a famous law suit against the architect) that it was uninhabitable!

The Fox River house is located in one of the most difficult climates on earth, with an annual range from sub-polar winters to summers of Congo-like heat and humidity. Comfort, indeed survival, under such extremes as these would dictate an architecture of flexible response, of accommodation to environmental change. Miës's design makes no such concessions. All the exterior walls are identical, all are of glass, and none of the glass is shaded. Hence (so ran the owner's testimony) glare was often severe inside the house, especially in winter when the ground was covered with snow. Drawing the curtains won some relief but also, of course, cut out the view—which was the reason for the glass in the first place.

In fact, control of light and heat through the glass walls posed all sorts of related problems of comfort for the tenant. Direct sunlight penetrated the unshaded glass, sharply raising the temperature inside the house, even in winter. Again she was advised to draw the curtains; she observed (quite correctly) that they could only modify the light. They could not reduce the heat which, in radiant form, had already penetrated the glass.

All the glass in the house was fixed. There were no openable windows and only a single pair of doors. Natural ventilation was therefore impossible: yet the house had no air conditioning, not even an attic fan. To escape this hot-weather dilemma one could move out to the beautiful porch and famous floating terrace—except that without insect screening they too were uninhabitable at that time of year.

From the point of view of comfort and amenity, the house raised other problems in acoustics, privacy, odor control. It is needless to re-

Entrance, Fox River house, Illinois, 1950. Ludwig Miës van der Rohe, architect.

Cooking area looking toward sleeping areas (above), and living room seen from covered porch.

capitulate them here, since we have already the main outlines of the Miësian paradox. The controversy about this famous house, unfortunate as it was for all concerned, is now history. The owner has made certain modifications in it which presumably make it more comfortable to live in. But it cannot be held, alas, that they make it more pleasant to look at. In fact, in screening the porch, even with the care that was obviously exercised, Miës's beautiful creation has been not merely maimed but destroyed. Where once pure space flowed between and around those hovering marbelline planes there is now a solid black cube, heavy and inert. This necessary modification of his design constitutes an exquisitely painful demonstration of the dilemma with which he confronts us: his architecture is literally Utopian.

It is a dilemma of which Miës is not altogether unaware; and there is something at once admirable and ornery in his Olympian refusal to lift a finger to help us. The *size* of his talent is so immense that, from an esthetic point of view, it confers an air of classic nobility upon almost everything he does. But the *shape* of his talent is so Platonically narrow and restricted that it exposes many of the same buildings to serious challenge from an operational point of view.

To acclaim Miës for the monumental purity of his forms and yet deplore their malfunction as organisms is rather like praising the sea for being blue while chiding it for being salty or admiring the tiger for his beauty but urging him to become a vegetarian. Miës's genius is elemental and indissoluble. The fact is that he accomplishes his ambition of an absolute purity of form *only* by doing exactly what Plato did— that is, by ruthlessly disregarding many of the dictates of social and physical reality. There is no chance of changing Miës; in a certain poetic sense, it would not even be proper to do so if one could. He is a force of almost geological dimension. But responsible criticism for too long has allowed certain consequences of his architectural philosophy to go unremarked, unchallenged. If future architects are to profit from his immense contributions, these consequences must be analyzed and understood.

PART III:

The Field of Vision

11. AMERICAN PLEASURE GARDEN

Despite the fact that it is descended from all the great garden traditions of the world—Chinese and Japanese, Persian and Arab, Classic and Renaissance—the American pleasure garden is unique. Never in its three centuries of development has it been immune to foreign influence. And it has been quick to respond to external stimuli, to absorb new designs, new plants, new horticultural techniques. Moreover, these gardens have evolved in a wide range of climates—coastal, alpine, steppe, desert, subtropic, rain forest. It is little wonder, therefore, that a wide range of special forms have evolved. Another great factor in their development has been the special conditions of American life itself. The few gardens which remain to us from early Colonial days remind us that though the European found many important new plants when he landed in the New World (e.g., tomatoes, corn, marigolds, and zinnias) he found no indigenous garden forms. These latter he brought with him; and though they differed somewhat, depending upon whether the settler was English, Dutch, French or Spanish, they all belonged to one basic type—the walled, geometrically patterned plot of the Renaissance.

Upon this basic skeleton, all seventeenth- and eighteenth-century American gardens were constructed. The dooryard herb gardens of New England no less than the cloistered courtyards of California monasteries, the patios of New Orleans as much as the boxwood parterres of Williamsburg, all show this immediate Renaissance parentage. There are, naturally, variations. The Spanish had learned from the Moors to place the garden in the center of the house—as excellent a device for the climate they found in the Southwest as the one they had left in Spain. The Bostonians would use English lilac, while the Louisiana French would accommodate themselves to oleander and magnolia. Philadelphians might use holly where Charlestonians would use camel-

Two attitudes toward nature: a Japanese garden, in which man's intervention in her processes is carefully minimized; and a Western garden, in which man's mastery over nature's forms and processes is the basis of the entire design. The seventeenth-century garden at Kyoto, Japan; the seventeenth-century Fountain of Saturn at Versailles, André Le Nôtre, architect.

lia or azalea imported from the Orient. But these were all local variations on the basic scheme with which American gardens began.

Time has fogged the clear outlines of these old gardens. For one which is maintained with truly archaeological precision—such as Mount Vernon, where all the plant material is kept to its original scale —there are dozens of so-called shade gardens around Natchez or Mobile, which were once just as sunny and tidily clipped as George Washington's. As a matter of fact, few old gardens even in Europe are maintained at their original scale. Versailles is one such—its pleached *allées* and *tapis vert* are the same size as Le Nôtre envisaged them in 1661. But most old gardens owe their present charm to the fact that they were not kept in scale. One has only to compare Villa d'Este in Tivoli as it is today with seventeenth-century drawings of it to realize how much more effective it is with sixty-foot cypresses than it would have been when those same cypresses were clipped to a six-foot hedge. Only the Japanese have consistently followed the tradition of planting a garden at full scale and then keeping it that way with continual pruning. This is essential because, for all their apparent naturalism, their gardens are as carefully composed as a Cellini salt cellar. Many an honored old Japanese pine tree, receiving pilgrims as though it were a religious shrine, is pruned with tweezers, needle by needle!

The central characteristic of the Renaissance garden is its explicitly formal organization. Its planes, patterns, and forms are those of geometry, not nature; its structure is that of architecture, not botany. But this, in turn, is merely the expression of a very specific set of ideals for the landscape—one of technical origin, the other cultural. The beginnings of the pleasure garden are, of course, functional. It derives from horticulture, is a kind of cultural superstructure erected upon the basic process of food production. Hence its essential order and rationality grow directly out of such gardening necessities as easy cultivation, good exposure, irrigation, and drainage. But at a higher level, as a work of art, the Renaissance parterre is a mark of man's rational victory over the undisciplined and unpredictable energies of the natural world. It is easy to see why it became the very symbol of civilization in the New World, for here the European settler was immured in a primeval landscape which was at once a source of unimaginable wealth and unimaginable

Chinese landscape architects and painters celebrated the peace that nature offered troubled man.

dangers. On both counts it had to be liquidated, and it was not possible for Americans to "love" nature until the wilderness had substantially disappeared. Such precocious figures as William Bartram and James Audubon, with their scientific passion for the flora and fauna of the New World, seemed at best amiable crackpots to their contemporaries.

Actually this attitude of Americans toward nature had its origins deep in the European past, whose primitive folk had peopled the wilderness with all sorts of dangers, many of them supernatural, all of them malign. (German and English folk lore is full of such figures. The Italian word for foreigners, even today, means "people from the woods.") This attitude toward nature is the reverse of the Oriental, as Loraine Kuck tells us in *The Art of Japanese Gardens:*

Bandits and brigands have infested lonely spots in the Orient quite as often as in the Occident, yet this fact has never prevented the Oriental from going into the wilds when he desired. . . . [The Chinese] have created another host of demons, jinns and devils, but these evil genii are seen to be more menacing in the cities. . . . Oriental demons do not haunt rocks and streams and trees; there is, rather, a feeling that rocks and trees are themselves, in some dim way, sentient beings and possess a sort of kinship to humanity. No Oriental, therefore, fears Nature itself. Instead of wishing to escape from it, there has been, rather a yearning to fly to it when life becomes too pressing.[1]

This Oriental attitude, so closely allied to both Taoist and Buddhist conceptions of man as being but one manifestation in the unbroken chain of nature was, however, very late in appearing in Western thought. Athenian gentlemen left the city only to visit their farms, and then only to check up on the olives or the vineyards. Roman gentlemen like Pliny the Younger delighted in their country villas, but these were set in landscapes of intensively cultivated farmlands and almost suburban villages. Renaissance men enjoyed nature only from the amenities of a villa at Fiesole or the policed hunting park at Chambord.

The concept of the untouched natural world as being a source of beauty and delight begins to appear in Europe only in the latter half of the eighteenth century. Jean Jacque Rousseau with his philosophy of the "natural man" in a real sense prepares the way for the naturalistic gardens of the great English landscape designers Lancelot ("Capability") Brown (1715–1783) and Humphrey Repton (1752–1818). These

Before (above) and after (below) views of a proposed reconstruction of a Georgian garden by Humphrey Repton, Brighton, 1808.

men, in response to shifting upper class taste, began to rip up the axially balanced parterres of the preceding centuries and to replace them with the casual, plan-less lines of nature. The distinguishing mark of this new school was the *concealment* of man's handiwork. Theirs was, of course, an idealized version of nature. Their rolling lawns only *seem* to be natural—they actually required maintenance as continuous and expert as the *tapis vert* at Versailles. And the plantations of specimen plants which they grouped so artlessly (in reality, so artfully) are also idealizations of nature. Often they were not indigenous, many were delicate and all needed continual attention to produce the compositions planned by the designers. In the sense that it imitated a more perfect state of nature than nature herself ever achieved, this school of gardening can be quite properly called Romantic.

The similarity to the Oriental attitude is not accidental, for this was precisely the period of the European discovery of China and Japan. Along with porcelain and wall papers and tea, the ships brought back exotic seeds, bulbs, and cuttings. They also brought back shrewd observations on the theory and practice of garden design, as the architect William Chambers makes clear in his *Dissertation on Oriental Gardening:*

[The Chinese] compare a clear lake to a rich piece of painting, upon which the circumambient objects are represented in the highest perfection; and say, it is like an aperture in the world, through which you see . . . another sun and other skies.[2]

This attitude, so different from the diamond-sharp materialism of the Renaissance (and so startlingly anticipatory of Claude Monet's poignant ambition to paint "the illusion of an endless whole, of water without horizon or bank") began to permeate English landscape design and led during the next century to the creation of that ravishing combination of waters, woods, lawns, and herbaceous borders that the world came to call the *jardin à l'anglaise.*

This process was far removed in time and space from the contemporaneous American experience. American art in all its aspects always tended to lag behind European developments owing to the cultural backwardness of many of the settlers, the brutalizing effects of frontier life, and the enormous isolation from the metropolitan centers of

Western culture. But the pleasure garden was tardy in appearing in the Colonies for the further reason that it was, from a social point of view, a great luxury—always one of the last to appear in any new culture. Our first gardens were strictly utilitarian. William Wood, writing in 1634 from the new town of Plymouth, says that its gardens were planted in "sweet sorrel, perrenial [sic] yarrow, hempe, and flaxe, besides turnips, parsnips, carrots, radishes, musk mellions [sic] cucumbers, onyons." In Boston we are told that guests of Governor Winthrop could have "a private walk in his garden" as early as 1646 but we are not told what grew in it. Charleston's first formal garden did not appear until 1730, when a "Mrs. Lamboll excited great interest in the science of horticulture and gardening by planting a large and handsome flower and kitchen garden upon the European plan." The flower garden does not appear in the Virginia Tidewater until the eighteenth century. Of course, people grew flowers before then. Captain William Byrd was growing anemones, crocus, and iris in 1684, but his son's famous house, Westover, was not built nor the gardens laid out until the 1740s.

Nevertheless, in the older and richer colonies great houses with pleasure gardens are a commonplace after the mid-eighteenth century. Without exception they are Renaissance layouts, deriving largely from the estates which Andrea Palladio had laid out for the Venetian aristocracy along the banks of the Po and the Brenta in the sixteenth century. Large estates like those of Monticello or Mount Vernon often included a whole complex of facilities—lawns, bowling greens, flower and cutting gardens. These are sometimes so large in scale as to seem from this or that vantage point to be naturalistic in design. But the fact is that they are still elements in an axially balanced composition around the great house.

The appearance of the naturalistic garden—the *jardin à l'anglaise*—in the United States was the result of a complex cultural process involving the American in a basic reassessment of his relationship to nature. Many media played a role in this process (and it is necessary here to do no more than indicate them): literature of esthetic theory, landscape painting, increasing travel abroad, and technical developments in horticulture itself. A group of English writers, widely read in this country, were dedicated to the exploration of the sources of beauty in nature: Edmund Burke in his *Philosophical Enquiry into the Origin of Our Ideas of the Sublime and Beautiful,* Sir Uvedale Price and Thomas Gilpin in their writings on the picturesque in the landscape. Then, too, there were the more technical publications on the works and theories of the great English landscape architects, Brown, Repton, and Langley. In the early years of the nineteenth century there began to appear such "travel" books as Joshua Shaw's *Picturesque Views of American Scenery* and William G. Wall's *Hudson River Portfolio,* both of them engraved by the Englishman Hill, and both of them celebrating the primeval majesty of the mountains, plains, and gorges of the continent.

The painters were making the same discovery. John Vanderlyn was at the Falls painting the "sublime Niagara" as early as 1802. Samuel Morse was in Cooperstown painting the scenery around the Cooper estate in 1827. But the full impact of the Hudson River School of landscape painters was not felt until the 1830s when Thomas Cole, Thomas Doughty, and Asher Durand began painting the glories of the great river. Just as these books and pictures gave Americans new insight into romantic standards of landscape design, natural and man-made, so travel was also giving them firsthand contact with them. Washington Irving and James Fenimore Cooper would have had ample opportunity to see the great naturalistic gardens of the English gentry. Americans were even beginning to travel in America to "see the sights." Thus a fashionable resort hotel, the Catskill Mountain House, drew throngs of stylish New Yorkers up the Hudson to its Greek Revival colonnades, where there was nothing to do but imbibe the splendors of the mountain scenery. And Margaret Fuller spent the summer of 1843 touring on the Great Lakes; the steamboat carried mostly freight and travelers on business, but tourists like herself were no longer a novelty, even in Chicago.

The impact of these new perspectives of the natural world would inevitably be reflected in American garden design. As early as 1827, Sir Basil Hall wrote home to England that the great houses around Natchez had gardens "some laid out in the English, others in the French style." But it was well into the 1840s before the informal style began actually to replace the axially developed parterre. As might be expected, the

Two engravings from an early nineteenth-century treatise on landscape architecture demonstrate the difference between the "beautiful" (above) and the "picturesque" (below).

movement was initially urban or, more precisely, suburban; and one of the influential figures in the movement was the Newburg nurseryman-turned-gentleman-landscaper, Andrew Jackson Downing. An able horticulturalist and facile designer, though an ineffably ambitious snob, Downing achieved fame and fortune as the landscape architect associated with the New York firm of Town and Davis. He died heroically and young (37 years old), in a steamboat explosion on the Hudson; but not before he had associated himself with Calvert Vaux, later to be the partner of Frederick Law Olmstead, and not before he had conceived the design for the first upper-class suburban community along naturalistic lines, Lewellyn Park in East Orange, New Jersey. Both acts were pregnant for the future: in the one, he made an important contribution to the climate that led to the creation of that prototype of great metropolitan parks, Central Park in New York (begun in 1858); in the other, he created the prototype of the wealthy American suburb of large landscaped grounds, streets curving gently to conform to the contours, with the shade trees and natural features carefully preserved. These two projects served to fix the direction of American landscaping for the following century.

From the English experience we inherited a heightened interest in horticulture per se. Plant material, after all, had been of comparatively little interest to Vignola or Le Nôtre; for all their visual splendor, the gardens of Villa Lante or Versailles were executed with a very limited range of quite ordinary plants. One often has the feeling that the Renaissance gardener would have preferred foamed plastic sponge to live plant material, had it only been available; then the topiary work could have been executed once and would never have needed shearing again. But the English, like the Orientals, placed a much greater value on the individual characteristics of the plants themselves. One invention of this period, the herbaceous border, displays English talent at its highest level; it permits the massing for display of a wide variety of flowering plants while at the same time dramatizing their individual qualities of form and color.

Another English specialty which the Americans adopted with enthusiasm was the lawn. Veblen might ridicule it as a fatuous example of conspicuous waste; and so, from a strictly utilitarian point of view, it was—fat pasture land taken away from the cattle who, in Veblen's

The American discovery of nature, in the first half of the nineteenth-century, led to both the publication of engravings of "natural wonders" (like Niagara Falls, above) and to the erection of hotels (like the one at Saratoga, below) from which to view them.

view, were its only logical tenants. But the shaven lawn is an indispensable feature of the English garden, and the lawn, as employed in American suburbs by Downing and his successors, had a very specific esthetic function. It served as the universal background against which the upper-class house, like a jewel in its case, could be displayed to the world. In these suburbs the lawns of one establishment flowed, almost without visible boundary, into those of its neighbors. A high fence or an opaque wall would have been unneighborly; in many of the most exclusive suburbs they were actually forbidden by law.

Whatever the merits of this urban landscape, it is unique in the world. The fact is that it expresses a socially peaceful landscape. It is the setting for an economy which is not only relatively prosperous but one in which at least the necessities of life are sufficiently well distributed to hold petty theft and housebreaking to a minimum. We deserve no credit for this; it is an accident of history which has permitted us, almost alone among the people of the earth, the luxury of an "open" house, in a landscape secure against marauders. Most other peoples would find it intolerable, an impermissible sacrifice of privacy even more than an open invitation to thievery. And, indeed, the typical American house plan is centrifugal, with all rooms opening out upon the world, while the typical Mediterranean or Oriental plan is centripetal, with all rooms opening inward to a private garden. The American plan has a two-fold significance: on the one hand it indicates an active interest in the outside, social world, a desire to "see what's going on"; on the other hand it displays the less admirable desire to be seen and admired (envied, respected) by the neighbors.

With the rise of the urban middle class since the 1850s, the house became an increasingly important symbol of status. This symbolic function has been very clear in all the literature on the subject, beginning precisely with the *arriviste* polemics of Andrew Downing's very successful books. It led to architectural postures which time has exposed in all their grotesqueness; but it was perhaps endurable so long as houses sat upon large, spacious plots of ground. Then sheer distance insulated each house (and the passerby) from the more egregious errors of the others. But with the steady compression of house and lot size in recent times, this ambition to be seen reaches the level of caricature. In the current use of the "picture window" it often verges on crime. In the

185

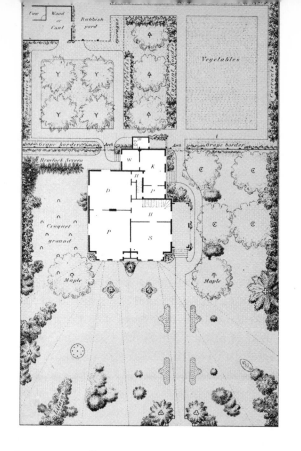

The extroverted Victorian house (left), centered in its own spacious grounds, cannot be compressed. The introverted Pompeian villa, looking into its own private courtyard, is much better suited to urban conditions (below).

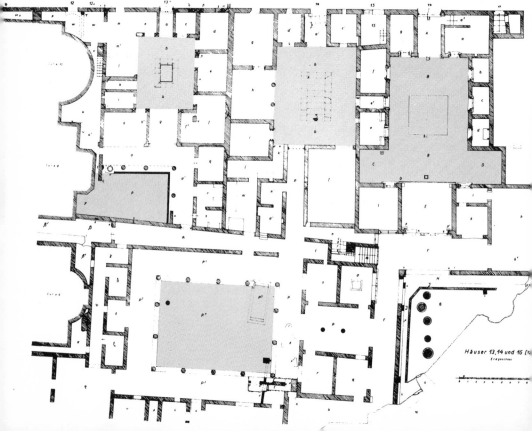

Häuser 13, 14 und 16 [...]

hands of the Japanese or of Frank Lloyd Wright a picture window was a marvellous device for uniting indoors and out, but they always placed two conditions upon its use: (1) that there be a picture to look at from inside the house, and (2) that it be a private, irreversible view—i.e., that under no circumstance could strangers look in. Both of these conditions are violated in most American "picture windows" today. They have no view from inside out and become show cases, draped and furnished like a department store's, with the family possessions put on brightly lit display. These windows afford one of the sorriest views of American life. What profound insecurity breeds such exhibitionism?

Actually, the conditions of American life are forcing the reappearance of one of the oldest house-and-garden plans—the centripetal inward-turning plan of ancient Athens, Peking, Rome, and Memphis. The demand for urban land makes the lot size steadily smaller and the free-standing house, even though greatly reduced in size, occupies a larger and larger proportion of it. Meanwhile, the street has become as unsafe and dangerous as it ever was in ancient times, thanks largely to the automobile. Since the house is umbilically tied to the street, with its auto and its municipal services, it cannot move far away. "Front" and "back" yards, under such circumstances, become pathetic anachronisms. The house would obviously be better if it surrounded the periphery of the lot, concentrating any open area in the center and making that the focus of family life, as in the atrium of the ancient house. The garden of such a courtyard house could quite as well follow Japanese as Pompeiian precedents; indeed, the Oriental way of abstracting the essential elements of the landscape into small rock and sand gardens seems ideal for such situations. In any case, such tendencies as these will have the obvious advantage of returning some decent reticence to the house.

It may be too much, at the present stage of development of American society, to expect the secure and unpretentious houses and gardens of earlier times. After all, such status symbols as the picture window and the tail-finned motor car are but the manifestations of a profound inner uncertainty, of a corrosive lack of self-identification. In this light, it is obvious that the disappearance from the stage of history of such excrescences will be more a matter of social than of architectural design.

The window-wall of a Japanese house (above) and that of an American house (below).

12. SKYSCRAPER:
SKIN FOR ITS BONES

As the term is used nowadays in the United States, "curtain wall" describes the nonstructural sheath or skin which encloses our skeletal structures. In appearance, this new wall is quite unlike its predecessor, the load-bearing wall of history; and this novel appearance is not deceptive, for the new wall marks a big conceptual advance over the old one. The specialization of members involved in this separation of building skeleton and building skin corresponds to the specialization of tissue in biological evolution. And it has had equally powerful consequences, for the evolutionary step from the load-bearing to the non-load-bearing curtain wall has made possible a new order of performance in buildings.

Any architectural structure has two distinctly different tasks to perform. The first is simply that of carrying vertical and horizontal loads. The second is that of providing an enclosure which can regulate the flow of heat, cold, light, sound, air, and water between the building and its external environment. These two tasks create the age-old paradox of architecture because, generally speaking, they are mutually exclusive. That is to say, a material suitable for one function is not adaptable to the other. Steel and concrete are excellent load-bearing materials, but they are exceedingly poor thermal insulators. Mineral and glass wools make excellent thermal and acoustical insulators, but they have no structural value at all. Glass is transparent to light and heat and, for that very reason, is useless an an insulator. Wood is strong in tension and compression but vulnerable to fire and rot. There is, in short, no such thing as a universal building material.

The only way to escape this paradox is the way of nature—i.e., through structural specialization. But before the appearance of steel and reinforced concrete the only natural material available for spe-

Train sheds, Newcastle Station, 1846–55. Dobson and Prosser, architects.

Palm House, Kew Gardens near London, 1845. Decimus Burton, architect.

cialized skeletal use was wood. Wood has been scarce in most of Europe for centuries; even in those areas where it was still plentiful, the hazards of rot and fire tended to limit its use to upper floors and roofs. Thus masonry remained the basic building material of western Europe. Since it was undifferentiated tissue—serving both for support and for enclosure—masonry could not perform either of its tasks very well.

American experience proved to be somewhat different. In the new world the English settlers found limitless supplies of virgin timber. They brought with them a familiarity with the relatively advanced, wood-framed house of the seventeenth century. These two factors combined to make wood the dominant building material on this side of the Atlantic. The English frame was subjected to steady refinement and produced, by the mid-eighteenth century, a highly specialized structural system: a light wooden skeleton sheathed in two skins—overlapping wood shingles or siding on the outside, plaster on wood lath internally. This familiarity with skeletal construction was to stand Americans in good stead when iron and steel became generally available in the last half of the nineteenth century.

Nevertheless, all the early metal skeletons appeared first in Europe. The English train sheds of the 1830s and 1840s, like the Library of Ste Geneviève in Paris (1843), employed metal skeletons to achieve huge vaults of practically no mass and no weight. And this principle was shortly to be carried even further in two English structures of breathtaking scale and lightness—Decimus Burton's Palm House at Kew Gardens (1845) and Joseph Paxton's Crystal Palace in London (1851). Here the consequences of structural specialization, of the separation of building tissue into skeleton and skin, were clear for all to see. Although the vitreous skin did not yet protect the ferrous skeleton, the concept of the curtain wall had appeared in full flower.

Its origins were European, yet the subsequent development of the curtain wall was largely to be carried on by the Americans. There were many reasons for this. The first was, as we have seen, our familiarity with skeletal structures in wood. The second was our discovery, during the nineteenth century, of immense supplies of coal and iron ore. These made the metal skeleton as cheap, relatively speaking, as the wooden ones. But the third and greatest reason was undoubtedly the

191

skyscraper. This characteristically American building type has dominated our skylines and our thinking since the 1880s, when the rapid growth of our cities made necessary—and the elevator made possible—this peculiar form of urban concentration.

As a matter of fact, the demand for multi-story office buildings was so great, during those early days, that the first skyscrapers were not skeletal at all. Root's Monadnock Building (Chicago, 1891) climbed to a height of 16 stories with solid, load-bearing masonry walls. To reach this height, the walls had to be 6 feet thick at sidewalk level. But this was the absolute limit. Someone had to perfect a stable, self-supporting steel skeleton which could rise indefinitely, independent of enclosing walls. As a matter of fact, someone already had: William Le Baron Jenney built the Home Insurance Building in 1883—the world's first completely articulated, multi-story steel skeleton clothed in a non-structural skin.

Once this structural system had been invented, architectural attention could be focussed on the further refinement of its parts. It must be confessed that during this period the architects' principal concern was with the skin; even here they saw the problem as more esthetic than functional—i.e., the emphasis was more on its *appearance* than on its *performance*. The principal walling materials then available—cellular terra cotta tile, brick, plate glass— produced walls which were weatherproof, fire-resistant, and relatively lightweight. Such architects as Root (in his Reliance Building, 1895) and Sullivan (in his Schlesinger Building, 1899) used them with great distinction. But for the climates of North America such walls were far from ideal. A typical Chicago year presents temperature extremes unknown in Europe—from one hundred degrees Fahrenheit to twenty or thirty degrees below zero; a typical day can easily have extremes thirty, forty, or even fifty degrees apart. Solar radiation is intense in summer; heavy snows, high winds, and months of frost mark the winters. An American wall must be designed to meet both subtropical and sub-Arctic conditions. All this implies a high degree of specialization *within the tissue of the wall itself* (again the biological analogy!)—thermal insulation, *soleil brise,* waterproofing, vapor barriers, ventilation, daylighting, etc.

Another negative aspect of these early curtain walls was economic. While incomparably lighter and less massive than load-bearing masonry, they were still built up of relatively small units (brick and tile), whose assembly required a lot of hand labor in contrast to the skeleton itself, which was largely prefabricated. The next logical step, therefore, would have been to abandon masonry altogether and prefabricate the curtain wall in story-high, bay-wide panels. Only thus could the advantages of industrial production, already applied to the fabrication of the skeleton, be brought to bear upon the fabrication of the wall.

Yet half a century elapsed between the Schlesinger Building and the first prefabricated curtain wall. The reasons for this delay were two: the trade unions and the municipal building codes. The mason crafts, early and powerfully organized, were umbilically tied to the old techniques and naturally resisted technological change. The building codes, drafted during those same years, had a built-in prejudice in favor of masonry and ceramic walling materials. Their specifications were all written in terms of how a wall should be *built,* rather than in terms of how it should *perform.* It took decades of pressure to overcome these two obstacles, with the result that a nonmasonry curtain wall has become legal in most American cities only since the Second World War. Thus only in the last decade has it become possible to clothe the American skyscraper in skins of stainless steel, aluminum, porcelain enameled steel, and plastics.

Progress since the war, however, has been spectacular. The new metals, together with the new thermal and acoustical insulations, synthetic finishes, and insulating glasses, are yielding walls three inches thick (instead of 12 to 15 inches) which weigh 12 pounds per square foot (instead of 125 pounds). The panels are so large and light that one entire twenty-three-story skyscraper in New York was sheathed in a single day!

In terms of its total area, glass has always played a dominant role in the curtain wall. Today's "crystal towers" employ only slightly more glass, perhaps no more glass, than some of Sullivan's buildings of sixty years ago. The glass itself has been importantly modified, however. The industrial production of rolled glass in large sheets was accomplished by the early 1880s, and the Chicago architects were quick to use it—in fact, big plates of fixed glass were originally called "Chicago windows." But ordinary glass, for all its remarkable properties, displays many deficiencies when used in the skyscraper. Its transparency to

193

visible light and infra-red radiation is both a blessing and a curse. In the bitter American winters, large areas of ordinary glass are uncomfortable, wasteful of heat, and cause serious condensation. In the torrid summers, on the other hand, they admit too much solar heat. To correct this the insulating glasses were developed—sandwiches of two sheets of glass separated by a hermetically sealed air space. They are 51 percent more efficient as thermal insulators than ordinary glass.

Another limitation of ordinary glass is its optical properties. Under most conditions, it is *too* transparent to visible light, offering no means of modulating its intensity or distribution. Early skyscraper architects soon discovered that, if the window was to be enlarged to cover the whole wall, then interior blinds or curtains or outside awnings became more important than ever. To meet this difficulty, glass manufacturers began to modify the light-transmitting qualities of the glass itself: the current tinted glasses reduce light transmission by 27 percent. When these glasses are used as the outer leaf of an insulating sandwich, a reasonably good control of heat and light is achieved. This sandwich was used in the first post-war skyscraper to have a completely nonmasonry curtain wall—Belluschi's Equitable Building in Portland, Oregon. It is this glass which gives so many recent skyscrapers their characteristic blue-green color.

This particular formula, far from being the final solution to the curtain wall, has proved to be merely the beginning. During the years when men were advancing the use of glass, many things were happening *inside* American buildings which were placing ever greater demands on the performance of the wall. New standards of human comfort and of industrial efficiency were demanding ever more precise control of the thermal, acoustical, and luminous environments. Since, as we have seen, the fluctuation in most American climates is so immense, the concept of the hermetically sealed wall appeared. In some factories, this concept went so far as to eliminate glass altogether—i.e., the skin was made as nearly opaque to all environmental factors as possible. The sealed-envelope concept has certain virtues for such industrial processes as pharmaceuticals (where absolutely sterile air is mandatory) or radio broadcasting (where control of sound must be very precise). Even in the skyscraper, it has certain advantages. It makes the wall easier to fabricate, and it eliminates such troublesome elements as movable sash, with its leaks, heat losses, and rattles. For reasons such as these, the sealed wall has been used in many recent skyscrapers.

Nevertheless, the sealed curtain wall—especially in its all-glass version—raised a whole new set of problems for skyscrapers. A simple thing like window washing, difficult enough with movable sash, now becomes a major operation. More fundamental, in these completely sealed and air-conditioned buildings, was the problem of solar heat loads—especially in summer. Even the insulating glasses described above are relatively transparent (62.1 percent) to solar infra-red radiation and, contrary to popular belief, shades and blinds *inside* the glass do nothing to reduce heat; the air conditioning has to absorb the added heat and can only do so indirectly. The simplest solution is to interrupt this radiation *outside* the building skin, as the South Americans do with *soleil brise*. But icing and corrosion have so far prevented the widespread use of this technique, at least in the northern United States. It is for reasons such as these that the designers of many of the most recent curtain walls have felt themselves compelled to return to movable sash and much smaller glass area.

The dominant esthetic problem of the skyscraper has been seen by the architect, from Sullivan's day to the present, as being the "truthful" expression of its peculiar properties. In practice, this has usually meant the expression of its skeleton, and this, of course, has depended upon where the skin or curtain wall was placed. From a purely logical point of view, one would expect it to be always stretched *outside* the skeleton, since the latter needs the skin's protection almost as much as the enclosed volumes of the building proper. In practice, however, we find the curtain wall located in any one of three vertical planes: (1) outside the skeleton, (2) between the interstices of the skeleton, (3) completely recessed behind the skeleton. Generally speaking, the decision as to where to place the skin seems to be made on a purely esthetic basis. Since it radically alters the external appearance of the building, it is indeed an important esthetic decision.

In the first case, the curtain wall appears as a continuous skin, stretched tight and unbroken around the entire structural frame. The sense of internal articulation is lost. And the odd thing is that glass or metal curtain walls, because of their reflectivity, seem just as opaque as

Crown Hall, Illinois Institute of Technology, Chicago, 1955. Ludwig Miës van der Rohe, architect.

masonry. Thus, for all the actual lightness and thinness of their walls, these buildings appear as solid cubes of glass or solid rods of hammered metal.

In the second case, the curtain wall fills the interstices of the skeleton but is kept on the same vertical plane as its outside edge. Here the esthetic intention is to delineate the skeleton on the façade. How effective this delineation is depends upon the colors and specular qualities of the surfacing materials used. If there is great contrast in color and texture between skeleton and skin, then the delineation is inescapable. If, on the other hand, the skeleton is surfaced in a material similar to the skin, its visual importance will be diminished—may, under certain circumstances, disappear. In any case, it should be noticed that the expression of the skeleton is, at best, diagrammatic and two-dimensional.

Miës van der Rohe is the leading exponent of the third technique— that of depressing the wall plane behind that of the columns. He has done this in Crown Hall at the Illinois Institute of Technology (where the steel frame, being a single story, requires no fireproofing), and in his earlier Lake Shore apartments (where the steel skeleton, of necessity fireproofed, has an armature of flat steel plates bolted on the outside to make the "steeliness" of the skeleton explicit). Where these exposed columns are structural and mark the true bay, the cellular nature of the enclosed volume is apparent. But, where the bay is divided by a number of equally sized, equally spaced verticals, as in his Seagram Building, this nature again disappears. What results is a richly textured surface with a strong vertical emphasis. The building appears as a solid, fluted column.

The reader is free to decide which of the above techniques he prefers as the most satisfactory expression of the structural character of the building. However, it must be observed that all of them share a common esthetic characteristic: they become, ultimately, mere textural manipulations of the surface, like the weave of a fabric. They exist almost independently of the mass or profile of the building as a whole and give scarcely any clue to its internal organization. Moreover, since the panels on a given building are identical, on a big façade they establish a kind of irresistible rhythm which no architect seems able either to interrupt or to halt. Thus the handsomest (though certainly the coldest and most noncommittal) of our curtain walled skyscrapers are those,

Price Tower, Bartlesville, Okla., 1955. Frank Lloyd Wright, architect.

Reynolds Aluminum building, Detroit, 1959. Minoru Yamasaki, architect.

like the Lever and the Seagram, where plan, profile, and volume are tailored to fit the modular pattern of the curtain wall. A permissible analogy might be that men's clothing be tailored, not to fit men but rather to fit the woven or printed pattern of the cloth!

How difficult it is to do otherwise, to bend the curtain wall to meet the plastic requirements of the total design, is amply demonstrated in those buildings where it has been tried. Here the architects have attempted to maintain a monumental quality for the building as a visual whole by framing or containing the powerful pattern of the curtain walls. Esthetically, their efforts can scarcely be called successful. In fact, of all recent efforts along these lines, only Frank Lloyd Wright's small skyscraper in Bartlesville, Oklahoma, can be called successful. Here one feels it is the architect, and not the curtain wall, who is in control.

A close examination of this building reveals some possible explanations for its success. In the first place, it is neither regular nor rectangular in plan. Secondly, in addition to office space, part of each floor is given over to apartments, whose more complex space requirements introduce a contrapuntal movement into the composition. Finally, each of the façades of this air-conditioned prism has a different kind of curtain wall designed to handle the climatic conditions of that particular exposure. Wright, with his usual mastery, has converted each of these functional requirements into esthetic assets.

As we have seen, the development of the curtain wall has been umbilically tied to the growth of the skyscraper. And the skyscraper, of all American building types, has been the most generalized and abstract in plan and function. It has housed only one type of commercial activity— office work—and this activity had relatively simple requirements. Moreover, the skyscraper plan developed within the gridiron street pattern, inheriting its rectangularity. This was given a third dimension by the zoning laws requiring stepped setbacks as the building rose in height. All of this led to a building composed of a basic cubical bay which could be indefinitely extended both vertically and horizontally. Thus, esthetically, the paradox of the skyscraper involves the entire structure and not merely the skin alone. Perhaps the way to get more variety and flexibility is to abandon the rectangular plan and the single-purpose occupancy, as Wright did in Oklahoma.

199

The third aspect of the Wright tower, a different wall for each exposure, shows the most pregnant area of the entire design. Here, for the moment, we must return to purely functional considerations. The typical skyscraper today is a free-standing monolith whose curtain walls are identical on all its façades. This represents a purely formal response to the facts of climate. The buildings are designed as though for an environmental vacuum or—at best—a stable and unchanging set of environmental conditions. In actuality, of course, few climates in the world (and none in the United States) offer anything approaching this state of affairs. Logically, one would expect different types of curtain walls for different exposures and different climates. But this is seldom the case in America—north and south walls, whether in Texas or Chicago, are identical in design.

This sort of unimaginative and inefficient standardization is possible only because of the relative cheapness of fuel and power, as well as of heating and cooling equipment. But it becomes increasingly hard to defend from the points of view of human comfort and mechanical efficiency. Air-conditioning equipment is expected to meet undeviating physiological criteria (e.g., 72° F. air temperature, 50 percent relative humidity) throughout the enclosed volume of the building. Yet around the periphery of this volume, conditions would vary immensely. Thus, on a cold, bright, windy day in December, the north wall—chilled by the wind and untouched by the sun—would have the climate of Canada. At the same time, the south wall of the same building, protected from the wind and exposed to the sun, would have a climate like that of South Carolina. On a hot July afternoon, the west wall would have the climate of the Arizona desert, while at the same time the east wall would have the climate of Massachusetts. Thus the thermal extremes within which the air conditioning is operating might be more properly expressed in thousands of miles than in tens of feet! Within this continuously shifting pattern of unequal thermal stresses, the air conditioning is expected to maintain a set of stable and uniform conditions.

From a conventional point of view, the most urgent problem in tall buildings is protection from excessive solar radiation in summer. The simplest (though not necessarily the best) is to make the sunny walls, especially the western ones, opaque to solar energy. This alone could reduce the cooling load by as much as a ton of refrigeration for each one hundred square feet. Since many plans do not permit this, architects are increasingly using the *soleil brise* of Le Corbusier and the Brazilians. However, these heavy fixed sunshades become progressively less feasible as one goes north and the length (if not the intensity) of the summer decreases. Hence we find another type of sunscreen appearing—a lightweight metal screen mounted out beyond the curtain wall, dense enough in its depth and perforations to exclude most of the high summer sun yet open enough to be unobjectionable in winter. In several of the new buildings this sort of sun screen has been wrapped around the entire building, becoming in effect another specialized membrane of the wall itself. These are not only sensible correctives to the too-transparent wall but also yield some extremely handsome decorative textures to a building type which is all too cold and dull in appearance.

Ultimately, of course, we must demand much more than this of the curtain wall. A technology which can achieve the thermonuclear bomb and the moon rocket should give us a wall which behaves like the epidermis of the animal body—i.e., which responds actively and automatically to changes in its external environment. It is not too difficult to imagine such a wall. In the first place, it should have a capillary heating and cooling system built into it, much like the skin of a warm-blooded mammal. The function of these capillaries would not be actually to heat and cool the interior volumes of the building so much as to provide a thermal symmetry inside which the air conditioning could more effectively operate. A building with such a capillary system would then find its sunny walls cooled with circulating chilled water, even on the coldest winter day, while the solar heat thus picked up would be used by the system to heat the much colder walls on the shaded side of the building.

We can imagine still more efficient and sophisticated building skins than these. For example, in all but polar and subpolar latitudes, enough solar energy falls upon any free-standing building during the course of the year to power that building—i.e., to heat, cool, and light it. The problem, of course, is to trap and store that energy against the hour of need. So far, most solar heat and storage devices are very inefficient, or limited to regions of intense insolation, or both. Though many of these devices could be vastly improved, a new contender, the solar battery, offers interesting possibilities. Assuming that their efficiency could be even modestly increased, the solar batteries might be imagined as forming the outer membrane of sunny walls; they would then pick up sunlight, convert it directly into electrical energy to power the building, storing any surplus of power in conventional storage batteries. Even this system might prove inadequate, however, for the long sunless periods of cloudy climates or high latitudes. If men ever master nature's process of photo-synthesis, we might imagine architectural tissue, built on an analogue of the vegetable, which manufactures starch and then stores this energy in the stable form of alcohol for fuel. A range of such possibilities lies theoretically open; by exploiting them intelligently, men might design buildings which would approach the animate world in their operational efficiency.

Of course, some technological break-through of a quite higher order may override such developments. For example, if the thermonuclear reaction is finally domesticated, it will supply the energy for a whole new order of environmental control. We can then think of air conditioning entire cities; with such energies at our disposal we could change the climate of whole regions.

Obviously, such developments will radically alter the appearance as well as the structure and performance of our buildings. It need not be for the worse, though the area in architectural design in which personal taste can freely operate will undoubtedly be circumscribed—circumscribed not merely by structural necessities (that has always been the case) but by our vastly increased knowledge of man's physiological and psychological requirements, as well as by the new technological processes he employs to meet them. This in truth will demand a new order of esthetic competence.

13. AT PEACE WITH THE PAST:
THE UNFINISHED CHURCH

On St. John's Day, 1892, the cornerstone was laid in New York City for what was to be the world's largest cathedral and second largest church. Today, a full two-thirds of a century later, this church, the Cathedral of St. John the Divine, is still not more than three-fifths complete, with its most difficult and expensive part (the crossing) not yet begun. This is not a good record, even as cathedrals go. Chartres took only 64 years to complete, Notre Dame 72; even St. Peter's in Rome required only 120 years between Bramante and Maderna. By American standards, of course, 69 years is an unheard-of time to erect a building—few of ours last that long from birth to death—and the end of St. John's is not yet in sight. Conservative estimates are that it would take 14 years and up to $20 million to complete the church if the plans of the last architect, Ralph Adams Cram, were to be followed.

But the question now is: Should they be followed at all? Decades have elapsed since the last work was done on St. John's; Dr. Cram is himself years dead; and in the interim the most profound revolution in architecture since the Renaissance has been completed. To pick up the operation where it was dropped, to continue as though nothing had happened, following designs as archaic conceptually as those for the Lincoln Inaugural—this is inconceivable to the modern temper. And yet, sooner rather than later, in one fashion or another, the Cathedral must be completed. The question is: *How?*

The inherited task of completing a building left unfinished by a previous generation is not in itself new. And it must always have posed certain problems for the heirs. Even with the slow pace of development of Gothic times, and certainly with the acceleration of the Renaissance, there would always have been that subtle change in belief and attitude, that shift in intellectual perspective, which inexorably distinguishes one period from the next. Thus, after each lapse of work on a cathedral, there would have been the question of whether to resume in the exact stylistic idiom at which the work had stopped or to begin again in a thoroughly contemporaneous (i.e., "modern") style. Discussion and controversy there probably was, though we have no record of it; yet we do know, from the buildings themselves, that always after each lapse the architects carried on in their own personal styles, expressing the points of view peculiar to their own epoch. The remarkable thing is the way in which, despite this, they managed to maintain an organic continuity between the old work and the new. Even when the project spanned great stylistic change, as did Chartres in the years between 1194 and 1260, a basic esthetic unity was maintained. Here, Henry Adams exclaimed, "the quiet, restrained strength of the Romanesque [is] married to the graceful curves and vaulting imagination of the Gothic [and] makes a union nearer the ideal than is often allowed in marriage."[1] For the modern taste, wearied of industrialism's endless repetition of a few basic forms, it is this related yet constantly shifting focus which makes the Gothic cathedral so appealing. It is this quality which makes Chartres seem so much richer than the coolly identical and mechanically consistent passages of Salisbury Cathedral, built by one architect in the incredibly short span of 38 years.

Can we, in the twentieth century, carry on in this noble tradition? St. John's confronts us with this question in a form that admits of no evasion. For, as we shall see, a whole series of developments make it mandatory that the structure be completed and unlikely that it will be completed in the mock-Gothic manner envisaged in the 40-year-old designs of the architect. We must recognize that the question is not local; its implications extend far beyond this one structure into the very fabric of contemporary life. It poses the problem of our connections, not merely with some remote medieval past but with our own immediate tradition. It exposes a live nerve of present controversy: how do we contemporary architects propose to come to terms with our own past?

Generally speaking, we avoid this question as we do so many others of equal gravity (e.g., the obscene talk of providing civilian "shelters" against thermonuclear war) by refusing to recognize it. In day-to-day life, in the design of individual secular buildings, this policy of neutralism is possible though ultimately disastrous (an entire historic landscape is being wiped out with no real effort either to evaluate its cultural significance or preserve its finest monuments). But in church design the architect cannot refuse to deal with tradition since in organized religion tradition is the actual vehicle by which the cult is preserved and transmitted. He cannot evade the issue; he must offer some responsible formula for the architectural expression of tradition. Of course, if the church is a new structure on raw land, he will have a certain degree of expressive leeway. How much will depend upon the liturgical and iconographic requirements of the congregation involved. But here at St. John the Divine—in a half-finished cathedral on which so much time and money have already been lavished, in a building which is already a national shrine of the Episcopal church— here the past cannot be bull-dozed or ignored: it must be squarely faced. The next architect must complete a fabric begun by others—begun, moreover, in one of the most confused periods of all architectural history and further developed by a correct but bloodless eclectic. He must complete it esthetically as well as structurally, so that it reads as a satisfactory, organic whole.

What remains unfinished at St. John's today is, ironically, the very heart and climax of the design—namely, the crossing and the transepts. This odd state of affairs is not the result of any planned or normal sequence of cathedral building—traditionally, construction begins at or near the crossing and moves steadily west towards the entrance front—but is due to a series of misadventures which dogged the project from its inception. To understand them, it is necessary to know the history of the church, which began in 1891 with a great national competition. A prize so large and carrying such prestige won the attention of most of the country's architects. There were many entries, and they ran a stylistic gamut which today seems well-nigh incredible. Some of them, like Carrere and Hastings's proposal for a church in the Spanish Renaissance manner, were merely platitudinous; some of them, like Halsey Wood's grotesque mimicry of H. H. Richardson's Trinity, make one flinch at their awfulness; while others, like Buffington's bold Romanesque, have a rude yet admirable vigor.

L. S. Buffington of Minneapolis submitted the design shown above; the New York firm of Carrere and Hastings proposed that shown below.

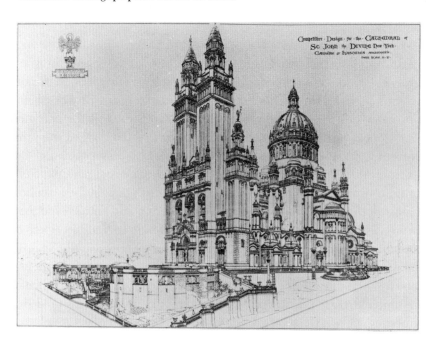

Elevation (above) and main floor (below) of prize-winning design by Heins and La Farge.

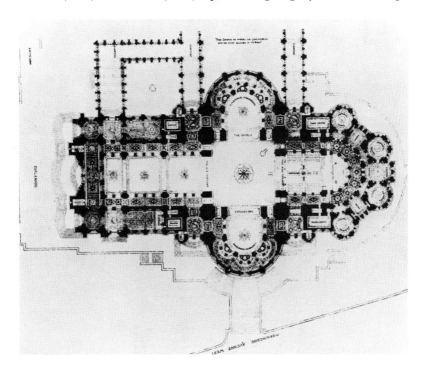

The crossing of St. John's, as visualized in the competition drawings submitted by Heins and La Farge.

The prize went to the design of the New York firm of Heins and La Farge. It was a complex and florid piece of eclecticism—more Byzantine than Romanesque within, more Gothic than Romanesque without. The plan was very compact and un-Gothic, though the scale was immense, with wide, stubby nave and transepts. But the central feature of the design was a paradox possible only in an age which had no artistic language of its own: the crossing was to be celebrated by a great Byzantine dome (when seen from within) topped by a great pyramidal "Gothic" spire (when viewed from without). No two forms could have been more antithetical: the one was the essence of the empty, glowing vessel sheathed with golden mosaics; the other, the essence of solid, crushing weight. This central feature was to prove the nemesis of both Grant La Farge and Ralph Adams Cram after him. It is still unsolved today.

However inappropriate his superimposition of solid on void, La Farge's proposed structural solution was ingenious. He enclosed the crossing with four gigantic arch-ribs of granite, these arches to be braced against the thrust of their great loads by eight buttresses. This system would support both the dome over the crossing and the tower over it; but, hybrid that it was, La Farge proposed to conceal it completely in the finished fabric of the building. Although he completed the arches and buttresses, he was unable to go further because he ran into subsoil conditions (quicksands and subterranean springs) which were in those days insuperable. His design therefore proved unfeasible, and he began casting about for alternatives. Meanwhile, work proceeded on the choir and the apse with its ring of small chapels.

Eighteen years after the cornerstone was laid the crossing was still unroofed, and it was at this juncture that a temporary enclosure was decided upon. A brilliant Italian mason with a patented system of light terra cotta tiles, Rafael Guastavino, was called in to enclose the crossing with a light, self-centering dome. A remarkable structure in itself, this dome was guaranteed by Guastavino only for ten years. It has outlived its guarantee by five times, but it cannot last much longer; it is this fact which gives urgency to the completion of the church.

Guastavino completed his dome in 1909, and the same year La Farge was discharged as architect. Whatever the merits or shortcomings of

The unfinished church of St. John the Divine as it stands today (above) and as it would look if completed according to the 30-year-old design of Ralph Adams Cram (below).

his design, it had become a victim of the rapidly shifting taste of his time. He must have been aware of the danger, for in 1907, fifteen years after the start, he had felt it necessary to publish his longest and most detailed defense of his church.[2] It is a moving document and reflects, however indirectly, his understanding that the tides of fashionable taste were shifting beneath his very feet. His intuition was correct; the next month *American Architect* published the famous "Candidus letter." This anonymous communication was a thoroughly hostile document, challenging the La Farge design on the bases both of historic precedent and esthetic congruity. The Cathedral was wretchedly lit and badly heated and disproportionately expensive, Candidus charged. "Much of the huge structure is a needless outlay, superfluous in a Gothic [sic!] cathedral," and "a great mistake has been made by changing a possibly good Byzantine design into a bad Gothic one." Candidus admits that "matters have gone too far to rectify them in choir and crossing" but urges that "a reconsideration of the nave should be made before it is too late, to save money and avoid a still more hybrid effect."[3]

Whoever Candidus was, he obviously spoke for an influential body of opinion, both ecclesiastical and secular. Shortly after his thunderous attack, Ralph Adams Cram, that paragon of archaeological precision, was appointed consulting architect. This insulting process was completed in 1911 when La Farge was removed from any connection with the project, and the task of completion was handed over to the firm of Cram and Ferguson. "A harsh divorce," the *Architectural Record* tartly observed, which put St. John's in the hands of a " 'consulting architect' whose own works show an entire lack of sympathy with what has thus far been accomplished."[4]

La Farge's inability to solve the problem of the crossing may have played some role in his dismissal. In retrospect, however, it seems inevitable that the taste of the time would have preferred the impeccable scholarship of Dr. Cram to La Farge's more vigorous but more Victorian eclecticism. In any event, the Cram office immediately discarded the unbuilt portions of the design. The nave, the transepts, the west façade, even the roof of the already complete choir—all were recast into High Gothic, irreproachably accurate though rather thin and cold, especially on the exterior. But the problem of the crossing remained to dog the footsteps of Dr. Cram. He was committed to the 100-foot square by the overwhelming presence of La Farge's choir and by his indestructible cage of granite arch-ribs; and he was committed to some sort of vertical accent by the sheer logic of the composition.

Cram's first proposals, submitted in 1913, showed "twin towers with lofty spires located at both north and south transepts, accompanied by a massive but rather low square tower at the crossing." But he abandoned the idea of the transeptal towers, and later designs showed a return to the tower at the crossing. "The next two completed designs were of polygonal towers of varying heights, followed by a third (1920) whose base was similar to the former two but was topped by a richly panelled, lofty spire."[5] But this did not solve La Farge's original dilemma, and years were to elapse before the new architects could publish a solution which did accomplish that. Finally, in 1927, they evolved an ingenious new design for the crossing which was hailed as a solution which "had never before occured to Gothic architects from the twelfth century to the present time."[6] This was a scheme for inserting a set of four smaller arch-ribs inside the square created by La Farge's originals and locking them together egg-crate fashion. In addition to reducing the vaulting problem to manageable proportions, this design would keep the crossing open and furnish support for the huge flat-topped tower.

Yet the difficult foundation problems and rising building costs led finally to the abandonment of this tower, too. In the 1940s it was replaced by the flèche of the current design, a flèche of such un-Gothic size that some wag has identified it as being a copy in rubber of Notre Dame but inflated to the American proportions. Thus the confident Dr. Cram (Could *he* have been the author of the Candidus letter?) got no further with the crucial problem in 30 years than had poor La Farge in 20.

And now history has overtaken the Cathedral again. Its story to date may seem to us a tale of sincere if mistaken effort, but it has the great merit of being still unfinished. It thus presents still another generation of American architects with a challenge. The challenge should be accepted; St. John's should be finished in a thoroughly contemporary idiom, just as cathedrals have always been. But it is one thing to decide to move and quite another to decide in which exact direction to do it. If the cathedral authorities have shown qualms about moving away from Cram, their qualms are not hard to understand. American architects have seldom dealt imaginatively or sensitively with the past —their own or anybody else's. Generally speaking, they have shown a consistent tendency, when a change in bath water was indicated, to throw out the baby, too. If St. John's is to be brought to a satisfactory completion, then the architects, whoever they may be,are going to have to display more historical perspective, more sympathy for and at the same time more detachment from the forms and symbols of the past, than they commonly do. They must produce a new work consistent and congruent with the old. And this consistency, this congruity, cannot be merely literary. It must be real, tangible, visually apparent.

Like most esthetic problems, those at St. John's have their roots in simple reality. For example, costs: unlike most Gothic Revival structures which merely hang a skin of Gothic forms on a skeleton of brick masonry, reinforced concrete or modern steel, St. John's is exactly what it pretends to be—a load-bearing, hand-crafted, cut-stone masonry fabric built precisely like its medieval prototypes. This has made it an extremely expensive construction in the past and would make it almost prohibitive in the future. It is estimated that to build the crossing and tower according to Cram's last designs would cost $5 million and take five years. Thus from a purely practical point of view, a less costly, less time-consuming method of construction is indicated.

This need for economy reinforces the Episcopalian demand for architectural honesty of expression. Steel and reinforced concrete are the two basic materials of modern structure, and one or the other should be used at St. John's. Thus the crossing might be enclosed in a great prismatic parasol of folded concrete slabs. Or it might be wrapped in a glass and metal cage like a great baldachino. Externally, this point might be marked with a great open-work spire of stainless steel, in whose interstices the iconography of the church could be displayed in bronze, lead, and copper sculptures. Alternatively, it might be marked with a ring of metal masts, from which the baldachino could be hung. The possibilities are rich and wide, as is indicated by a range of modern churches across the country. But whatever the forms or

213

materials, the new work must be congruent with the dominant features of Cram's steeply pitched roofs, grey stone, stained glass, and crockett-edged pinnacles.

Other possibilities must be considered also. There is, in Cathedral circles, some talk of moving the high altar down from the choir into the crossing, in which case La Farge's original conception of this as a great light-filled vessel would be more valid than ever. There is also some feeling that the south transept might be entirely omitted. If this were done, the south wall of the crossing would automatically become a gigantic window. Since it would be 100 feet wide and 150 feet high, it would require heavy wind-bracing. (The building is exposed to high winds and carries heavy insurance against glass damage.) This bracing would necessarily constitute a tracery; and though no one would expect it to mimic Gothic motifs, it would have to live at peace with La Farge's and Cram's handsome stained glass windows.

These are a few of the problems the new architects must face; there are many others, some of them tantalizingly complex. For example, the western towers—at present awkwardly truncated at an insignificant belt molding—must be completed. What materials will they use, what form will they take, how will they accommodate the great bells which the Dean and the Chapter hope some day to have?

Then there is the problem of what to do with the little Greek Revival building which stands just to the south of the Cathedral. Dating from the 1840s, it housed the old Leake and Watts Orphanage which formerly occupied the site. Although a handsome structure of some historic and artistic significance, its demolition to make way for the South Transept was always envisioned. But if there is to be no South Transept, what then? Can it be left where it is? Should it be razed? Is it worth moving to some other site on the grounds?

The new architects of St. John's will confront one of their thorniest responsibilities when they come to the matter of selecting the artists for all the sculpture, stained glass, metalwork, and liturgical furniture that will be required. Here tradition is at its strongest; the church comes out of the past, its iconography and liturgy have been molded by the centuries, and its requirements are specific and relatively inflexible. How these will be met by contemporary artists is a real question. Nowhere has taste undergone so profound a revulsion against the eclecticism represented by La Farge and Cram, yet nowhere is the spectrum so wide and contradictory. At one end lies the new academicism of abstract expressionism which, if it deals with objective reality at all, employs a symbolism so private and subjective as to be useless liturgically. The other end is represented by the anecdotal cemetery art of Mestrovic, so untouched by modern sentiment as to be equally useless. Somewhere between these two extremes, presumably, St. John's will find the artists to interpret its symbols with conviction and taste.

All the above are limitations, no doubt about it: they are problems of real substance which surround—indeed, *define*—our artistic dealings with the past. But limitations never prevented artistic accomplishment; on the contrary, they often seem a necessary precondition to it. One sort of limitation we are mercifully spared: that peculiar slavery to tradition, to historic precedent, which crippled Le Farge and his generation. Since these men had no genuinely contemporary language of their own, they could only express themselves in the dead idioms of the past. The tragic consequences of this are very clear in La Farge's 1907 defense of his design.[7] He cannot propose *anything* without citing historical precedent to justify it. He is opposed to flying buttresses because he does not think they could long withstand "the ferocious attacks of our climate." But that is not a sufficient argument to omit them; he must find a medieval church without them. He finds his precedent at Albi. He wants a big crossing, domed and light-flooded from above. But he cannot justify it on merely functional grounds— that it makes a better auditorium—or on a frank esthetic basis—that it creates the sort of splendid intersection of nave and transept which he desires. No, he must also cite precedent, Gothic precedent at that. He can only find two (the Cathedrals at Ely and Gerona), but these, he wryly hopes, will prove "good enough." Every aspect of his design is thus firmly grounded, not on Greenough's "manly use of plain good sense" but on eclecticism's only crutch, historic precedent.

It would be grotesque, at the middle of the twentieth century, to see architecture justified on any such grounds. This of itself is proof that our position is sounder than La Farge's. Moreover, this new position, bitterly fought for and newly won, should give us precisely a new perspective of the past, a new ability to live with tradition on terms of equality and respect.

215

14. IN DEFENSE OF THE CITY

The mechanization of American life in all its major aspects has gone far towards equalizing the historic disparity between the material conditions of urban and rural life. A whole range of amenities which had been hitherto the monopoly of the city has been extended into the countryside—amenities of which the public school, the paved road, the ambulance, and the powerline are merely symbols. Mechanization has also made possible the decentralization of manufacturing, thereby introducing new modes of work and thought into the rural hinterland. Thus the countryside has been opened up as the theater of a much wider and more varied life than was conceivable in preindustrial times.

These same developments have, of course, affected the function and the form of the metropolis. Mechanization makes possible the unprecedentedly fluid movement of people and goods. This has meant that many of the commercial and industrial activities historically concentrated in the city could be moved out of it; with those activities could go the populations connected with them. These shifting populations and processes have, especially in recent decades, left ugly vacuums and imposed dreadful strains upon the physical and social fabric of the central city. The resulting confusion and squalor have driven further sectors of the population out to the suburbs, even though their economic and cultural focus remained in the city.

The result of all this has been the blurring of the physical and cultural distinction between the city and the countryside. Indeed, urban amenities have become so widely distributed beyond the urban area that a whole new set of misconceptions, as well-intentioned as they are misinformed, has come into being about the city. Not only is the countryside now described as a more pleasant place in which to live (The urban elite, Virgil no less than Vanderbilt, have often felt this way during epochs of social peace.), but now, for the first time in West-

216

ern history, it is seriously being argued that the city itself is no longer viable. A whole literature on "the disappearing city" has appeared. Following that special brand of social Darwinism which is endemic in so much current American thought, it is argued that the central city is "doomed" and "obsolete," its disappearance from the stage of history ineluctable. According to this interpretation of the "law" of survival of the fittest, the city is destined simply to dissolve, distributing its amenities in a thin film of suburban houses, shopping centers, and country day schools across the landscape.

This is a grotesque misreading of the city's historic function. As the etymology of the word suggests, the city has always been not merely the vessel but the actual generator of civilization. It is not at all accidental that such words and concepts as civil, civilized, citizen, or urbane and urbanity cluster around the word and concept of the city. Urban experience is their point of origin. They represent mankind's distilled experience with the city as a special instrument of social organization. It has always been the lodestar of farmer, herdsman, hunter, sailor. It offered them steady employment and the food, clothing, and shelter that was statistically so uncertain elsewhere. It offered them paved streets, lighted taverns, and buzzing markets instead of barnyard mud or storm-tossed ocean nights. It promised them music, dancing, theater, and spectacle. Even more precious, it gave them relative safety from war, a place of sanctuary, an asylum for dissent. But beneath all of these was the city's most splendid gift: *a range of choice,* an entire spectrum of possible lines of action. This was the lodestar that pulled them—the chance of escape from the routine idiocy of life on the farm, the steppe, the sea.

The attractive power of the city is somewhat obscured in contemporary America by the surface glitter of universal mechanization. But one need only visit such such underindustrialized countries as Egypt or Greece to see the process still vividly at work. The peasantry flees the stupefying poverty and monotony of a countryside ravished by centuries of ignorance and neglect. This instinct is correct, however inadequately or unevenly Cairo or Athens may live up to its promises, for the amelioration of the material conditions of life can be accomplished only by the science and technology of the city. Even the regeneration of agriculture and the countryside is, culturally, an urban task.

Of course, the advantages which the city offered the citizen were a kind of cultural superstructure erected upon its basic economic function. As an instrument of production, it was unique—the only conceivable habitat of merchant and banker, craftsman and artist, because it afforded them three factors, critically important and available nowhere else: proximity, predictability, option.[1] The city constituted a common reservoir of raw materials and finished goods, of manual and intellectual skills, upon which everyone engaged in production could draw. This was a reservoir of absolutely incalculable value, one which no individual could conceivably afford to maintain alone. And its concentration, in both time and space, meant that any producer had immediate *proximity* to all the goods and services upon which he depended as well as to those which, in turn, depended upon him. Because there was always duplication of every type of goods and skill, there was always *predictability* of supply. And, finally, because of both of the above factors, the city offered that last essential of the market, *option,* a range of choice within a given type or category.

Out of such quantitative relationships grew the qualitative phenomena of civilization. If such a process was true of the city of antiquity, how much more characteristic it is of the infinitely more complex fabric of modern industrial society. Today, when we speak of financial centers, garment centers, publishing centers in a great metropolis like New York; or when we refer to Detroit as the center of one industry or Hollywood of another, we are not dealing in metaphor but the most concrete of social realities. Such a center represents a unique concentration of cultural forces. Personal, face-to-face contact; daily exposure to the friction of competitive ideas; continual cross-fertilization from various elements within related fields—these are the essential properties of the center. This is precisely why the center cannot be decentralized. Modern technology may permit the dispersal of this or that phase of production. Modern telecommunications may make it possible for a single national center to control a national industry. But the creativity of the urban center will no more survive subdivision and dispersion across the countryside than would the human brain survive a similar distribution across the nervous system.

These are some of the fundamentals ignored by the literature of the "disappearing city." For those who seem to think that paved roads and electric refrigerators are equivalent to urban culture we can present other fundamentals. A law of urban development, analogous to laws which operate in the physical sciences, dictates that human communities must pass beyond some quantitative minimum in order to effect that qualitative change which we call social invention. This qualitative difference is not directly (or at least not mechanically) proportional to simple physical magnitude. The Athens of Pericles was never larger than Yonkers, New York. Renaissance Florence was smaller than New Haven. Chicago, on the other hand, is three times the size of Imperial Rome and has not a fiftieth of her power and substance. It seems logical to suppose that, for a given level of technological development, there must be an optimal size for the metropolis. But on the basis of present knowledge it does not seem possible to say what that optimum size should be. It may well be that the great metropolises of the world are too large to function effectively. It may well be that the future will see a planned reduction in their size. But this is a far different thing from declaring them "obsolete" and rejoicing in their dissolution.

Yet that is what large and influential sectors of American opinion are doing today. They describe the desiccation of the central city (and the parallel urban sprawl which pollutes more of the landscape every day) as inevitable. Some of them go much further, hailing the process as good:

We have been able to disperse our factories, our stores, our people; in short, to create a revolution in our living habits. Our cities have spread into suburbs. . . . The automobile has restored [sic!] a way of life in which the individual may live in a friendly neighborhood, it has brought city and country closer together, it has made us one country and a united people.[2]

In so far as the future of the city is the subject of any responsible thought, that thought seems dominated by a kind of mad laissez faire. Subjected to a whole set of anarchic and destructive forces, the city is expected to prove itself, medieval style, in a trial by fire and water. If it survives, this theory seems to go, well and good; if it succumbs, good riddance. This preposterous policy of nonintervention permits the subsidy of all sorts of forces hostile to the city's well-being, yet forbids any defensive response on the part of the city—as if attrition were inescapable, but conscious resistance inconceivable.

219

This is especially clear in the field of transportation, where the dominant attitude is one of macabre *non sequitur*. Responsible men see nothing improper in the expenditure of tens of billions of dollars to build new highways to bring automobiles into the cities. Yet they are outraged at the obvious corollary—that there should be free, tax-supported parking garages to receive the cars that are thus dumped into the city. Respectable opinion finds it unobjectionable to subsidize the movement of people and goods by motor, plane, and barge—none of which could move a mile without stupendous public expenditures on highways, airports, and rivers. Yet this same opinion boggles at the idea of subsidy to the railroads, grows apoplectic at the mention of nationalization (though the USA is the only nation on earth which still clings to the polite fiction that privately owned railroads are consonant with national welfare). The central city is being throttled by such paradoxes. Its streets are drowning in a rising tide of vehicular traffic at the same time that public mass transportation systems are declining. Rail passenger service between cities, and especially commuter service into the city, is collapsing without a finger's being raised to prevent it. The large investment represented in interurban and trolley systems has been junked piecemeal, with no effort at planned rehabilitation. Side by side with this private bankruptcy, billions of public funds have been pumped into insatiable highway schemes which, whatever they may have accomplished in the countryside, have only led to steadily worsening traffic conditions in the central city.

Transportation is only one aspect of the urban problem but, like the circulatory function in the animal body, it is a critically important one. Our current irrational manipulation of it reveals our lack of understanding, at both national and local levels, of the cultural function of the central city and of the minimal conditions for its survival. The physical expression of this function (proximity, predictability, and option) is the street. The street, and not the buildings on it, is the secret of the city. Unless the street is healthy the city dies.

Part of the American mismanagement of the city is due to our persistent inability to see the difference between the street and the road. Our long exploitative experience with land as a commodity leads us to act as if every country lane was destined ultimately to become a profitable city street. Many of them have, of course; and this very process has served to conceal the essential difference between the two. A road is for moving people and goods from where they are to where they want to get to, while a street is for people who are already where they want to be. Thus the road can be almost indefinitely widened or extended. Since transport is its only function, it can be designed to accept any type of vehicle, in any quantity, moving at any rate of speed. But a city street, to be successful, must meet the incomparably more subtle assignment of facilitating commerce in ideas and goods. It is therefore primarily a pedestrian facility and must be designed to man's scale in time and space.

Of course, the foot has always had to share the street with the wheel, and conflict between the two is not new. Already in Cicero's Rome, wheeled traffic was so heavy on the main thoroughfares that it was restricted by law to late night hours (much to the annoyance of the tenants of the apartment houses on either side). This conflict has steadily sharpened, especially since the Industrial Revolution. Only Venice, with her unique separation of water-borne transport from all pedestrian traffic, has escaped; it is to Venice that one must go today to comprehend how wonderful a space is a street without any wheels!

But what was merely conflict before the automobile appeared has become a mortal dichotomy since. Its impact upon the central city has been disastrous throughout the world, but its most destructive effects have been most acutely felt in America. This has been due not only to the fact that we have made the widest use of the auto as a means of personal transport but also to the fact that most American cities have been greatly extended, if not indeed largely built, since its introduction fifty years ago. Some of the newer metropolitan areas (Houston, Los Angeles) have been structured upon the private auto as the only form of transportation.

No other form of wheeled traffic has ever approached the auto in destructiveness. (No reference is here intended to its destruction of human life, though that is murderous enough. It is the nation's seventh most important cause of death and fourth highest cause of disability; and it is now coming under suspicion as contributing to the alarming rise of lung cancer.) The auto has not merely taken over the street, it is dissolving all the connective tissue of the city. Its appetite for space

221

is absolutely insatiable: moving and parked, it devours urban land. In Los Angeles, where the process is perhaps most advanced, the spectacle is frightening. George H. Hildebrand, a long-time student of the city, says

Two-thirds of the land area of Los Angeles is now devoted to streets, freeways, and parking lots. A recent semi-official projection of future public investment, amounting to several billions for the next decade, commits over half to the motor car. Not one cent is set aside for public transportation. Between 1949 and 1951 an invaluable nucleus for a rapid transit rail system was deliberately abandoned in favor of exclusive dependence upon freeways and the private automobile.

It would be dismaying enough if these freeways, which cost from $3 to $15 million per mile, solved the problem. Unfortunately, says Professor Hildebrand, they do not:

Already they are so clogged with traffic at peak hours that one can say of them: as a means of transportation they are always available except when you need them. The center of the city is dying. There are no poper facilities for opera, symphony, or theater. . . . All civic energies are devoted to the sole purpose of "relieving" automobile congestion—by encouraging it further. Each day the atmosphere is poisoned by smog, two-thirds of which is attributed to automobiles. What has emerged is an endless waste of suburbs, yielding an impression of chaos and ugliness. . . . If this is the image of the American future, it is not a pleasant one.[3]

Much the same picture can be seen (and with especial clarity from the air) in any American city. The public groundspace has been rendered largely uninhabitable. Esthetically it has been destroyed, lost beneath a tide of moving, stalled, and parked automobiles. Gas-filled, noisy, and hazardous, our streets have become the most inhumane landscapes in the world.

Under such circumstances, it is not surprising that the social and cultural effectiveness of the central city has dropped alarmingly. To restore it, the street must be redeemed. And this, as Louis Kahn has pointed out, can only be done by unscrambling the traffic.

Today's city streets carry half a dozen different, contradictory types of traffic —pedestrians who want to stroll along; busses that want to go-stop-go; private cars that want to go at an even rate without stopping and then find a place to park; other cars that want to pass the city altogether (but cannot);

trucks, trolley cars, delivery boys on bikes, each with a different mission, each with a different rate of movement.[4]

To funnel all these kinds of traffic through the same street at the same time is as absurd to Kahn as trying to funnel gas, hot water, cold water, sewage, and electric current through a single tube. This makes it impossible for the street to function effectively as a traffic artery. And there is an even more disastrous effect upon the buildings along either side, for no building can "work" satisfactorily at two different time-scales—one for pedestrians lazing along at a speed of two miles per hour or stopping altogether to window-shop, talk, or sit; and the other for automobiles moving at 50 miles per hour.

With its heavy wheeled traffic, narrow crowded sidewalks, solid walls, and open ends, the typical American street acts like a simple conduit. This form sets up a strong, linear current which is hostile, both physically and psychologically, to the full development of urban life. It creates a rip tide along the street face of the buildings where there should be quiet water, coves, and bays. The very nature of social intercourse requires the cul-de-sac, the enclave, the shaded portico, and sunny court—in short, that transitional zone between the full openness of the street and the full enclosure of the building.

The first step in the reconstruction of the street would be to restore a healthy circulation between the city and the surrounding hinterland from which it draws its nourishment. And it should be apparent to any rational observer that this can be accomplished only by mass rapid transit. Whatever the proper uses of the private automobile (and they are many and real) urban transport is clearly not one of them. It does not matter what form this mass transit takes—subways, surface trains, aerial trams—technology makes the solution of this problem simple. Nor, in terms of the stakes involved, does it matter what the necessary subsidies will amount to. The cost of the present urban chaos is quite literally incalculable.

When this fundamental task is accomplished, the reconstruction of the central city becomes possible. What precise lines this reconstruction should follow is still a matter of discussion among planners and architects. But there is general agreement that all surface transportation, public and private alike, would terminate at a ring of stations and storage garages (Kahn calls them "harbors") around the periphery of

223

Architect Victor Gruen's famous plan for the reconstruction of the center of Fort Worth (above) and architect's sketch of typical pedestrian way (below).

the central district. Subways, local busses, and taxis would handle local passenger traffic within the center, moving in channels strictly segregated from pedestrians. Trucks would have their own separate times and lanes of movement. This is the schematic substance of the now famous Fort Worth plan of architect Victor Gruen. Although it now seems unlikely that the Texas city will ever enjoy the benefits of this plan, it has already become a classic. It visualized the conversion of the central city streets into landscaped pedestrian malls, with the existing gridiron pattern of intersecting conduits converted into a series of snug, pedestrian-scaled cul-de-sacs. This pedestrian world was to be connected, by a dense network of shuttle busses, to a ring of bus terminals and parking facilities around the periphery. By its concentration of office buildings, stores, theaters, and public buildings of all sorts in this district, the Gruen plan sought to reestablish it as the locus of centers of the interacting social, cultural, and commercial activities of the city.

The Gruen plan is perhaps the most mature American response to date to the crisis of the central city. It does not, of course, stand alone. As a result of Congressional legislation and appropriations for so-called urban renewal and redevelopment, we begin to have the means for this type of intervention in the urban crisis on a national basis. The means, but not yet the policy: enough of these redevelopment projects are taking shape to make it evident that, though we are becoming aware of the need to act, we have a very unclear image of what should be done. Aside from the ineffable scent of profiteering and graft that surrounds some of the projects, most of them seem to be structured upon makeshift or improvised plans. Too often they appear as mere by-products of complex traffic arteries whose validity is open to question. Too many of them assume the form of luxury apartment towers standing in the midst of expensively landscaped deserts. Very few show any real grasp of the essential qualities of urban space.

Since few American architects and planners have ever had the opportunity to design projects of such dimensions before, a certain amount of initial fumbling was perhaps to be expected. But by now we should understand that one source of the exhilaration we experience in the great urban spaces of the world comes from the variety they always afford the senses. This variety is the expression of multiplicity and diversity of tenancy and building type. Thus, though neither could be called beautiful, both London's Trafalgar Square and New York's Times Square are almost always rewarding experiences for the pedestrian, at almost any time of day or night. On the other hand, a large single-use project, like New York's Lincoln Center, is not apt to yield the maximum of metropolitan excitement because its specialized use will lead to part-time, monochromatic activity. Traffic jams at curtain time will alternate with wasteland emptiness at other times.

A second precious quality in successful urban space is its pedestrian scale. Most architecture is experienced (seen, heard, felt, smelled) along a plane five feet above the ground. That—not an aerial vantage point— is the point of view from which urban spaces should be conceived. They need not be small—there is nothing small about the scale of Piazza San Marco in Venice or the Tuilleries in Paris—but they should afford the pedestrian that sense of comprehensible organization, that delicious feeling of embrace and enclosure, which all the great urban spaces of the world provide.

A coherent policy toward the city, based upon a clear understanding of its cultural function, will also enable us better to regulate its relations with suburbs and hinterland. One of the first objectives of such a policy would be to restore and preserve the special social and physical characteristics of each. It will not be enough to rehabilitate the center; the mindless squalor which today surrounds and isolates it must also be cleaned up. The endless semi-slums of South Chicago, the miles-long decay of Euclid Avenue in Cleveland, the ugly spoilation of the Jersey Meadows—all of these are symptoms of the same disease of urban sprawl which must be halted and then reversed.

If we are to preserve and extend the values we most cherish in our culture we must act to save their generator. The task will not be easy, cannot be quick, and certainly will not be "automatic." We must relinquish that childish American faith in laissez faire which assumes so delicate a mechanism as a city will repair itself, like those reptiles which are supposed to grow new tails to replace dismembered ones. The task demands considered policy and planned and resolute action. The sheer magnitude of the issues involved permits nothing less.

PART IV:

Problems of the Day

15. THE ENGINEER:

FRIEND OR FOE?

The American engineer is no longer content with merely "conquering Nature," said a recent European visitor; he is, instead, "intent on occupying the very Throne of God." Americans may flinch at his verdict, but it is increasingly the reaction of many foreigners to our rockets, space medicine, and earth satellites. As a matter of fact, one need only look at the bull-dozing operations for the nearest supermarket or housing project to get much the same impression. Trees are being pushed over, topsoil buried, contours altered with a calm and bloodless ferocity which can suggest only a glacier or a lava flow. The analogy is not amiss, for the American engineer has so enlarged the scope of man's action that he now becomes a major force of nature. He has raised the order of magnitude of human capacity to literally geologic proportions. What he does with that power, in what directions he employs it and to what ends, thus becomes a pivotal question not only for Americans but for the entire human race.

The conquest of nature, especially in Western history, is a very old ambition. In one sense or another, it furnished the motive power to the Roman engineer and Renaissance architect alike. Its nucleus was a noble concept: man did not have to exist as the hapless victim of blind natural forces; he could, by understanding them, master them and thus remake the world to his liking. The paintings of the Renaissance, even more than its gardens and palaces, reveal the kind of landscape aspired to: a system of organized vistas in which the materials and furnishings of handsome rooms are extended right out into the garden and street. And this was the kind of urban (and urbane) landscape that Leone Battista Alberti had in mind when he wrote in *De Re Aedificatoria* that our cities should be "healthy, wide, pleasant, various, fruitful, secure and abounding in plenty of fruits and great quantities of water."

The nature which engineers like Leonardo and Le Nôtre sought to conquer was, in a certain sense, quite different from our own. Europe, emerging from the wars and plagues of the Dark Ages, presented frontiers as wild and savage as any the Romans had known. These dark landscapes were filled with forces hostile to man: wolves and werewolves, witches and bandits, malaria and hobgoblins, typhus and bears. The conquest of the wilderness, therefore, was the conquest of darkness and death itself. It was in a walled and barbered garden, beautiful *and* safe, that the *jeunesse dorée* of Boccaccio sat out the plague. But it is in the gardens of Versailles, grandest of all Renaissance landscapes, that we can see the fullest symbol of victory. There is no raw nature here—the tamed and disciplined lawns and trees run right over the horizon.

Our own concept of nature is today quite different. What is left of the wilderness is no longer dark. With airplanes we have already mapped it; quinine, penicillin, and snake serum will cope with any dangers we meet there. We can thus think of the natural world as beautiful, for perhaps the first time in Western history. We can see the forest primeval as a cultural and recreational resource and can preserve the Olympic Rain Forest and the Grand Tetons, not to landscape them but to keep them exactly as they are. The other side of this new attitude is, of course, our X-ray vision of nature's resources. In the light of modern chemistry every square inch of the earth is potentially rich in something. This new knowledge threatens the little undisturbed nature remaining to us.

The main instrument of this profound shift in the balance of forces between man and his environment has been the engine, and its pilot has been the engineer. Every field of human activity has felt the impact of his appearance on the stage of history, and none more so than architecture. The engineer altered both the kinds of buildings which the architect was to design as well as the materials out of which he was expected to build them. Even worse (from the architect's point of view) he has increasingly invaded the field of architecture itself. Although the American architect today may be at least nominally responsible for the vast majority of our schools, hospitals, and commercial buildings, the engineer has won full control of industrial installations and the whole field of such civil and military activities as ports, docks, dams, airfields, and the like. And if we consider all the engineering specialists directly involved in the individual project—structural, mechanical, illuminating, acoustical, sanitary—it is obvious how pervasive a role they play even in the buildings directly under an architect's control.

Qualitatively, too, American architecture has come to be dominated by concepts from the fields of engineering and technology. Standards of efficiency and economy, first accepted in plan and construction, have come ultimately to find their expression on the esthetic plane. Thus our concepts of architectural beauty have, in the past hundred years, been radically modified in the light of the engineer's discoveries.

For this we can be grateful. There is no need here to recapitulate the sorry state into which American architecture, indeed all Western architecture, had slipped by 1860. Clearly it was the engineer who rescued the architect, for it was he who, by his bridges and towers, railroad stations and exhibition halls, first demonstrated the great new esthetic potentials of technology. (That he often did so unwittingly is beside the point.) And we must admit that the architect was slow to see the significance of the proffered assistance. Half a century after Paxton's Crystal Palace, Montgomery Schuyler could still lament

. . . the artistic irrelevancy of the modern architect. In general, engineering is at least progressive, while architecture is at most stationary. And, indeed, it may be questioned whether, without thought of art, and, as it were, in spite of himself, the engineer has not produced the most impressive as certainly he has produced the most characteristic monuments of our times.[1]

He would have no such cause for complaint today, for there has seldom been a period in history when problems of pure structure have so prepossessed the architect. Structural logic, structural clarity, honesty of structural expression—these have become controlling values in design. They have, beyond doubt, purged architecture of much of the irrelevancy against which Schuyler protested. But they have also produced what a physician would call "unfortunate side effects." Obsession with structural "purity," at the expense of other and equally important problems of satisfactory function, has recently led in the direction of less

231

totally effective architecture. Nor has this interest in structure produced the rich and wide variety of structural systems one might have expected; on the contrary, the skeleton of the skyscraper has dominated all building types, including even those which are not multi-story and hence need not be cubical. This form has been cultivated at the expense of all others. Structural inventiveness has leveled off, the captive of the handbook and rationalized mass production.

As a result, American structural engineering seems increasingly stereotyped in contrast to such work as that of Italy's Pier Luigi Nervi or Mexico's Felix Candela. And, in parallel fashion, American architecture as a whole seems timid and cold when compared to the buoyancy and imagination of such projects as Le Corbusier's capital city of Chandigarh, or Oscar Niemeyer's of Brasília, or the new University City in Mexico. When we ask why we see so little of this sort of thing in the United States, we are told they are too costly! Only the "poor" and "backward" nations of the earth can, it seems, afford this kind of richness. It is true, of course, that the formwork for a parabolic shell runs higher than that for a flat slab, and that Nervi and Candela work with a cost ratio of labor to materials which is the reverse of ours. But it was the engineers themselves who have taught us that everything is too costly until it is mass produced but that nothing remains too expensive once it gets into serial production.

Here we confront the paradox of American engineering, especially as it is conjoined with American industrialism. The factual and "practical" bias of engineering theory tends toward conservatism in design. Characteristically the engineer has neither the intuition of the artist nor the speculative daring of the scientist. Furthermore, his rationalization of industrial production, in conjunction with the trustification of industry itself, tends to restrict the range and variety of articles produced. Though the union may well be the most productive on earth, it is increasingly the most monochromatic. The situation is not wholly frozen, of course, though it is certainly less fluid than it was even a few short decades ago. Technological break-throughs are still possible, though the opposition to basic change seems stiffer. We are told that the new thing is too expensive, the cost of the change-over prohibitive. Yet, if the demand continues, the log jam finally breaks: color comes to television, summer cooling to houses, welding to steel construction, atomic generators to electric power, even smaller cars appear. But the whole apparatus seems less flexible, less responsive than it was.

Much that is humdrum or inexpert in structural design may be due to sloth on the part of architect or engineer. Much more of it is directly related to the existing situation in professional fees. It takes time (and hence money) to design complex structures, especially concrete shells; somebody has to foot the bill. Since the architect normally has to pay the engineer out of his already inadequate fee, there is a natural inclination to settle for routinized procedures. Obviously, a larger portion of the project cost should be allotted to the design process. (It is ironic, to phrase it mildly, that architects often find themselves today accepting smaller fees than Latrobe was demanding in Napoleon's day!) Nor does it much help to cite the much greater amounts spent on research and design by industry for certain types of industrial products. When these costs can be prorated over millions of identical units, they become relatively unimportant. There is, unfortunately, scarcely any parallel in the production of buildings. Only the speculative house builder and the prefabricator operate on a comparable scale; and few of them have found it worthwhile to engage really distinguished architects and pay them the fees necessary for really thorough design.

The problem of mediocre design is, however, more than a simple question of low fees or lazy engineers: it is ultimately a cultural phenomenon. Specialization alone accounts for much of the confusion, as Fred Severud, one of our leading engineers, has pointed out:

Many factors operate in the selection and development of a structural system. [On a big project] owner, tenant, banker, even lately the advertising agency all have a finger in the pie. To meet all their often conflicting requirements is no simple task.

Too often the engineer is merely called in to "figure out" a cut-and-dried scheme. It may or may not be the most appropriate structural solution, but "in either case, it's not much of a challenge to a creative engineer. If he suggests an alternate scheme, at this late stage, the architect is apt to take umbrage." Generally speaking, says Severud, the most felicitous results are achieved when the engineer is brought into the design process at the conceptual stage. "That is the only period, actually, at which all possible alternatives can be freely weighed and the best solution adopted."[2]

And yet, no matter how complex the problem or dismaying the task, the ultimate responsibility is the architect's. Unless he knows what *kind* of structure he wants and can reasonably demand from the engineer, he will get the lowest common denominator. And that, under current conditions, is apt to be fairly low, relative to what is possible.

The American architect today draws heavily upon the resources of another type of specialist, the mechanical engineer. Just as there could have been no skyscraper without the structural engineer's steel frame, so was it also dependent upon the elevators, heating plants, and sanitation systems of the mechanical engineer. But what is much more important is the fact that without him we would not have the concepts of comfort and safety which distinguish contemporary architecture and city planning from all the epochs of the past. He has made possible our current standards of comfort and amenity. Le Corbusier's tower-studded urban parks or Wright's beguiling country houses—neither is conceivable without all the hidden services of the engineering specialties. Remember the cumbersome and ugly paraphernalia of preindustrial houses: privies, wells, and cow barns; slop jars and ash bins; unsafe candles and inefficient lamps; red hot stoves and ice-cold rooms. The new architecture could not rise until the engineer had banished all of them.

But there is, alas, another side to the engineer's story. In his anxiety to save us from labor and discomfort, he has carried us to grotesque extremes. He has given us kitchen ranges with control panels like military planes, television sets which can be operated from across the room with electronic guns, automobiles like Martian circus wagons whose size and power has made necessary a whole secondary hierarchy of mechanisms to make them operable at all. The illuminating engineer learned all about electric light decades before he paid any attention at all to the eye. (The foot-lambert, which is the measure of the brightness the eye actually sees, as only recently replaced the foot-candle, which is a theoretical unit unseen by the eye.) He gave us a range of new artificial light sources and forgot all about the sun. (The largest lighting demonstration center in the nation is windowless!) The air-conditioning engineer is apt to be much more concerned with degree-days than with comfort, or to know much more about how to get a given air velocity than its effect upon health. He has perfected the electrostatic air filter, but he uses it largely to cleanse our air of the impurities that his faulty combustion engines have placed there. The sanitary engineer perfected the water closet in the 1870s; he has done little to it since then except to lower the tank and change its colors.

You cannot "blame" the engineer for all this, any more than you could blame an undertaker for not carrying a line of baby clothes. These limited perspectives are, so to say, the occupational hazard of the various engineering specialties. The very training that makes them valuable as specialists renders them consistently unable to cope with the whole biological man. If anyone is ever to put the pieces back together again, to reorganize them in *man's* favor, it will be a generalist like the architect. Yet it must be admitted that he is presently in no position to call the kettle black. All too often he forgets what Vitruvius and Jefferson could never forget—the decisive effect of orientation upon architecture. Too often he designs arbitrary façades and then hands them over to the air-conditioning engineer to make them habitable. He uses microphones and loudspeakers, as the Greeks never could, to correct faulty acoustics which he himself has made inevitable by faulty design. He uses artificial light to make up for bad fenestration and electric fans to correct poor ventilation.

Too often, in fact, the architect abdicates in favor of the engineer. It is in this sense that the engineer has harmed him almost as much as he has helped. He has proffered so many fascinating *means* of doing things that the need or needlessness for doing them is often lost sight of. Just because he is there at the architect's shoulder, with all his wonderful panaceas, the architect can be weaker, less effective, than he ever could before. By the very majesty of his powers, the engineer has blinded us as to what actually is possible and proper.

Recognition of this fact, however, is not confined to any one sector of the building field. One is just as apt to find an air-conditioning engineer as an architect who understands that the sun still gives off real heat or a tree still casts real shade. As a matter of fact, the more advanced engineers realize that, all too often, they are merely called in "to pick up the pieces." Understandably, they resent this. They would prefer to be consulted early in the design process, conceptually as well as chronologically. As Walter Fleisher expresses it,

The air-conditioning design engineer is usually placed in a straight-jacket of pre-set building plans and rigid specifications. He is not consulted on such basic questions as orientation, fenestration, insulation—in fact, he's lucky if he gets adequate, uninterrupted space in which to run his ducts. He is thus in the position of being handed prefabricated space and told to make it habitable.

Air conditioning, as Fleisher admits, is far from being an exact science. "It is full of all sorts of imponderables and, to protect himself in a situation of which he has only partial control, the engineer is forced to use ridiculous factors of safety." Qualitative standards are needed—*performance specifications,* such as one finds in testing laboratories where equipment is tested under extreme environmental conditions. Here, he points out, the engineer would be asked only to *produce a specific environment.* "This sort of specification details only the end result, not the means to be employed to obtain it. This method takes full advantage of the engineer's ingenuity and experience."[3] If the same principle were applied to architecture generally, a far higher performance standard would be possible.

Like Severud, Fleisher is in effect asking to be consulted earlier in the game, to be used by the architect as a colleague and not merely as a crutch.

The acoustical engineer presents us with a somewhat different picture. Because so much of his work has been in the field of telecommunications—where the end product is, so to speak, salable sound—he has been compelled to show more interest than his colleagues in the human being, or at least the human ear. Thus his interest in sound will sometimes extend beyond the decibel to an appreciation of music itself. From such a specialist, the architect has much to learn. Professor Richard H. Bolt of the Massachusetts Institute of Technology's Acoustical Laboratory puts it this way:

Man cannot be expected to exhibit a standardized esthetic judgment. . . . Into this apparent confusion the acoustical scientist is supposed to bring some degree of predictability. Basically, his dilemma is this: science cannot be applied rationally to the engineering of acoustics without a set of standards, and yet the final judges, the audience and musicians, don't seem to subscribe to any such set. In spite of this, the answer must somehow be found in those judges. If they will not all respond alike, one can at least look for an average response.[4]

This is a point of view not commonly associated with the engineering specialties and one which any architect should be glad to accept. Indeed, it is from this point of view that some of the most distinguished of recent concert halls have been created. Musician, engineer, and architect have designed them acoustically—i.e., to yield a certain agreed-upon type of sonic behavior—before the architect put pencil to paper. But this is clearly not a philosophy which can be applied, like a coat of paint, to a finished building. It calls for functional collaboration between specialists from the very inception of the project. And it is, in point of fact, the only policy which can conquer the sheer gadgetry whose efflorescence corrupts so much of American design today.

One conclusion should be apparent: for better or worse, the engineer has forever altered the *scope* of the architect's task. He has catapulted him into a new and higher order of responsibility. Design has become a business of manipulating, not "raw" materials like bricks and two-by-fours, but entire systems of highly specialized prefabricated elements. Supervision involves not merely masons and carpenters but whole schools of extremely skilled specialists. The architect, in short, must specify environment and not materials. It is he who must specify safety, not fluorescent tubes, as the criterion of good industrial lighting; comfort and health, not radiators, as the object of school heating; intelligibility, not acoustical tile, as the measure of the good auditorium. If the architect does not assume this crucial responsibility, who will? The engineer cannot be expected to; he does not deal with the whole client, only some specialized part of him.

Does this mean the architect should "take over" the work of the consulting engineers? Not at all. To begin with, he couldn't: these fields are all complete scientific disciplines in themselves, with a higher proportion of graduate degrees than in architecture itself. But in the second place, he shouldn't: detailed competence in any one specialty would only be won at the cost of over-all architectural wisdom. What

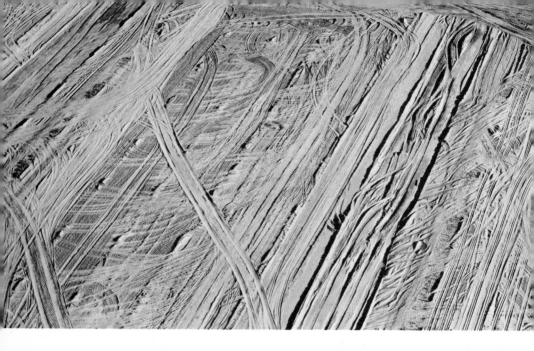

Modern technology has raised the power of the modern engineer to literally geological proportions, but there has been no commensurate increase in his wisdom. Modern earth-moving techniques (above) preparing for tract housing in California (below).

the architect should be, is already in fact becoming, is the informed arbiter of the conflicting demands of these specialists and their systems. Each has his own set of demands and criteria of judgment and, from the very nature of the problem, they will not coincide. These conflicts must therefore be resolved at the highest possible level, not merely of appearance (though this too is important) but of total behavior or performance. This implies standards, and these can only be derived from the needs of the actual users of the building. The architect, then, must arbitrate not between one machine and another but between all machines and *man*.

The engineer has also made it impossible for the architect to limit his attention to the individual, isolated building. The sheer scale of the engineer's operations, his immensely increased capacity for good or evil, is forcing the architect out of his ivory tower. For no tower is safe when modern earth-moving equipment shows up in the neighborhood; a whole landscape can vanish in a twinkling, irrevocably, beneath a sea of asphalt drive-ins or jet-bomber runways. The engineer is committed to the proposition that a straight line is always the shortest distance between two points. Let him drop an interchange in your community and it goes up, literally, in a cloud of dust. George Washington may have slept in building "B"; Bullfinch or McIntire might have designed it. But if it happens to lie along a line connecting the engineer's point "A" with his destination at "C," then "B" is not long for this world, no matter what its artistic worth or historic significance.

The American landscape is full of such examples today. The structural engineer throws a beautiful span across the Golden Gate—and the beautiful residential landscapes for which the Bay Region is famous are drowned in automobile traffic. The sanitary engineer begins to deflect his sewage away from the Hudson River, to return its waters to their original state of purity. (It was he, of course, who polluted them to begin with.) But while his attention is turned to the disposal plants, *another* engineer (chemical, this time) dumps enough industrial wastes into the stream to undo all the good work of the first. The engineer must be watched not because he is ignorant but because, in a sharply limited way, he is so smart; not because he is dishonest but because his honesty has all the limits and rigidity of the slide rule. Left to his own devices, he threatens the whole race with disaster.

It would be arrogant nonsense to claim for the architect the right to police these busy colleagues of his. Only the American people can, in the last analysis, tell the engineer what to do with his bulldozers, dishwashers, and space frames. But the architect (along with the city planner and the landscape architect) has been assigned a peculiarly strategic position by society. His training, if anyone's, should teach him to balance trees against asphalt, historic patrimony against selfish expediency, human happiness against mere efficiency. He can show the American people how to use our splendid technology to build houses and cities worthy of our country. And he can show the engineer how to channel his energies in this direction, how to convert his technical units of measurement into the broader scale of great architecture.

16. THE USES OF HISTORY

We are all aware of the general cultural benefits, not to say the civilizing effects, of the study of history. But even professional historians might hesitate before so sweeping a claim for their métier as that offered by a contemporary American novelist: "Man has no material other than his past out of which to make [his] future." Yet this does not really overstate the case, for the greatest natural resource of the human race is its experience. Both conceptually and materially, our past is our principal building material. And the science of history is a tool which we can use, like the Geiger counter in prospecting for uranium, to discover and exploit the great deposits of our cultural past.

Today's architect has, in his schooling, been exposed to a certain amount of the history of his profession. Rather too much history, some of the older men would say, bearing in mind the esthetical and antiquarian overtones which architectural history carried until the very recent past, or remembering the disastrous stylistic eclecticism into which the study of history carried us in the nineteenth century. Such protests, however, are the result not of the proper study of history but of its misunderstanding; such protestors are the victims of a primitive phase of historiography. The past is not just one vast deposit of shining success and prefabricated precedent, as the Victorians fondly imagined it. On the contrary, it is formed geologically in strata of truth and falsehood, accuracy and error, cold fact and disappointed fancy. Modern history is the instrument with which we can analyze and separate the two—bearing in mind, of course, the odd fact that the past, viewed in this light, is often quite as valuable for what it warns us against duplicating as for what it advises us to repeat.

That the study of history has immediate practical utility is being demonstrated in many fields other than architecture. Dr. Henry E. Sigerist, the famous historian of medicine, studied the practice of

Alexandrine medicine, not out of esoteric scholarship but in search of guides to modern psychosomatic theory. Dr. Lazlo Schwartz, the historian of dentistry, investigates the mechanic-craftsman origins of his profession to demonstrate how they led to certain mechanistic, anti-physiological tendencies in modern dental thought. The pharmaceutical industry launches extensive research into the folk pharmacopeia of primitive peoples, first to discover drugs of known effectiveness, and then to isolate them from the medicine man's brew. And archaeologists since Schliemann have learned to study myth and folk tale attentively as guides to new sites.

In one way or another, these are all planned expeditions, scientific treasure hunts, into the past. Their results are known: they serve to illuminate general theory in their respective fields at the same time that they yield discoveries of real and immediate practicality. When the architectural past is similarly exposed to the light of modern historical investigation, equally new and fruitful discoveries are revealed.

Of course, the study of the artistic past does present some rather special complications. The history of science or medicine, for example, has little or no esthetic dimension. Sigerist can discuss Hellenistic medicine, or Schwartz can study Confederate dentistry, without becoming enmeshed in a network of esthetic value judgments. Moreover, the history of science shows real development and records objectively provable advances. There is no such progression in the field of art. Each epoch differs from all others. The artistic production of one may be rated higher than another (though this always involves subjective judgments) but no continuously rising curve can ever be plotted (though many an art historian has tried to in the past).

Not only do architectural historians have more disparate materials to work with than historians in other fields, they also have a more difficult audience to address. American architects today tend to display one of two characteristic attitudes toward the past, both of them highly charged with emotion. The older generation, generally speaking, tends to look at it through the rosy glasses of romantic antiquarianism. The younger men, on the other hand, wear the blindfold of simple prejudice and refuse to look at it at all. Both attitudes, are, of course, mistaken. Both prevent our exploiting the great resources of history for the enrichment of the future. Fortunately, there is an escape from the cul-de-sac into which such attitudes have led us, and it should be the task of the historian to point it out.

For example, the historian might well act as guide to the architects whom the rise of American power has catapulted into global activity and international prominence. These men are being called upon to design buildings for the Arctic, the Middle East, South America, Polynesia. They are confronted with cultural and environmental conditions of unprecedented complexity and diversity. In designing for them in a context of emergency (real or imagined) the architect is apt to protest that he has no time for a history of the place. Yet history is the first thing he should make time for, if his ambitions include genuinely successful architecture. He is being asked to design for unfamiliar cultures, geographies, climates. In such a context, the catalogs and handbooks of American technology are of surprisingly little value. A first-rate historical analysis of the local culture and its architectural response to local conditions—its materials, structures, and design principles—would be of much more immediate utility.

Thus, when the American designer, floundering in the Arctic, is confronted with such problems as building on permafrost or resisting Arctic gales, he should be given not a Detroit handbook on insulation or structural steel but a first-rate analysis of traditional Eskimo building practices. For, as Stefansson long ago pointed out, the igloo is an example of an extremely sophisticated regional architecture, quite remarkably adapted to the climate, resources, and needs of the area. Its combination of ice-lined snow blocks, fur-lined spherical form and pin-point radiant heat source constitutes a comfort formula which stands up to the strictest scrutiny of science. These principles, though naturally not necessarily these materials, should be the springboard for Arctic design.

Or again, when an American architect builds new oil towns in the Middle East, he should study first the traditional forms of Arab building and only after he has mastered them turn to texts on air conditioning. In the high heat capacity of Arab mud and masonry construction, he would find the best thermal formula for handling the diurnal temperatures extremes of the desert.

Finally, when the architect is called upon to build in the South Pacific, with its continuously high humidity and heat, the historian should provide him with factual studies of the local architecture. No better comfort formula could be found than its airy, stilted, wide-roofed pavilions. These primitive buildings represent not forms to be copied but principles to be understood. They are principles distilled from millenia of experience on the part of men quite as intelligent as ourselves. It is a matter of elementary culture (as well as of technical proficiency) that the architect master these principles before he begins to design. Who but the historian should discover them for him? It can, of course, be argued that these are farfetched examples or that American architects have no business being in such outlandish places anyway. This may well be true. But the same thing holds for our own country as well. The technical problems of building around the world are duplicated, in climate if not in culture, right here at home. We also have Saharas, tundras, Melanesias, and steppes all around us. Furthermore we have behind us from three to four centuries of experience in dealing with them—our own "primitive" period. This indigenous experience constitutes a real wealth which goes largely unexploited because of blindfolds and rose-tinted glasses.

One of our richest regional architectures, for example, lies in the deposit of eighteenth-century houses in and around New Orleans. It has been fairly well explored by historian and amateur antiquarian alike; and while much of the resulting literature many seem either snobbish or parochial, there is no need to belittle its importance. It has proved necessary and useful work, and many an important landmark has been preserved, either in records or reality, because of it. Yet despite this work, the true significance of this architecture goes largely unnoticed by practicing and student architects alike.

It happens that this same body of work can be analyzed from quite another point of view, a much more fruitful and exciting one—namely, the point of view of social and technical invention. An examination at this level will reveal an impressively sophisticated design for comfort and amenity in a very difficult semitropical climate. Here are the characteristic features of these eighteenth-century houses:

1. Elevated living floors, raised above floods and animal and insect pests and offering maximum exposure to prevailing breezes.
2. Huge, light-mass, parasol-type roofs to shed subtropic sun and rain.

244

3. Continuous porches and balconies to protect walls from slanting sun and blowing rain.
4. Large floor-to-ceiling doors and windows for maximum ventilation.
5. Tall ceilings, central halls, ventilated attics for warm-weather comfort.
6. The louvered jalousie, providing any combination of ventilation and privacy.
7. Building materials highly resistant to water, fungus, or insect attack.

In short, the characteristic features of this architecture show a deep understanding of the local relationship between climate and comfort and a most intelligent use of a limited range of simple materials and technique to manipulate this relationship. Neither the climate nor the people of this region are much changed today, a century and a half after the Louisiana Purchase brought an abrupt end to this particular architectural idiom. There has been much subsequent invention, both social and technical. But to what sort of use has it been put in the New Orleans–Gulf Coast region? Can we honestly say that the level of contemporary architecture measures up to its historic precedent? Unfortunately, we cannot. Instead, we find a qualitative deterioration in standards. The antiquarians mimic the *forms* of the past, with no real comprehension of their content and function. The younger men display a hostility which is little short of psychotic to the parasol roof and the wide overhang, the balcony and the jalousie. And the average level of domestic architecture is lower in grace and amenity than it was in Napoleon's day.

It is currently argued (by the blindfold set) that modern technology has made obsolete the principles on which this earlier idiom was based. But this is patently untrue: the Louisiana sun shines with undiminished ferocity, and a moment with a slide rule should convince any architect that an air-conditioning system requires a cool roof and shaded walls even more urgently than he does. Such a vulgar underestimation of the value of tradition and overestimation of the powers of technology is exactly what explains so many current American failures. Such an attitude is not only not scientific, it is not even civilized.

245

So here we face a paradox: a rich tradition, valid by all objective tests, useful for the present, yet abused or ignored by all. It is the task of the historian to intervene in this absurd situation, to place the past into a new perspective. We must admit that historians are themselves largely responsible for this paradox since, until recently, they have tended to paint the past as a vast treasure trove of prefabricated architectures. The architects of this century have been right to reject this approach. We all know now that the past does indeed have its riches but only, so to say, in the form of raw materials: tested principles and proven concepts which must be distilled by modern knowledge before they can take useful form. Of course, not all of the past will prove immediately useful; nor is the immediately useful the only goal of the historian. On the contrary, he must organize scientific expeditions to every region of the past, irrespective of its apparent promise at the start. Only thus will his new histories achieve the combination of depth and comprehensiveness so needed today.

What will the criteria for the writing of these new histories be? The first will obviously be that they observe the same standards as those of modern historiography in other fields. The work must be objective, precise, factual. It must have a comprehensive knowledge of the forces at work not only in its own but in adjacent fields. It must have a truly world point of view, not a parochial one, no matter how restricted the epoch or locale involved. What happens to history when these standards are not observed is painfully apparent in a great nineteenth-century work like Banister Fletcher's *History of Architecture on the Comparative Method*. This was the first attempt in English at a comprehensive picture. It is still unique: ten or twenty specialized works would be required as a substitute. It is certainly factual—the production of the measured drawings alone would grace the lifetime of a lesser man. It is precise to the point of dullness. It is, within certain limits, objective: Sir Banister obviously loved all architecture and showed no particular bias for or against the great European styles. In its method, his *History* marked a real advance. One gets a first glimpse in English (though Viollet-le-Duc preceded him in French) of the evolutionary process at work in architecture, of the conditioning effects of time, climate, and resources upon each great style.

Yet this monumental work is today not merely obsolete, it is actually harmful. This is due not so much to subsequent historical and archaeological research as to a fundamental flaw in its conception. The *History* is not, as its title clearly suggests, a world history. It is a history of the Western world alone, begining with the Egyptians and ending (in the most recent, 15th edition) with the Empire State Building. It classifies the stylistic epochs between these two points as the "Historical Styles." In its earlier editions, it neglected entirely the architectures of Asia, Africa, and pre-Columbian America. It omitted any consideration of primitive or prehistoric building. And it ignored the folk or popular building of the West itself. In recent years, efforts have been made to correct some of the more glaring of these omissions. But the basic structure of the book remains unchanged; thus it still defines the great architectures of India, of China and Japan, of Mexico and Peru, as the "non-historical styles"!

The mortal flaw in Fletcher is thus the very parochialism which has marked most of the dealings of the West with the rest of the world. Of course, this flaw can now be seen in its own historical context as being nothing more than the esthetic aspect of nineteenth-century imperialist policy. Culture, civilization, and history itself were taken to be the exclusive property of the white man. If we no longer run the risk of such egregious errors, it is largely due to the hard, continuous work of the art and social historians, the archaeologist and anthropologist, even the explorer and the psychologist. Such men have given us a broader and deeper perspective of the field of architecture. Thanks to them, world history is coming into focus as a unified whole. The day seems safely past when another "world" history will devote 887 pages to the West and 46 to all the rest of mankind's total experience.

From the scientist we have much to learn in terms of the criteria of scientific research. But we should be careful not to make a totem of him in the abstract. We have seen that the same physicist who can split the atom is somehow able to deny any responsibility for exploding the hydrogen bomb. Architectural history should remain in the hands of the humanists: if the historians' work is not characterized by certain attitudes, illuminated by certain convictions, it is not apt to have permanent value. These necessary attitudes seem to me to be optimism and humility, imagination and realism, esthetic maturity.

Of all professions two at least have need of optimists—medicine and architecture. To be effective they must be optimistic, for they deal with life and living processes. Architectural history has certainly been made by optimists: it should be written by them. Giotto and Brunelleschi in Florence; Leonardo with his garden-city satellites for Milano; Le Nôtre with his gardens at Versailles; Le Corbusier with his design for rebuilding Paris—these men and all like them are characterized by confidence in the utility of their work. They believed that the earth could be made a better place for men to live in (the "garden" that Bacon visualized) and were determined to make it so.

And who should chronicle the works of giants like these if not historians who share their point of view? Viollet-le-Duc in his *Habitations of Man in All Ages* goes so far as to create two protagonists through which to view the evolutionary process in architecture. One of them, Doxius, is the prototype of pessimism. For him, man moves around in aimless circles, no progress is observable, or possible, or even desirable. Things were always better in the good old days. His partner Epergos (for fictional purposes Viollet-le-Duc has them living forever) is both realist and optimist. He observes man in the filth and peril of the cave. He watches man slowly invent the roof, the wall, the window, the chimney. He sees the laborious and uneven rise in levels of comfort, cleanliness, nutrition, and security. Epergos does not deny that the task is difficult, that mistakes are plentiful and disaster all too frequent. But he does see man gradually conquering his physical environment, changing himself from the slave into the master of nature.

This was the source of his optimism, and of Viollet-le-Duc's also. Nor was it a shallow optimism. It was soundly grounded on scientific fact. Viollet-le-Duc was among the first in our field to turn to archaeology and anthropology for assistance, just as he was among the very first to apply the principles of Darwinian evolution to the problems of architectural development. It is true, of course, that Victorian technology cast no such terrifying shadows across his landscape as does ours today. But, he might well retort, neither did it hold such glowing possibilities for the future.

Parallel with optimism we will find humility in all good historians. This has nothing to do with lack of power or principle but merely recognizes the plain fact that history has proved more historians wrong than right. This is, one might almost say, an occupational hazard of the field. For though the past never changes, the point from which we view it does so constantly. The historian who rewrites history to suit his own narrow ends had best remember this. Poor John Ruskin is a classic example of the danger of forgetting it. The way in which his arrogance vitiated his real powers as a critic is sad to contemplate. He was right in seeing grievous flaws in Victorian art and life, wrong in thinking that a return to medievalism would correct either one. Yet he stopped at nothing (least of all the willful distortion of the facts of history) to prove his point. Since his was an immense audience—probably the largest of any art critic who ever lived—his bigoted myopia was no laughing matter. In the process of proving that Gothic art and architecture were the pinnacle of human achievement, he did violence to all other epochs, including his own. But he also did immense damage to Gothic itself. By his mechanical analogies between medieval art and medieval life, by magnifying the virtues and minimizing the faults of Gothic art, and by his ignorance of the real conditions under which it was produced Ruskin made it difficult for whole generations to appraise it correctly.

We have his exact antithesis in Greenough. They were, for a while at least, contemporaries. Yet seldom have two spectators of the same event brought back more divergent accounts. If Greenough makes rewarding reading today it is because he was, among other things, humble about his own great powers. His formal education was equal to Ruskin's, his actual experience in art much wider. He too was aware of the evils of his day, but, unlike Ruskin, he saw that two ways at least lay open, forward as well as back. Unlike Ruskin, he had no vested interest in any single kind of art; his vested interest was a grander, more durable one—that of man himself. Thus Greenough could find praise for any period, any style, any idiom which had enriched the lives of its users. On the other hand, he was able to see that none of them could ever be literally revived. All that remained viable in them was the *principle* on which they had been erected.

Modesty did not weaken Greenough's powers as a critic. Many things around him struck him as unworthy and he had his own robust way of saying so. (Versailles was "a royal mushroom," Barry's new Houses of Parliament "colossal geegaws." He found Boucher "a chaos of bombast, falsehood, and clogging sensuality" and distrusted the "prolific silliness of Borromini" and the "royal whim-whams" of Baroque sculpture at Munich.) Yet modesty did compel him to turn to authorities in other fields for guidance and advice. In his effort to understand the basis of beauty in nature—the body of man, the silken coat of the tiger, the color and scent of the flower—he turned to comparative anatomists, zoologists, botanists. Thus, if so many of his judgments seem astonishingly up-to-date, it is because he had the good sense to use the intellectual resources of his time. Around him was that enormous constellation of Victorian scientists who were remaking man's concept of the world. Ruskin, neurotic and self-centered, was contemptuously ignorant of their work, but Greenough drew upon it hungrily, using it to deepen and enrich his understanding of his own field.

Imagination is still another quality essential to the historian—not the kind of imagination which invents facts where they do not exist but the kind which discovers new relationships which explain hitherto inexplicable problems. The astronomer who postulates a new planet before the telescope picks it up is using the same kind of imagination as Greenough when he says that, in nature, form is the expression of function. Lewis Mumford shows the same sort of intuition in such pregnant studies as *Sticks and Stones* and *The Brown Decades,* which first turned the attention of his generation to a "lost" period in American history. And Siegfried Giedion demonstrates the power of imagination when, in *Mechanization Takes Command,* he turns to such unorthodox sources as the United States Patent Office and the catalogs of long-dead factories to write a new and revealing history of American technology.

This historical imagination must, however, be disciplined by a strong sense of realism. In approaching the men of the past, the natural tendency is to read into their actions motivations which were in fact not theirs. Such misconceptions lay behind all the great stylistic revivals of the nineteenth century. Ruskin was not alone in idealizing the past. The Greek Revival, stunningly timed to coincide with the Greek War of Liberation against the Turks, read into Greek democracy all sorts of dimensions which unfortunately did not exist; noble it might have been but limited it certainly was. Even Jefferson, the best-informed

American of his day, was able to overlook the very grave shortcomings of Roman republicanism just as he was misled by the faulty scholarship of the period into thinking that he was emulating Republican architecture when in fact his cherished prototype at Nîmes was a temple of the Augustan Empire. Such mistaken emphases can perhaps never be completely avoided in writing history, but they should be held to an absolute minimum.

A final requirement of the architectural historian is that he be esthetically mature. Whatever his private convictions, he must bring to the scrutiny of past styles a maximum measure of comprehension, even of compassion. He may, for example, feel that late Gothic wall painting often confused the essential clarity of Gothic interiors as in the case of the magnificent brick Cathedral at Albi. But that should not blind him to the plain historical fact that it appeared eminently satisfactory to the people who did it. He may, himself, infinitely prefer the naked brick vaulting of Roman structure today to the marble-skinned state in which Augustus was proud to have left it. But he gives the student a distorted view of Roman reality if he does not show him the way the Roman preferred Roman buildings to appear. He may prefer the luminous and buoyant materialism of Venetian painting to the static mysticism of Byzantine mosaics, but this affords him no basis for trying to prove the one superior to the other.

The ability to make such objective analyses, to break down into their component parts the periods of history, to understand the complex of technical, esthetic, and cultural forces which acted upon them and gave their art its characteristic form—this ability is relatively new and marks an absolute gain in the science of history itself. No previous period has had such tools to work with. It enables us, for example, to understand something which troubled our predecessors—namely, the two distinct aspects of the history of our field. The first is the cyclical path of development of art; the second is the objective and fairly steady rise in the material condition of man's life. This new power makes it easier to understand why the Etruscans please one man, Michelangelo another; why Giotto satisfies some tastes and Hiroshige delights others. It explains, in short, the absolute relativity of taste. We deal here with relative values, and—what is more interesting to the historian

—they have always been relative values. What one epoch adores, the next will despise.

This is a disturbing discovery for those who are only comfortable with absolutes. They seek to discover some sort of progression in the history of art, some continuously rising line of artistic accomplishment (with themselves, of course, at the apex). When they find that history offers no such tidy consolations, they are apt to turn pessimist. Since there can be no objective proof that Periclean art is "higher" than Minoan or that Baroque is "better" than Ming, such absolutists are apt to jump to the conclusion that the same thing is true of the societies which produced them. This impermissible leap from esthetics to sociology goes unremarked. Yet in just such a fashion one might argue that the America of Jefferson was a lower social form than that of the cave dwellers of Southern France since, by modern standards, the latter were incomparably the better painters!

Modern historiography permits us to see that the material condition of man follows quite a separate pattern from the evolution of his art. In materialistic terms, there is clearly cause and effect, accumulated momentum, progression forward (and sometimes, alas, movement back!). Yet, oddly enough, man's art and artifacts offer the best record of this movement, so different in nature from that of art itself. Today's historian will have no difficulty proving that the level of life was higher in the Etruscan city-state than in the Italiote societies which preceeded it. He need only turn to a monument like the Tomb of the Stuccoes at Cerveteri to document his case, for here are portrayed, in accurate, full-scale bas-reliefs, all the furnishings and equipment of an Etruscan household. These demonstrate, among other things, that culinary and dietary levels must have been quite high, so varied is the range of culinary tools displayed.

This same historian will have no difficulty in showing that the seaport city of Ostia, in its turn, marked a further advance over the earlier Etruscan towns. He can show this by her monuments—libraries, theaters, temples, and arenas. He can show technical advance from her fire stations, public baths and toilets, water and sewer mains; industrial development from her workshops, warehouses, harbor installations. Even the commercial signs in her sidewalks show the reach and variety of her commercial contacts. Here he moves in a realm of fact, deals with elements subject to measurement and comparison. But there is no possibility of establishing parallels in the art history of these towns. Modern taste would find the Etruscan preferable to the Ostian and might well find the primitive Italiote preferable to both.

Architecture is exasperatingly composed of sculpture and cesspools, frescoes and frigidaires, beautiful motifs and ugly motivations. We cannot judge a beautiful fountain only by the typhoid it might spread. Fountain and plague have each their own law of development. Our standards of history, to accommodate this paradox, must therefore be compound and not simple.

17. THE CRITIC'S SHIFTING VIEW

It has always been easier for the critic to analyze the past than the present. When he deals with contemporary events, his task is immediately more difficult, often more hazardous. He is himself involved in the event, and the judgments he makes and positions he takes may affect the outcome, as they could not possibly do with past events. Yet criticism plays a decisive role in the formation of the attitudes and standards of judgment of modern society. On the one hand, it introduces the public to the new event, prepares it, so to say, for the future. At the same time criticism reflects the public's reaction to the new event, and in this sense modifies its subsequent evolution. The critical mechanism is the same whether the field be politics or drama or—as in this case —architecture. And it has had a far wider impact on our field than most architects realize. A few novels by Sir Walter Scott; a couple of thin, acidulous tracts by Augustus Welby Pugin; two incandescent sermons by Ruskin—and the centuries-old Renaissance tradition was overturned by the creaking literary machine of the Gothic Revival. Here was a classic case where the critics spoke over the heads of the profession to a new middle-class audience; and the architects had no choice but to follow, bringing up the rear.

The battle for contemporary architecture was fought and won, on both sides of the Atlantic, as much by the pen as by the drawing board. The polemics had, of course, to be documented by pictures which illustrated the main points of the argument. Sometimes these were photographs of actual buildings; more often they were merely the architect's sketches of what he hoped to build. It did not seem to matter much, from a polemical point of view. In any case, tens of thousands of people could learn the rationale of the new architecture from the critics where only tens would ever be likely to see it in reality, The critics themselves came from disparate backgrounds. Some of the most effective were the architects themselves: Sullivan and Wright in this country, Adolph Loos and Le Corbusier abroad. But many of the protagonists came from other fields—Mumford, Hitchcock, Giedion, Johnson (who later become an architect). Whatever their point of departure, it was critics like these who eventually convinced the public of the validity of the new style.

The battle was late in reaching American shores. Or, to be more precise, it was late in reerupting on American shores, for in a real sense the battle had begun here. Sullivan and Wright had been among the very first to formulate both the theoretical base and the actual forms of the new style. Their work had fed the flames of revolt abroad. But here at home the vast eclectic apparatus of official architecture, piloted by such ineffable figures as Charles Follen McKim and Ralph Adams Cram, had succeeded in silencing the first, exiling the second, and suffocating their polemics. Thus it was that as late as 1924 even so alert an observer as Lewis Mumford, then as now architecture's most perceptive critic, could be largely unaware of the modern movement, either here or abroad. When he was writing that remarkably prescient book, *Sticks and Stones,* as he says in the Preface to the 1954 edition, "The story of American architecture after 1850 was a pathless waste. By 1924, the work of the Chicago School, historically speaking, had dropped out of sight completely."[1]

The isolation of American architecture during the 1920s from the revolutionary developments abroad seems, in retrospect, incredible; it was as complete as had been that of American painting prior to the Armory Show of 1913 and it was exploded by a very similar event— the Museum of Modern Art's famous show, *The International Style,* in 1932. If travelling American architects during the twenties saw the radical new architecture of Holland, France, or Germany, their work did not reflect it when they returned. If any American critics saw its significance, the journals did not print their reports. One of the few men during that period who showed either knowledge or understanding of the new movement was Henry-Russell Hitchcock. In a little-known and long-forgotten book[2] he described the European scene accurately and completely, including even such peripheral figures as the Spanish architect and builder, Antonio Gaudi (whose Sagrada Famiglia in Barcelona, he felt, was "surely neither fine nor important"[3]). It was Hitchcock also who, with Philip Johnson, organized the famous Museum show and wrote the famous book of the same name. Only a handful of Americans could actually have seen the show in New York, but thousands studied the book. Whatever else they did, these two events put the subject of the new architecture back on the American agenda of public controversy. After this it was no longer possible to be unaware of the issue, no matter what stance one took.

The vast range of social, economic, and technical forces which gave rise to the new architecture needs no recapitulation here. Yet, overwhelming as they were, these forces still required a literature of criticism to prepare the way for the acceptance of the new idiom. This literature furnished the philosophical substructure upon which the new architecture was to be erected. And it is fascinating today to study the rationale it offered at the beginning and to see how profoundly that rationale has shifted since. It was called by different names in different countries but the label that Hitchcock and Johnson attached to it proved to be, in this country at least, the more durable.[4] A rereading of the literature of the period will show us, however, that it was not defended primarily because it was "modern" or "contemporary" or "international" but because it was efficient, effective, economical or, as the phrase went, "functional." Actually, of course, an entire hierarchy of values was involved, and different critics assigned them different emphases, creating a structure so intricate as to defy encapsulation. Generally speaking, the values were primarily ethical and utilitarian and only secondarily esthetic. Some architects like Loos and Hannes Meyer all but denied the validity of esthetics as a criterion of the new style.

The very adjectives used confirm the ethical emphasis. Modern architecture was "good" because of its "integrity"; it was "honest" in its expression of structure; "frank," "pure," or "simple" in its forms. It was politically admirable because it was "democratic," "unpretentious," "unassuming," devoting its attention to the problems of the common man instead of, as in past epochs, the aristocracy. It was consonant with the technological realities of industrial mass production. It used not only the tools of industry (Gropius's Bauhaus) but also its organizational methods (Gropius's theories of group design). The conceptual identification with the machine was made explicit visually. Le Corbusier not only considered the house a *machine à habiter* but literally modeled his railings and gangplanks on the machine he admired so much, the ocean liner. Finally, as it was all these things, the new architecture was socially desirable because of the qualitatively new total environment it gave to men: the Swiss and German *siedlungen,* Le Corbusier's Utopian reconstruction of Paris, Patrick Geddes and the English Garden Cities, Frank Lloyd Wright with his Broadacre City.

Since the Modern Art Museum show and the controversy it enkindled occurred in the depths of the Great American Depression, when apple-selling Americans were being told that grass would grow in the streets if they took political action against the disaster that engulfed them, it is not surprising that the new style became associated with the social objectives of the New Deal. (Hitler, at the same time, was denouncing the new style as Communistic, exiling its architects, and camouflaging with steeply pitched gables the flat-roofed modern buildings that he found it convenient to confiscate.) The task of discrediting traditional idioms was made easier by their identification, whether real or apocryphal, with the old order under whose regime the debacle had occurred. This lent a note of moral fervor to much of the writing of the period. Interestingly enough, the productive capacity of the machine is seen as both the source of plenty and the measure of excellence. Even Wright, ordinarily isolated from social and political movements, was stirred by the possibility that the New Deal would make "our machine power and our millions democratically beneficent." And Mumford was stirred by the same potentials: "The great mass of housing erected since the industrial revolution . . . was unhygienic, ugly and inadequate. . . . The machine has endowed us with new powers and created new needs; the hygiene of the body, the care of health, the wide-spread interest in athletic recreation, the education of children, the use of leisure—all demand an environment differently ordered from that with which our ancestors were content."[5] The Cheneys, in another influential book of the 1930s, saw "the community of tomorrow as a place unified and harmonious: an industrially-designed machine age entity. Its considered patterning of buildings and spaces, its landscaping, public and private, are a coming realization of the universal utility of the machine."[6]

So sharp was the struggle to free architecture from the dead hand of tradition that even the most esthetically minded of the critics accepted this moral reference frame. "It were better," wrote Hitchcock and Johnson in 1932, "that the world build only according to the rigid anti-esthetic theories of the extreme European functionalists than that 19th Century debauchery of design shall continue."[7] The new style, they admitted, "sets a high but not impossible standard for decoration; better none at all unless it be good. . . . It aims as much at making monstrosities impossible . . . as at assuring masterpieces."[8] Such Draconian advice was historically quite appropriate. The task of winning the American people to a wholly new kind of beauty would not make much headway until they were convinced of the bankruptcy of the old forms of beauty. Hence the protagonists of the new style were proceeding, consciously or not, on Emerson's proposition that the good and the true become ultimately the beautiful.

The problem of beauty in the modern style, while subordinate in its hierarchy of values, was not altogether ignored by the critics. But such was the temper of the times that the word itself, beauty, was suspect. Hence modern buildings which the critics saw as beautiful were described in elliptical terms. Thus Hitchcock and Johnson:

The esthetic principles of the International Style are based primarily upon the nature of modern materials and structure, and upon modern requirements of planning. . . . The technical and utilitarian factors, in the hands of designers who understand the inherent esthetic possibilities, have resulted in an architecture comparable in integrity and *even* beauty to the styles of the past.[9] (My italics, JMF)

Generally speaking, the critics confined themselves to more factual criteria. The Cheneys illustrate this approach very well. The basic principles of modern design, they wrote,

are broad and general. The resulting style marks are few and simple. Honesty, simplicity, and functional expressiveness are the primary values involved. . . . Materials are used honestly, each in accordance with its own properties, its adaptation to machine processes. . . . Simplicity in the number and kinds of materials employed. . . . Functional expressiveness . . . insistence upon engineering integrity . . . is accepted as the basic design fact,

and the artist's undertaking is to bring out of this fact a characteristic and expressive appearance . . . as beautiful in its own Machine Age way as the dy-
namo and the ball bearing . . . or the clean bright surgical instrument.[10]

But there was a strong current of antiesthetic opinion in those early
days, especially in Europe. When Adolph Loos called ornament "a
crime" he was, by extension, calling beauty itself a crime; and intellectuals like Siegfried Giedion and Hannes Meyer were equally strin-
gent. "They claim," said Hitchcock and Johnson, "that interest in proportion or in problems of design for their own sake are still an
unfortunate remnant of 19th Century ideology. For these men, it is an
absurdity to talk about the modern style in terms of esthetics at all."[11]

Finally, there were those who, while admitting that the esthetic factor was important, still insisted in measuring it against an over-all social
reality. Mumford was one of the most eloquent of these: "The esthetic
arises out of the actual. The eye is gratified by the new architecture, not
alone because its order and composure is the essence of all sound architecture; the eye is likewise happy because every other function of the
mind and body is in effective rhythm."[12]

All these polemics are history now. The dust and clamor of battle
have ended, and the modern idiom is left as the undisputed victor in
the field. There can be little doubt that the victory was due as much
to these polemics as to the actual architecture which they espoused.
Before dismissing as old-fashioned the hierarchy of values upon which
this criticism was erected, it might be worthwhile to recapitulate its
accomplishments. It was one of the boldest attempts in the whole history of esthetic theory to liberate architecture from the prison house
of formalism. It aimed at reaching a unified and coherent theory of
architectural design, based upon an objective analysis of the field itself, and not upon a patchwork of analogies drawn mechanically from
the two-dimensional esthetics of music, painting, and literature. It attempted to integrate, in a single hierarchy of values, the social, ethical,
technical, and esthetic criteria which it felt to be indispensable for an
effective evaluation of architecture. These values were not always congruent or equivalent: consequently, this criticism never succeeded in
erecting as elegant and balanced a theoretical structure as the professional philosopher demands. But, given the composite nature of the
field, this may itself be an unrealistic demand. In any event, the fer-

259

tilizing effects of the theory are evident, and there is no actual proof that its fecundity has been exhausted. Yet important American critics are today rejecting it *carte-blanche*.

This rejection takes two forms. They appear diametrically opposed to each other, but they spring in fact from an identical ideological position—a subjective prepossession with problems of form, a hostility towards problems of function (content, as the painter would put it). One of these schools of criticism advocates an "architecture of pure form"; the other, an "architecture of taste." Both tend to isolate esthetics from its social matrix—a familiar phenomenon during periods of political reaction; and both maintain a posture which implies that architecture—having accomplished all its assigned tasks, socially and technically—has no task left except the visual refinement of accomplished forms.

Miës van der Rohe is the paradigm of the architecture of pure form. Writing of him and a group of younger men of similar tendency, Aline Saarinen (an outstanding critic and the wife of a distinguished architect) tells us that this group feels "that structure is the dominant element in architecture, and that if it is used in the most direct, reasonable, and economical way, it will automatically produce beauty. In even simpler terms, it has been called the dogma of 'less is more.' "[13] Other critics have carried the proposition still further. One describes Miës as a "pioneering purist" who has given us an architecture "of implacable calm."[14] And another writes that Miës, "fixing with a hard stare on a single thing, has eliminated so much that seems irrelevant that what is left stands forth with unexpected significance. . . . With Miës, architecture leaves childhood behind."[15] In these evaluations the standards of judgment are formalistic and narrowly visual. Compared with the much broader and more complex values of twenty years ago, there are significant omissions: no reference to efficient plan, to functional problems of adaptation to site and climate, to biological well-being or sociological desirability.

This tendency toward isolating form from content, of replacing multi-dimensional performance with a single-dimensional appearance, has far more serious implications for architecture than it does, for example, for painting. Buildings which are open to criticism on functional grounds will be defended on the grounds of their "beauty." People who venture to point out that a building is uncomfortable, no matter how beautifully it photographs, will be dismissed as vulgarians, with no understanding of the "higher" qualities of the building involved. And the whole level of criticism will descend to the sort of irrational subjectivism which has all but destroyed contemporary art criticism. The danger is not imaginary. In 1957, in Chicago, the doctrine of "less is more" was carried to its logical conclusion: *None is most of all.* There, in an architectural competition for a memorial auditorium to the late atomic physicist, Enrico Fermi, the award went to architecture which was, quite literally, invisible! The auditorium itself was buried *below* a white marble plaza one block square—its implacable calm undisturbed by either architecture, art, or so much as a single tree. The memorial function was to be fulfilled nonvisually by an electric carillon, whose music, the jury explained,

will be able to reach out and touch the lives of many more people than would be possible through vision alone. . . . This brilliant conception of using sound as a unifying principle for the entire project has produced the most beautiful and dignified memorial . . . particularly appropriate since it achieves a unification of Art and Science.[16]

Symbolism admittedly is not the private property of the visual arts: Napoleon could be memorialized in the music of Beethoven's *Eroica* quite as well as by Chalgrin's Arc de Triomphe. The aural dimension is always a component in our total response to architecture. In some buildings, it is a very important component: choir and organ, for example, add a splendid sonic dimension to buildings like Chartres Cathedral. Their music, reverberating down those great masonry-wrapped perspectives, breaks over one in waves, very much like the light from the stained glass windows. Liturgical music is uncannily well designed to reinforce the emotional impact of the church. But the moving experience of a visit to Chartres is merely intensified by the music; it is not dependent upon it. Transfer choir and organ to the meadows outside the town and you might still have pleasant music. But only inside the silent church would you find the tremendous symbolism of architecture.

Thus, while it would be wrong for the critic to condemn the use of sound as a "unifying principle" in the premiated design, it is necessary

261

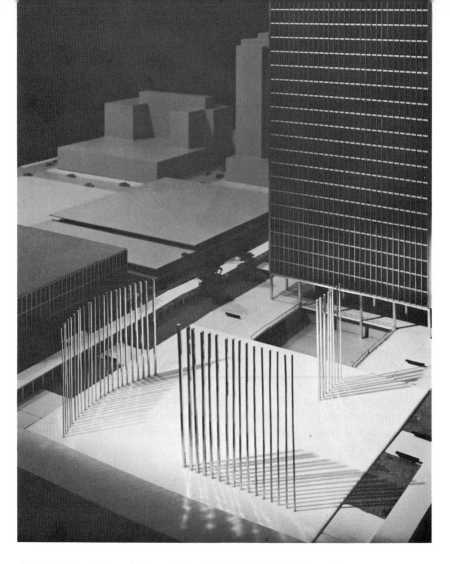

First Prize, Fermi Memorial Competition, 1957. Reginald C. Knight, architect.

Premiated designs in the Fermi Competition: (left) Box, Pratt, and Pratt, architects; (right) Jackson, Solmita, and Zalewski, architects, and Constantino Nivola, sculptor.

to ask if the competition was held to select a musical or an architectural composition, for he is being asked to respond to a set of commemorative symbols which visually do not exist. The great plaza is broken only by three files of tall stainless steel columns; they might be mistaken for flagless flagpoles since, housing electronic carillons, they are without even the recognizable form of bell and clapper. A lettered sign or a broadcast announcement would be necessary to tell us that they commemorate a great scientist, dead in his country's service. We are told that this carillon is appropriate because it memorializes "the unification of Art and Science." But this is verbal, not visual information. As a result, this design is empty and noncommittal beyond belief. It evades the central function (or what, at least, one had always thought of as the central function) of a memorial—namely, the celebration in intelligible, and hence moving, terms of some memorable person or event.

Of course, it is possible to understand the dilemma of both architect and jury, though it may be difficult to excuse their lack of candor. For the truth is that they are all prisoners of the larger fact that vibrant, vivid symbolism can grow only from a community of feeling, of concepts deeply felt and widely shared. American life offers few areas today in which this sort of agreement exists—least of all, in that Pandora's box of nuclear physics, with all its buzzing bees of threat and promise. Poor Fermi himself stands at the center of this paradox. Called "the architect of the A-bomb," he can symbolize either the frightful erasure of Hiroshima and Nagasaki or the peaceful application of nuclear power to the solution of mankind's problems. It depends upon one's point of view. Even the facts of his death are anomalous: as far as the layman can understand, cancer seems both caused and cured by the products of nuclear fission.

Little wonder, then, that all the contestants in this competition, including the runners-up, shied away from the explicit symbol. Only two ventured any use of sculpture at all and neither of these made any direct visual reference to the man or his work. One sculpture was a sort of sun-burst (a fission-fusion blast?). The other was a huge pair of human outstretched hands (Pontius Pilate's clean hands? Lady Macbeth's soiled ones?). Merely to list the possible interpretations is to indicate the hazards of symbolism in this particular area of American life. One may sympathize with the jury in sidestepping any commitment and admire the dexterity with which they transferred the task of symbolizing Fermi's life right out of their own domain into that of the acoustical engineer or the musician. But one can never say that this constitutes a serious confrontation of the problems of architecture.

As against the austere and limited range of visual experience permitted by the "architecture of pure form" there is now being raised the demand for the opulence and eclectic freedom of an "architecture of pure taste." The conflict between the two positions is, however, purely formal: the apostle of taste is merely demanding the right to use *any* set of forms his fancy dictates or his heart desires. This sort of reaction is no new phenomenon in Western cultural history, though its recrudescence in mid-twentieth-century America may seem surprising, for an architecture of taste has been traditionally the prerogative of a conservative elite. In the eighteenth century it was the idiom of the court (Marie Antoinette's rustic village in the Trianon gardens) and of the aristocracy (the "Chinese" pagoda for the Dowager Princess of Wales at Kew). In the nineteenth century it was variously the language of the new landed gentry (William Beckford's preposterous "gothick" pile of Fonthill Abbey), or of the resurgent Roman Church (Pugin's "Christian" Gothic), or of the new American millionaires (Richard Morris Hunt's "late French Gothic" châteaux for the Vanderbilts). But, whatever the place or the period, an ineffable air of snobbery surrounded both the architecture of taste and its critical rationale. Its accomplishments were always ephemeral, lying outside the main stream of architecture, like millinery or stage-sets, not only because its criteria were highly capricious and subjective but also because these criteria were based on factors external to the field. The decisive factor was always the power and prestige of the clientele, not the objective validity of the forms themselves.

Nor has scholarly competence ever saved the apostle of taste from egregious error. Pugin, after all, was an accomplished student of Gothic architecture and ornament; and no one ever measured the stones of Venice with more care than John Ruskin. Contemporary students of taste fare no better. An accomplished historian, Wayne Andrews, gives us this definition of taste: "the record of the ambition which leads the architect to spend more time and energy than is reasonable, and the client . . . to invest more money than common sense would dictate." Then, enthusiastically applying this definition to a history of American architecture, he outlines the odd historical perspective it imposes.

The Seventeenth Century will . . . not [be] explored. . . . Folk art will scarcely be mentioned. . . . There will be next to no talk of the home of the average citizen in any period. . . . Spanish civilization in the Southwest . . . fall[s] outside our scope. . . . Landscape gardening will not always receive the attention it deserves. . . . Very little will be said about our engineers.[17]

Nothing remains to be discussed, then, but the architectural vagaries of the very rich and especially the eccentric rich. But these can be lovingly dissected. We are allowed to overhear the architect Stanford White telling Clarence Mackay why the mooseheads for his library are so expensive or explaining to a Standard Oil bigwig, like a butler caught faking the wine bill, why the decoration of the "smaller rooms have added over a hundred thousand dollars to the price of the house." Since the architectural requirements of the rich are always far removed from brute necessity and since they seldom involve socially responsible goals, caprice and frivolity are bound to play a large role in their solution. The criticism which does not perceive this larger fact will handle the materials of history with the standards of the society gossip columnist.

Yet sycophantic attitudes are endemic in the current literature on an architecture of taste. A well-known book of recent years, *The Taste-makers*, opens with this anecdote:

Several years ago a friend of mine in a moment of husbandly expansiveness deposited $7000 in his wife's bank account. "There," he said to her, "you've been wanting to do over the living room. There's the money. Now do just as you please with it. And don't get in a decorator. Do it your own way, so that it expresses your personality."[18]

The nominal point of this is the friend's dilemma: to have or not to have a taste of one's own. Yet the implicit assumption is a prize example of snobism—i.e., that a $7000 budget for redecorating one's living room is a perfectly normal state of affairs, if not for all Americans (only 20 percent of whom earn that much annually), then at least for the author and his audience. The interjection of such attitudes into the literature of criticism can only act to debase the hard-won standards of modern

265

criticism itself. Thus Russell Lynes admits that modern estimates of
the Vanderbilt mansion are somewhat lower than those of the actual
contemporaries of that railroad-swapping millionaire and his parvenue
wife from Mobile. Yet he asks us to remember, as if it should be added
to the scales of balanced judgment, that that same mansion so impressed Ward McAllister, court jester to the fur-trapping Astors, that he
felt compelled to add the Vanderbilts to his guest list!

An extravagant subjectivism is, now as always, another characteristic
of this literature of taste. Henry H. Reed, in his book *The Golden City*,
illustrates this tendency quite clearly. After studying the monuments of
Europe—under the tutelage of "Signora Romoli, architect to Prince
Doria Pamphily [sic]," among others—"the work of other generations,
notably that of the American Renaissance began to appear superior
in every way and the Modern was questioned."[19] This new insight enables Reed to declare, with the imperturbable disdain for historic
process of the French Pretender to the throne, that "not everything
will pass muster, only that which has had the approval of time."[20] By
this test he finds that modern architecture is characterized by "indif-
ference to humanity, at worst [by] perversity to the point of being
evil."[21] By this test also he finds that the clock group of the Grand Central Terminal is "the best piece of monumental sculpture in America";[22]
that the Tribune Tower in Chicago is "now generally declared to be the
most beautiful skyscraper in Chicago and one of the most beautiful in
the world";[23] that "the World's Columbian Exposition of Chicago in
1893, with the independence which comes from being steeped in the
past" was a triumph.[24]

Apropos of the Chicago Fair, Reed brushes aside the testimony of the
expert Louis Sullivan, who "simply could not understand what was being done," and calls upon the graceful amateur Henry Adams "to set
the record straight." For Adams, the Fair was a triumph for the American business man who, if he had no taste, knew exactly where to buy it.
He had imported classical architecture from "Corinth and Syracuse,
over the heads of London and New York, to impose classical standards on plastic Chicago, just as he knew how to get his wife and
daughters dressed at Worth's and Pacquins."[25] Thus, with fatuous ir-
relevance, the standards of the hairdresser and couturier are substituted
for those of the professional.

At the level of personal liberties, any man is surely entitled to like whatever he pleases, for whatever reason he chooses. But the critic has certain responsibilities, one of which is to be aware of the hazards of applying a highly personal set of essentially literary values to so social an art as architecture, whose fabric is so durable, whose impact upon us all is so real. It is not that we demand neutrality from the critic—far from it. It is permissible that he "like" Richard Morris Hunt better than Frank Lloyd Wright or that he "prefer" Carrere and Hasting's New York Public Library to Miës van der Rohe's Seagram Building; but these are simple prejudices and afford no adequate base for a "new" theory of history. Yet upon just such a narrow pedestal some of the spokesmen for taste are now erecting the proposition that the whole great corpus of modern work is of no more historic significance than any of those petty stylistic revivals which tormented the surface of Victorian life. This is an essentially frivolous attitude toward history. It is not at all necessary to "like" their work to understand that the great makers of modern architecture—Wright, Gropius, Miës, Corbusier—did evolve the first authentically original idiom since the twelfth-century invention of the Gothic in the Île-de-France. And its originality arose, not from any isolated theory of form or taste, but in response to new forces which, convulsing modern life at every level, demanded adequate esthetic expression.

The architectural critic must constantly remind himself that, though he necessarily employs a literary form, he is not discussing literary phenomena. And though, in architecture, he deals with an act which has obvious analogies to painting and sculpture, the similarity is limited and the analogies are therefore of strictly limited utility. In such a context, the esthetic theories developed in the first four decades of this century seem especially valuable; the critic should seriously review them.

18. THE ESTHETICS OF PLENTY

The stylistic distance between the Platonic geometry of the new Seagram Building in New York and the absurd vulgarity of this year's automobile is a measure of the crisis in American design today. It would be hard to find another period in all history which presented such esthetic antitheses. These two objects do not even belong to the same spectrum of design: one is an aristocratic affectation of poverty, the other a *nouveau riche* ostentation of wealth. One draws its inspiration from Procrustean concepts of mathematical order, the other from the paperback literature of space-age warfare. Between these two poles, with no more apparent relation than the constellations of the Milky Way, lie all the other art forms with which our landscape is furnished— Tiffany glass and abstract expressionist painting, wagon wheel chandeliers and molded plastic chairs, Italian shoes and Danish furniture, Japanese screens and African sculpture, electronic cookstoves and open-pit braziers.

There are some odd and contradictory forces at work among us. And they have not gone unobserved. Indeed, there is a whole new literature appearing—a literature about American taste, taste-makers, taste-mongers and the like—the burden of which is that American design is in a parlous state. A wide range of explanations is offered, one of the more popular being that we are simply too wealthy. Our design is flabby because we are too rich. The corollary of this thesis, implied if not stated, is that our design would improve if we were poorer. Art thrives only in a garret. Artistic creativity requires the astringent touch of poverty. This theory has a fine mellow ring, even a surface gloss of plausibility, but history, unfortunately, gives it no support. High levels of artistic accomplishment occur only in wealthy cultures, or at least in those cultures which have surplus wealth to expend on art. Far from being the enemy of artistic productivity, social wealth is its indispensable prerequisite. However, this proposition cannot be read backwards; great social wealth is no guarantee of great art. If it were, the Roman record would be different, and we ourselves would not face our present dilemma.

Perhaps the question should be framed this way: if great wealth produced great art in fifth-century Athens, among the ninth-century Mayans or in fifteenth-century Florence, why not also and equally in twentieth-century Detroit? Could it be that the problem is not only wealth but the *conditions under which it is applied* to artistic production? To ask the question in this fashion is to answer it. Modern industrial civilization has produced unparalleled social wealth; but it has, at the same time, introduced several new and entirely unprecedented factors into the process of design. These have quite disrupted the traditional relations between artist and audience, craftsman and consumer, artist and patron. Only consider:

1. Industrial civilization, through mass production, has made material plenty a reality for mankind for the first time in history. It has, by the same process, robbed all of us of first-hand knowledge even of how the tools of daily life are made or how they work. It has correspondingly crippled our ability to evaluate critically their practical or esthetic value. It has made the citizen into an ignorant consumer, the designer into an isolated, powerless specialist.

2. Modern science and technology have given us a more imperious command of machinery for making things and materials from which to make them than Pharaonic Egypt, Augustan Rome, or Victorian London ever dreamed of. These machines and these materials confront both designer and consumer with properties, potentialities, and limitations of almost stupefying complexity.

3. Preindustrial limits of time and space have been destroyed. Modern transportation and communication, along with modern scholarship, expose us to the art and artifacts of all the present and all the past. Onto our unready retina they project the dazzling stimuli of all the art that men have ever made.

Any one of these developments, taken by itself, would have had an unsettling effect upon the esthetic equilibrium of a culture; their cumulative impact threatens to be disastrous.

269

Esthetic standards, in any period before our own, were strictly conditioned by what one might call the politics of handicraft production. The consumer, in buying an artifact, dealt with the man who was also the designer-producer of the artifact. Under such circumstances debasement of workmanship, adulteration of materials, or irresponsibility in design was difficult. Opportunity and incentive for it were greatly restricted by the very nature of the transaction. The consumer was literate in these matters; if the roof leaked or the shoe squeaked or the bread was moldy, he knew exactly where to lay hands on the craftsman. Moreover, he was apt to know quite as well as the craftsman what was wrong with the artifact and what was needed to correct it. In a pinch he could probably patch a roof, or sole a shoe, or bake a loaf of bread himself. At the very least, he would be armed with a firsthand knowledge of what the craftsman ought to do and how he ought to do it.

This intimate contact with the consumer was a happy situation for the craftsman as well. He would know intimately the limits and potentialities of the tools and materials of his craft. His esthetic standards would be firmly grounded on these, and they would be understood and accepted by the consumer. Any change in standards would come gradually with the slow evolution of preindustrial techniques; and when it came, it would have to be worked out with the consumer within mutually acceptable limits. In this essentially conservative relationship there was thus a constant, lively, and personal interchange between the two —a very fruitful relationship for both parties.

With modern mass production this relationship is radically altered. Milton Brown, the art historian, has described this change most succinctly: "The producer, who is more precisely designated by the old-fashioned term *entrepreneur,* takes over one of the functions of the earlier consumer, that of ordering and paying for production. The craftsman becomes a designer whose function it is to create an object that can be mass-produced. The consumer is confined to the truncated function of simple consumption through the process of rejection or acceptance of the finished product."[1]

Both consumer and designer suffer under these new circumstances; each becomes progressively more ignorant of the other's requirements and limitations. For the designer, surveys and market analyses are substituted for the give-and-take of personal encounter with the con-

270

sumer. The artifacts themselves become increasingly complex, involving a constantly expanding range of processes and materials. Less and less able to comprehend the complexity of modern technology, his function too is truncated; his designing becomes more and more superficial, less related to functional necessity, and thereby more vulnerable to the pressures of fad and fashion. And the consumer—removed by this same specialization from any possibility of first-hand knowledge of what he is buying—can only rely upon some expert's advice. He can only express his satisfaction (or dissatisfaction) by buying (or refusing to buy) from among the range of artifacts offered by mass production. In real life, it is difficult for this consumer to refuse forever to buy essentials—a house, a bed, an automobile. So he is forced ultimately to make his choice from a range of available products, some or all of which may be unworthy or unsuitable for his exact requirements. In accepting this new relationship, he largely abdicates his power—first his voice in the design process, then his esthetic capacity for coherent judgment of design.

It is true, of course, that this consumer can ultimately force a given product off the market by refusing to buy it. But this is a clumsy and purely negative response; since he is never given the opportunity to tell the designer precisely what features he objects to, the product can never be precisely redesigned to fit his needs. It is, instead, abandoned; and another one, also based on statistical averages, is rolled out into the market in its stead. The fantastic fertility of modern mass production conceals the fundamental wastefulness of this process. And while it may succeed in filling our material needs, it does so with artifacts whose esthetic quality is ordinarily quite low.

In reaction against this situation, advanced contemporary taste has turned more and more to the art forms of the preindustrial past—to folk, primitive, and prehistoric art. The reasons for this new interest are clear. Such art, for all its expressive richness and variety, is always based on a simple and limited range of materials and techniques. It displays an acute respect for these and thereby achieves a kind of "organic" unity of form and content, which is in refreshing contrast to the sleazy eclecticism of so much contemporary design.

This art is much admired for its "honesty" and "simplicity," and it is easy to leap from this to the conclusion that these admirable qualities

271

are the direct expression of simple poverty. But the fact is that any culture which can produce a thrown pot or a woven blanket or a carved canoe is already, by anthropological standards, an advanced and wealthy culture. Nor are the special qualities of this art due to what V. Gordon Childe, the British prehistorian, has called a "penury of raw materials." There was never any shortage of limestone in Yucatan, of potting clay in Etruria, or of wood in Japan. The "penury" confronting the primitive craftsman lay not in any absolute shortage of materials but rather in the narrow range or variety of those available.

In truly primitive societies conditions of trade and transport restricted artists and artisans to working largely in local materials. The desert peoples built of mud, the Siberians of skin and felted hair, the Melanesians of palm leaf and bamboo simply because that was all they had. Their energies and talents were thus focused on a very narrow range of materials and techniques. The wisdom, unity, and coherence of their designs are a direct expression of this fact.

Although the commerce and technology of the Classic world greatly expanded the range of materials available in its centers, the difficulties of transportation were still great and served to limit imported raw materials to the luxury trades. For example, the import of ivory, silk, gold, and tin by the Roman empire did not affect most Roman craftsmen. Roman architects of necessity continued to work in local materials, building of local brick and stone. Only a handful of the finest buildings could afford a few columns or a mosaic floor of imported marbles. And while Roman technology was very advanced for its time, it served largely to produce increased amounts of traditional materials. Waterproof cement was one of its few authentically new materials; small quantities of very expensive window glass was another.

Under such conditions, design could develop within a fixed palette of materials and techniques. Craftsmen would know it intimately, as would, from long exposure to it, the consumers. Everyone's critical capacities would thus be operating over an esthetic terrain which each knew exceedingly well. The rate of change would be so slow that accommodation to it would be easy.

All this has been radically altered by modern industrial civilization. The sheer range of materials and techniques with which it confronts the designer is staggering. Mechanized transport and communication have, for all practical purposes, made the material resources of the entire world available to him. The American can use Italian marble, African mahogany, or Javanese teak as easily as Louisiana pine or Indiana limestone. And this plenitude of natural materials is, of course, the least of the modern revolution. Technology has also supplied the designer with an every-widening supply of brand-new synthetic materials: steel, concrete, glass, aluminum, magnesium, and the whole huge family of the plastics.

This vastly increased palette of materials—natural and synthetic, imported and local—is not a "luxury line." Such materials have become the basic stock in trade, the newer ones often completely supplanting the older, more familiar materials. They are available everywhere, to everyone; not a craftsman or designer in the western world can be unaffected by their presence. And yet their presence is by no means fully understood. Their physical properties are very complex, their esthetic properties even more subtle and less explored. They are dumped upon the designer in such an accelerating flood that he has little opportunity to explore and master them in either practical or esthetic terms.

There are still some areas in the western world which are "poor" enough in raw materials for us to observe the benign effect of such poverty upon design. For example, it is not accidental that the most brilliant use of reinforced concrete in architecture occurs precisely in those countries which have no steel or wood and plenty of sand and cement—Italy, Brazil, and Mexico. Nor is it accidental that in those design fields where metal is indispensable (e.g., typewriters, automobiles, trains) a metal-poor country like Italy can lead the world. Here the scarcity and high cost of metal *forces* responsibility in design. Every ounce of material must be exploited to its fullest capacity. Anyone familiar with fine Italian automobiles must be struck by the care and imagination with which the metal is manipulated. The elegance of the final form is arrived at directly through a responsible handling of its raw materials. This condition may be transitory. As the Italians enter the American market, they are apt to cater to a corrupted American taste. But for the time being it is almost unkind to compare their finest cars with the American counterparts. Both the metal out of which our 4000-

pound monsters are built and the fuel with which they are propelled through the streets are so cheap that any design, no matter how preposterous, is perfectly practicable. Since neither economy, efficiency nor safety are permitted criteria, the American designer is forced into irresponsibility; he is as footloose and fancy-free as a pastry cook.

The traffic in raw materials has never been as fructifying culturally as that other face of commerce, the traffic in concepts and ideas. Societies, past and present, have always been subject to the cultural irradiation which follows trade. For artists and artisans the significant instrument has always been the artifact or art form, whose visual stimulus is indeed stronger than ten thousand words. Thanks to modern archaeology, the flux of these stimuli from one culture to another can now be traced in all its fascinating diversity. And it seems apparent that few designers have ever worked in absolute isolation from their colleagues; even in prehistoric times, the extent of cultural intercourse is amazing. It is true, nevertheless, that all designers before our age worked under conditions quite different from our own. The Etruscans afford an excellent illustration of this difference. This gifted people, because they possessed at Elba and Populonia the largest metallurgical complex in the Mediterranean, found themselves the focus of a lively trade with Greece, Phoenicia, and Egypt. In exchange for their metal, they imported the art and artifacts manufactured by these more advanced cultures. The impact of these stimuli is readily apparent in the development of Etruscan art. Yet the impact was always successfully absorbed and digested. The rate of irradiation of this foreign design was never high enough to overwhelm the Etruscan artist. We may speak of the Hellenizing or Orientalizing phases of his art, but these never obscure the basic identity of the objects themselves. They remain indisputably Etruscan.

Though this artistic irradiation was steadily to accelerate in Western history (witness the speed and thoroughness with which the idiom of the Renaissance was stamped upon the whole of Europe during the fifteenth and sixteenth centuries) it continued to be more or less successfully absorbed by the cultures involved. Even as late as 1800 a balance was somehow maintained. The architecture of Boston, Philadelphia, or Baltimore, for example, was still a model of esthetic homogeneity at this time. Despite increasing trade with such exotic areas as

274

Africa and Asia, despite a technological revolution which was by then already well advanced, architects and craftsmen were still confined to a narrow range of familiar forms (Greco-Roman and Renaissance) and to a very restricted list of traditional materials (wood, brick, stone, and plaster). All this has changed today; these same cities are now models of visual anarchy. And the change began just at that time, when modern technology (and its handmaid, modern scholarship) began to make available to Americans, designers and consumers alike, not only the whole world of contemporaneous art but also all the arts of the past.

The development of travel and communication in the nineteenth century was shattering. The steamship and railroad, the cable and telegraph, the book and magazine, most of all the photograph—these began to bombard the American eye with a dazzling, an unprecedented range of stimuli. No Etruscan eye had ever been so bedazzled, no Etruscan craftsman so disturbed by what he saw. And no man before the nineteenth century had ever been exposed to such unnerving knowledge as that now focused on him by the art museum, the art historian, the art critic, and the archaeologist. Their discoveries began, like acid, to eat away the very foundations of comfortable esthetic provincialism. They began to introduce the concept of relativity into an area of thought and feeling which had hitherto been governed by absolute esthetic standards. Nor was this experience confined to artist and designer. On the contrary, prosperous and literate consumers were reading the same books, making the same tours, visiting the same museums. Victorian discovery placed all standards, including esthetic ones, into what the chemist would call a state of solution.

Today scholarship continues this process apace, extending our literacy to unprecedented dimensions. We can be equally familiar with (and fond of) the paintings of the prehistoric caves at Dordogne and the canvases of Caravaggio, with the Japanese farm house and the Pompeiian villa, with Incan cast gold and Victorian cast iron. Meanwhile, the anthropologists and sociologists have been at work dissolving another set of provincialisms. We can no longer reject a war club because it was once the instrument of a cannibal or allow a prejudice against human sacrifices to color our judgment to the Mayan temple.

Intellectually, these accomplishments of scholarship are majestic but they are not always comfortable, and their impact upon design is not

275

always beneficent. To be sure, this sort of artistic irradiation has invigorated giants like Picasso and Wright. It often leaves us lesser men paralyzed. A news story which came out of Detroit in 1958 illustrates the situation pungently by telling us that automobile designers were turning for inspiration to "a pre-Incan vase . . . a Pennsylvania Dutch cookie mold, a leaf of a tropical plant . . . the art of Michelangelo and a wooden food grater from the Orinoco Indians"! Any of these images might of itself be beautiful, though its application to automobile design may not be immediately apparent. But it is certain that their superimposition in any design (least of all that of a car!) can lead only to visual anarchy.

To diagnose the causes of our present dilemma is, unfortunately, much easier than to prescribe a cure. The accomplishments of our industrial civilization are too real and too profound to consider relinquishing. In the light of modern knowledge, it is clear that the independent artisan cannot adequately feed and clothe and house the world; he can not now and never could. It is equally clear that the whole material base of modern life can be produced only on the assembly line: penicillin and space ships are not produced by village blacksmiths. Therefore, if the old, preindustrial balance between artist and audience, artisan and consumer is ever to be rewon, it will have to be accomplished at a higher level than before, basing itself on the incomparably more complex relationships of industrial civilization.

Modern mass production confronts the consumer with a whole spectrum of problems, extending from those of simple material quality to those of pure design. Although the two extremes are always umbilically linked, they are by no means identical. When the consumer faces a defective artifact in which materials have been deliberately adulterated or workmanship skimped, he deals with a manipulation of quantitative factors. Since these can be objectively measured, they can be legislated against and policed. But when he faces a corrupt design his problem is different, since value judgments are involved which, by their very nature, are not susceptible to objective measurement. Thus, in an automobile, the ratio between braking capacity, on the one hand, and power and weight, on the other, is a clear index of the car's safety. Here the irresponsible manufacturer can easily be detected. But the body design of the same car involves another and more complex kind of judgment, in which esthetic irresponsibility, while equally real, may be much harder to prove and impossible to punish.

Both the incentive to and the opportunity for adulteration of material quality and debasement of design seem to increase in direct proportion to the increasing centralization, mechanization, and automation of production. This specialization of the worker and the paralleled atomization of the work, the isolation of policy-making from product-making, the dwindling power and authority of the designer himself— all of these seem to be corollaries of modern production. But this specialization, so necessary to modern science and technology, is bought at a dear price; the process harms both work and worker, as Ruskin pointed out a century ago. Of the worker (whether it be physical or mental work) it demands precocious knowledge in the chosen field, while it permits sheer illiteracy in other fields of knowledge or experience. One sector of his abilities is enormously developed, the others tend to shrink and ossify. The very conditions of modern work act to limit generalized experience, to inhibit spontaneity, to restrict the intuition. Thus our standards of judgment, in art as in other areas, are stultified. The modern question clearly is: Need this be so?

Modern industrialism has raised the prospect—for the first time in man's history—of material plenty for all. In the West, this is already a largely accomplished fact; for the rest of the world it is only a matter of time. Though it may have proved its productive capacity on a quantitative scale, however, it has not yet established a parallel superiority on a qualitative plane. It may be an exaggeration to say that the ugly artifact, that ugliness itself, is the *invention* of the modern factory, but it is certainly true that factory production has yet to prove its esthetic supremacy over handicraft. This confronts us with the same question which troubled William Morris: Why do high rates of productivity and high esthetic standards seem so often to be mutually exclusive? Is it owing to some organic defect in the factory system itself? Or is it owing to the social order that runs the system? Is the qualitative gap between the promise and the reality of modern industrialism characteristic of all social orders today? Or is it limited to that sector operated by Western capitalism?

It is no simple question to answer—least of all in America, where the issue is most acute. It is complicated by the vastness of the vested interests involved and their unwillingness to encourage a basic examination of the issue. And beyond this lies the fact that, as the most advanced industrial nation on earth, we have no other body of experience against which to measure our own performance. Certainly, from a purely quantitative point of view, America leads the world in the production of goods and services. On a per capita basis, we are the nation best fed, best clothed, best housed. We have the highest ratio of doctors and dentists, automobiles and telephones, productivity per acre or mechanical horsepower per worker. A complex network of laws, codes, and ordinances has been erected to protect our health, safety, and general welfare: pure food and drug acts, sanitary regulations, fire and safety codes, zoning regulations, etc. These are designed to maintain a minimum level of material quality in the food we eat, the clothing we wear, the buildings and cities we live in. This whole system could doubtless be improved in both content and enforcement, but it nevertheless does maintain a high average level of material well-being in our country.

But this system, of itself, has not guaranteed comparably high esthetic standards. Thus it is that we can find sanitary and relatively nutritious food in American restaurants everywhere; but our regional cuisines have been all but destroyed by the spread of an industrialized "national" cookery, and it is difficult to find really distinguished cookery anywhere. Television may well have brought more professional entertainment to more people than ever before in history but its average esthetic level must mark an all-time low in terms of the banal and the vulgar. Our cities are almost certainly the most fireproof, our buildings the most sanitary, in the historical record; but they afford, from the esthetic point of view, some of the ugliest and most hostile landscapes on earth.

The very advances of mass production often seem, in America, to work out against high standards and wide variety in consumer goods. It is our boast that free competition guarantees the survival of the best of everything. The facts seem to indicate, however, an inexorable kind of "centrism," a movement toward mediocrity, toward the statistical myth of a national common denominator. This is very evident in all fields of consumption—magazines, movies, television programs; automobiles, houses, or skyscrapers. We find that competition narrows the particular field until only two or three stereotypes are available; these in turn conform as closely as possible to the "national" norm, differing in design only enough to make possible brand or trademark identification.

It is not easy to determine if these tendencies are unique to American industrialism or are an organic feature of mass production and mass marketing generally. However, one feature of this sorry picture is uniquely ours: the technique of "planned obsolescence" and its principal instrument, the annual or yearly "new model." Whatever short-range benefit this may have brought to business, its effect upon the design of American consumer goods has been disastrous. For, by mechanically equating real progress with mere change, it has fostered the wholly false concept that the rate of technological advance is so rapid and so steady as to necessitate a radical redesign of a product each year. Since no technology advances in this tidy fashion (and since no economy in the world could afford the resultant obsolence in plant and inventory if it did), the only real change in the "new" model is superficial.

Obsolescence is, of course, a fact of life; the rate of obsolescence under the conditions of modern industrialism is, objectively, the highest in history. But "planned" (i.e., arbitrarily manipulated) obsolescence has two faces, both of them ultimately hostile to the quality of the product. On the one hand, it institutionalizes the tendency toward adulteration of material and workmanship, so that the product wears out sooner than it otherwise might; on the other hand, it separates design from its base of functional necessity. Anyone who has watched the migration of tail-lights and brakelights over the rear end of American autos, or the ever-changing size and shape of the radiators, must realize that this kind of change is completely divorced from objective progress. Design thus isolated from reality can only weaken and die, like Antaeus when lifted from the earth.

Are these same forces at work in the industrial system of the Communist world? In theory, at least, the socialization of production (i.e., for use instead of for profit) should act to maintain high standards of quality in consumer goods. Whether it actually does remains largely to be proved. Judging from the stories in the Soviet press, the Soviet consumer has much to complain of in the merchandise offered him. He has denounced it as shoddy, high-priced and poorly designed, limited in range and short in supply. In view of the rising rates of Soviet productivity, this condition may change for the better. And certainly the Communist consumer seems safe, for a while at least, from the annual model, since his countries are in no risk of a glut of consumer goods in the near future. But even if socialized production should prove to be immune to the more venal pressures of capitalist competition, it has yet to give any evidence of built-in guarantees of high esthetic standards. If we are to take the Soviet record as indicative, Communist production has its stereotypes, too, and they turn out to be no more attractive than ours. Indeed, to date Soviet architecture and industrial design seem to have followed American experience quite slavishly, lagging behind it by a couple of decades and tending to mimic its lowest common denominator. Thus Soviet skyscrapers and automobiles—to cite two of today's most characteristic design forms—repeat almost verbatim some of our more unfortunate ventures in these fields.

It would be easy to conclude that (1) the Soviet consumer is even less demanding esthetically than his American counterpart; (2) that he has no more leverage on Soviet manufacture than we do; and (3) that the Soviet designer is just as much a prisoner of his management as ours is. On the basis of the scanty evidence at hand, this would seem to be the case in all Communist countries, though Czechoslovakia as the most highly industrialized and China as the least probably offer a whole spectrum of esthetic sophistication in industrial design. In any event, the crisis seems to be endemic in the very process of industrialism. It will appear in every social system that adopts it. Thus all the new nations of Asia and Africa which are busy industrializing themselves can expect to repeat at least this aspect of American experience—and probably in a telescoped and hence more poignant form.

The American people may have been the first to enter into this Arcadia of industrialized plenty. But it remains to be seen how constructive our aid and example will be to these new nations now preparing to leap from tribal and feudal societies into modern industrialism. Primitive and folk handicraft—whether pre-Columbian or merely

Colonial—have long since been crowded from the American scene. Only scholars and museologists have had recent contact with such artifacts. Yet, for the new nations, such handicraft constitutes a great natural resource, both economically and esthetically. It affords a wonderful opportunity, perhaps the last in man's history, to explore the possibility of a new kind of integration of handicraft and modern mechanized production. Aboriginal industry naturally offers no paradigms for electronics or chemicals: but for architecture and whole fields of consumer goods (furniture, fabrics, utensils) native practice is not only esthetically mature but also astonishingly rational in its understanding of functional problems.

As a matter of fact, it is dangerous to be dogmatic about native competence even in the design of technologically sophisticated products. It is fatuous to assume, for example, that automobile design must follow Detroit precedent. While a certain minimum of educated personnel and modern machinery is clearly essential, it is not at all hard to imagine that an African vehicle, designed and made by Africans, for African climates and conditions, might differ from its American prototype as radically in its standards of appearance as in its standards of performance. (Just about the only certainty one can postulate for a vehicle is that the wheels be round; and even this seems not too secure, since an inventor has recently patented a square-wheeled vehicle for wading through deep mud!)

The reservoirs of folk knowledge and folk skills must be preserved, not in museums, but in life. Such a task of social and cultural engineering could well be accomplished by the sophisticated scholarship of the West. Yet it is, alas!, the last thing we have any reason to expect of the West. If the past is any index, the new countries of Asia, Africa, and Latin America will be inundated not merely with the technologies of Detroit and Manchester but with their esthetic prejudices as well. And primitive art and artifact, subjected to the irresistible prestige of industrialism, will be corrupted and destroyed.

Whether the new countries will, in this respect, fare any better at the hands of Moscow and Peiping remains to be seen. Moscow's esthetic, as we have seen, seems to follow the West. As for the Chinese, the American observer has been so isolated from this third of the human race that any of his generalizations about them are apt to be ill-founded. As the people with the longest uninterrupted social experience on earth, they have enjoyed an incomparably consistent set of esthetic standards. Chinese art and handicraft, like the Chinese language, employed essentially the same grammar in the nineteenth century as in the fifth century B.C. It is as if the architectural language of Ictinus and Callicrates, largely unalloyed, were still in use in Athens today. But whether such an esthetic tradition can modify or even survive the massive industrialization of the present remains to be seen. At present it seems safe to say that, however different the political postures of the great industrial powers of capitalist West and Communist East, their esthetic positions seem very much the same.

Finally, as though his situation were not tormented enough, the American consumer is confronted with another dilemma. His plentitude of goods and increasing leisure time in which to consume them produces a kind of escalator effect in which satiety is never overtaken: as soon as one need is met, three others loom up behind it. Although long familiar to economists as a theoretical possibility (The need for food is limited by the stomach cavity, Adam Smith once said, but the appetite for ornament and conveniences seems to have no upper limit.) it is now a reality. How will we handle this new factor in human society? J. M. Keynes, the British economist, suggested that the struggle for the means of subsistence had actually become a genetic factor in the animal world. "We have been expressly evolved by nature—with all our impulses and deepest instincts—for the purpose of solving the economic problem," he says. "If the economic problem is solved, mankind will be deprived of its traditional purpose."[2] What will happen then, Keynes asks us. To illustrate the dilemma of this new plenty, he quotes the epitaph that on old London charwoman wrote for her own tombstone:

> Don't mourn for me friends, don't weep for me never
> For I'm going to do nothing for ever and ever

She aims at being the complete spectator: she will not even take part in the heavenly choir:

> With psalms and sweet music the heavens'll be ringing
> But I shall have nothing to do with the singing!

282

This is the age-long dream of the slave, the serf, the exploited laborer. But will he really be happy when someone else rings all the bells, does all the singing? We Americans have blandly assumed that the time wrested from the place of work by industrialism was literally free— free to be squandered on any leisure time activity, no matter how trivial or contrived. We have acted as though the gain were *net;* as though, having earned enough for our daily bread by our atomized labor on the production line, our responsibilities both as citizens and men were discharged. But, like that old charwoman, we forgot that in all preindustrial societies work had been quite as much the school as it was the scourge of mankind. Worse things could have happened to Adam than his expulsion from the Garden, for the sweat upon his brow was a mark of the work that made him human. Modern scientific technology through its fantastic productivity has freed us from all those bestializing aspects of labor which kept man in thrall so long. But it has simultaneously separated us from that multifaceted world of immediate experience which made wise and competent adults of the simplest peasant and fisherman.

If the nature of modern work experience can no longer develop this kind of common human wisdom, then it seems apparent that we must create new institutions which can. In them, as adults, we shall have to be prepared to devote part of that liberated time to a new kind of education—that of learning how to be adult—how, in fact, to be human. The alienation of artist from audience, artisan from craft, designer from client is but one aspect of a larger alienation: that of man from man, even of man from himself. In a world of increasing specialization, where more and more of adult work experience is focused on the narrow and the special, the other part of life must be devoted to mastering the broad and the general. The atomized responsibility of the assembly line, so essential to its performance and so destructive to the human psyche, must be somehow subsumed in a larger, more unified responsibility of the whole human being.

Even this may be too superficial a formulation of the problem which confronts us. For, once the technical means of subsistence have been perfected and the resulting material abundance made a reality to all peoples everywhere, the next stage of human development may well involve the reconstruction of society along quite other lines than those currently envisaged by social and political scientists. If we think of these productive processes as having been largely automatized, thus requiring very little of either our energy or our attention, then the problem confronting us is much more vast than the "wise" consumption of goods and services or the "proper" use of leisure time. The escape from "the nightmare of endless 'progress' and endless Faustian discontent"— the terms are those of the psychologist Norman Brown[3]—would involve the reconstruction not only of human society but of human consciousness as well.

Admittedly, this is a Utopian view of a situation which, for the majority of the human race, is not by any means an accomplished fact. But it is not too early to place it on the agenda of the earth's most advanced nations. The reconstruction of human society to conform to the new realities of industrial abundance may very well *imply* the appearance of a new state of human consciousness; but, by itself, it neither describes that new state nor prepares us for it. If, in this future that faces us, we are *not* "to do nothing for ever and ever"—what *are* we to do? The dilemma is not one of vacuums to be filled but of whole new systems of activity, thought, and feeling to be constructed.

Such a reconstruction, whether of our society or of ourselves, will certainly not be easy; but, in order of magnitude, the landings on the planets will pale in comparison.

NOTES

Notes to 3: ARCHITECTS OF DEMOCRACY:

JEFFERSON AND WRIGHT

1. *Autobiography* (New York, G. P. Putnam's Sons, 1959), p. 67.
2. *Ibid.*, pp. 6–7.

Notes to 4: HORATIO GREENOUGH, YANKEE FUNCTIONALIST

1. These essays, published in various periodicals, he collected in book form as *The Travels, Observations and Experiences of a Yankee Stonecutter* under the pseudonym, Horace Bender (New York, G. P. Putnam) in the year of his death, 1852. After almost a century the most significant were reprinted by the University of California Press (Berkeley, 1947) under the title *Form and Function: Remarks on Art by Horatio Greenough,* edited by Harold A. Small, with an Introduction by Erle Loran.
2. This isolation did not prevent his proposing that the quarrying of marble at Carrara be mechanized to improve quality and reduce cost. He suggests "a railroad of simple construction," in which "the weight of the product itself" would furnish the principal motive force, to enable the quarries to produce much larger blocks. Letter, unpublished, undated, in Carteggi Fenzi Emmanuele, Biblioteca di Risorgimento, Florence.
3. George Hilliard, *Six Months in Italy* (London, John Murrary, 1853), pp. 141–43.
4. Edward L. Pierce, *Memoirs and Letters of Charles Sumner* (Boston, Roberts Brothers, 1894), II, 116.
5. Ralph Waldo Emerson, *English Traits* (Boston, Houghton Mifflin, 1893), p. 9.
6. R. L. Rusk, ed., *Letters of Ralph Waldo Emerson* (New York, Columbia University Press, 1939), IV, 271.
7. *Form and Function,* p. 104.
8. Hiram Powers, Greenough's American contemporary in Florence, inaugurated the practice, in the early 1850s, of furnishing sets of daguerreotypes of his portrait busts to each of his clients. Each set consisted of four

views, and additional sets could be ordered for mailing to those friends who could not attend the unveiling. A portrait, Powers said, "should reflect, like a mirror, the very image of the original." *The Crayon, A Journal Devoted to the Graphic Arts* (New York), Vol. I, No. 5, p. 229.

9. Horatio Greenough, *Letters . . . to his Brother, Henry Greenough*, ed. by Frances Boott Greenough (Boston, Ticknor and Co., 1887), p. 129.

10. *Ibid.*, p. 116.

11. *Ibid.*, p. 121.

12. *Ibid.*, p. 169.

13. Pierce, *Memoirs of Sumner*, III, 110.

14. Greenough, *Letters to Henry Greenough*, p. 232.

15. *Ibid.*, p. 129.

16. *Ibid.*, p. 106. Now in the Massachusetts Historical Society, Boston.

17. *Ibid.*, p. 111.

18. Greenough, *The Crayon*, Vol. I, No. 6, p. 89.

19. Giovanni Dupres (Dupré), *Thoughts on Art and Autobiographical Memoirs*, translated from the Italian by E. M. Peruzzi (Edinburgh and London, William Blackwood and Sons, 1884), p. 117.

20. *Ibid.*, p. 100. *The Dying Abel* is in the Pitti Palace, Florence.

21. Now in the Smithsonian Institute, Washington.

22. Greenough, *Letters to Henry Greenough*, p. 108.

23. This was the same dentist to whom Washington drafted an apologetic description of the discomfort and embarrassment caused him by his bridgework and a plaintive request that he correct it in order to remove the "pouting and swelling appearance" they gave his lips. Letter, Washington to Greenwood, December 12, 1798, Collection of Old South Meeting House, Boston.

24. *Letters to Henry Greenough*, p. 106.

25. Greenough to S. F. B. Morse, May 1834 (New York *American*, August 5, 1834).

26. *Letters to Henry Greenough*, p. 180.

27. *Ibid.*, p. 183.

28. *Ibid.*, p. 185.

29. *Ibid.*, p. 184.

30. As did Emerson: he wrote to Margaret Fuller that the sculpture was "simple and grand, nobly draped below and nobler nude above." Rusk, *Letters of Emerson*, III, 121.

31. *Form and Function*, p. 8. The reference here is to the best known of the several "Spanish" dancers who toured the States in the mid-century: Lola Montez, the Irish-born mistress of the King of Bavaria whose appearance in New York in 1851 was an authentic sensation.

32. *Ibid.*, p. 75.

33. *Ibid.*, p. 84.

34. *Ibid.*, p. 109.

35. Horatio Greenough, "Dress," *The Crayon*, I, 177 *et seq.*

36. *Form and Function*, p. 77.

37. In July 1840, long after he had left it, the Accademia granted him a Diploma *per chiare prove della sua eccelenza nell' arte . . . tra le quali primezzia la statua colossale di Giorgio Washington."* This honor, Greenough acknowledged, came "like water in the desert to me." *Carteggi*, File 42B, Case 68, Anno 1853, Accademia delle Belle Arte, Firenze.

38. *Form and Function*, p. 89.

39. *Ibid.*, p. 90.

40. *Ibid.*, p. 98.

41. *Ibid.*, p. 93.

42. *Ibid.*, p. 76.

43. *Ibid.*, p. 118.

44. *Ibid.*, p. 119.

45. *Ibid.*, p. 91.

46. *Ibid.*, p. 118.

47. *Ibid.*, p. 83.

48. Robert Chambers, *Vestiges of the Natural History of Creation* (London, John Churchill, 1844).

49. Rusk, III, 283.

50. Chambers, *Vestiges*, pp. ix-xi.

51. *Form and Function*, p. 123.

52. *Ibid.*, p. 122.

53. *Ibid.*, p. 59. This war club was part of the collection brought back from the Fiji, Tonga, and Sandwich Islands by the first Wilkes Expedition to the South Seas.

54. *Ibid.*, p. 59.

55. *Ibid.*

56. *English Traits*, p. 10. Greenough's trenchant descriptions of famous buildings show his independence from the critical criteria then in vogue: St. Peter's was a "morbid development," Barry's Houses of Parliament a "gewgaw," Versailles a "royal mushroom."

57. *Form and Function*, p. 65.

58. It was not that Greenough did not admire the Greeks, it was that he wanted Americans "to emulate them like men, and not ape them like monkeys."

59. *Ibid.*, p. 63.

60. *Ibid.*, p. 61.

61. Greenough, "Fourier et Hoc Genus Omne," *The Crayon*, Vol. I, No. 24 (June 13, 1855), pp. 371–72.

62. *Form and Function*, p. 22.

63. *The Democratic Review*, Boston, Vol. XIII, August 1843.

64. As this writer has had occasion to point out elsewhere. See *American Building: The Forces that Shape It* (Boston, Houghton Mifflin Co., 1948), pp. 70–81.

65. *Form and Function*, p. 4.

Notes to 5: OUR DOMESTICATED UTOPIANS

1. Catharine E. Beecher and Harriet B. Stowe, *The American Woman's Home* (New York, J. B. Ford & Co., 1869), p. 42.

2. See Angelina E. Grimké, *Letters to Catharine Esther Beecher in Reply to An Essay on Slavery and Abolitionism* (Boston, Isaac Knapp, 1838), p. 37.

3. *Ibid.*, pp. 26–27.

4. Laura E. Richards and Maud Howe Elliott, *Julia Ward Howe* (Boston, Houghton Mifflin, 1916), I, 110.

5. Arthur W. Calhoun, *A Social History of the American Family* (New York, Barnes and Noble, 1945), p. 107.

6. Albert Brisbane, *The Social Destiny of Man* (Philadelphia, 1840).

7. Octavius Brooks Frothingham, *Transcendentalism in New England* (New York, Harper & Brothers, 1959), pp. 156–57.

8. *Ibid.*, p. 159.

9. Lydia Maria Child, *The American Frugal Housewife* (Boston, 1835), p. 1.

10. *Ibid*, p. 81.

11. *Ibid.*, p. 1.

12. *Ibid.*

13. *Ibid.*, p. 99.

14. Catharine Esther Beecher, *A Treatise on Domestic Economy* (Boston, Thos. Webb & Co., 1842), p. 271.

15. *Ibid.*, p. 262.

16. *Ibid.*, p. 259.

17. The best account of this phase of American industrialization will be found in Siegfried Giedion, *Mechanization Takes Command* (New York, Oxford, 1948), especially pp. 146 *et seq.*

18. For an early history of refrigeration see Richard O. Cummings, *The American Ice Harvests* (Berkeley, University of California, 1949).

19. Richard O. Cummings, *The American and His Food* (University of Chicago, 1940), p. 62.

20. *American Woman's Home*, p. 24.

21. An excellent bibliography of Catharine Beecher's published work appears as an appendix to Marie Harveson's *Catharine Esther Beecher* (University of Pennsylvania Press, 1931).

22. Harveson, *Beecher*, p. 204.

23. *Ibid.*, p. 200.

24. *American Woman's Home*, p. 24.

25. Edward Bellamy, *Looking Backward* (New York, Modern Library, 1942), p. 80.

26. *Ibid.*

27. *American Woman's Home*, p. 334.

28. E. Parmalee Prentice, *Progress: An Episode in the History of Hunger* (New York, Hildreth, 1950), p. 154.

Notes to 6: THE TWO MEN IN SULLIVAN'S TOMB

1. Louis Henri Sullivan, *The Autobiography of an Idea* (New York, Dover Publications, 1956), p. 259.

2. Louis Henri Sullivan, *Kindergarten Chats* (Washington, Scarab Press, 1934), p. 194.

3. *Ibid.*

4. *Autobiography*, p. 313.

5. *Ibid.*, p. 326.

6. *Kindergarten Chats*, p. 8.

7. *Ibid.*, p. 39.

8. *The Craftsman* (New York, November 1908), Vol. 15, No. 2, pp. 183 ff.

9. John Szarkowski, *The Idea of Louis Sullivan* (Minneapolis, University of Minnesota Press, 1957), p. 4

10. *Ibid.*, p. 7.

11. *Kindergarten Chats*, p. 194.

12. *Autobiography*, p. 194.

Notes to 7: FRANK LLOYD WRIGHT AND THE FINE ARTS

1. Among the artists who worked for Wright in the years before World War I were Marion Mahoney Griffin, Blanche Ostertagg, George M. Niedecken, and the sculptors Richard Bock and Alfonso Ianelli. See Mark Piesch, "Walter Burley Griffin" (unpublished dissertation, Columbia University, 1959), p. 64.

2. C. A. Mees, *The Life Work of the American Architect Frank Lloyd Wright* (Santpoort, 1913), p. 13.

3. Wright, though he often denied it, was extremely responsive to the stylistic currents around him. We are indebted to Dmitri Tselos ("Exotic Influences in the Architecture of Frank Lloyd Wright," *Magazine of Art*, April 1953, pp. 160–69) for a detailed examination of this aspect of his life.

4. *Frank Lloyd Wright on Architecture: 1894–1940*, ed. by Frederick Gutheim (New York, Duell, Sloan, and Pearce, 1941), p. 3.

5. *Ibid.*, p. 5.

6. *Ibid.*, p. 7.

7. *Ibid.*, p. 33.

8. *Ibid.*, p. 73.

9. *Ibid.*, p. 41.

10. *Ibid.*, p. 31.

11. *Ibid.*, p. 7.

12. *Ibid.*, p. 42.

13. *Ibid.*, p. 59 ff.

14. *Ibid.*, p. 64.

15. *Ibid.*, p. 33.

16. *Ibid.*, p. 42.

17. *Ibid.*, p. 71.

18. *Ibid.*, p. 72.

19. *Ibid.*, p. 67. Wright strikes this note repeatedly in these years— this call to architect and artist to exercise restraint. "The temptation to sweeten work, to make each detail in itself lovable and expressive, is always great." But to let the individual elements shine at the expense of the whole "is a betrayal of trust, for buildings are the background or framework for the human life within their walls." (*Ibid.*, p. 41)

20. *Ibid.*, p. 71.

21. *Ibid.*, p. 63.

22. See Ripley Hitchcock, *The Art of the World's Fair* (Chicago, 1893).

23. *Catalog of Objects in the Museum,* Art Institute of Chicago (Chicago, 1896).

24. *The General Catalog: Objects in the Museum,* Art Institute of Chicago, 1901.

25. *Catalog of the Art Institute of Chicago* (Chicago, 1906).

26. Aline Saarinen, *The Proud Possessors* (New York, Random House, 1959), p. 13.

27. Grant C. Manson, *Frank Lloyd Wright to 1910* (New York, Reinhold, 1958), p. 202.

28. A few months before his death, Wright told the author that he had never even seen the Japanese Pavilion at the 1893 Fair! Yet in his authorized edition of Wright's work, Frederick Gutheim, the editor, is permitted to say that "Wright's introduction to Japanese prints came at the Columbian Exposition in 1893." And Wright himself, in his introduction to the 1910 German publication of his work, said: "their debt to Japanese ideals, these renderings themselves sufficiently acknowledge." (*On Architecture*, p. 76)

29. *On Architecture*, p. 21. See notes 4–21.

30. *Ibid.*

31. Frank Lloyd Wright, *Autobiography* (rev. ed., New York, Duell, Sloan, and Pearce, p. 181).

Notes to 9: A LEVER LONG ENOUGH:
HOW GROPIUS MOVED THE WORLD

1. The contract was signed April 1, 1919. Alma Mahler Werfel, *And the Bridge is Love* (New York, Harcourt, Brace and Co., 1957), p. 134.

2. The contract, signed by King Faisel, was renewed after his assassination by the Republic of Iraq.

3. Personal Interview, Cambridge, February 25, 1960.

4. Gropius, *Programm des Staatlichen Bauhauses* (Weimar, 1919).

5. Walter Gropius, *Scope of Total Architecture* (New York, Harper & Brothers, 1955), pp. 18–19.

6. Gropius, *Programm.*

7. Herbert Bayer, Ise and Walter Gropius, *Bauhaus: 1919–1928* (New York, Museum of Modern Art, 1938), p. 27.

8. *Ibid.,* p. 29.

9. *Ibid.,* p. 127.

10. *Ibid.,* p. 30.

11. *Ibid.,* p. 28.

12. *Ibid.,* p. 24.

13. Bauhaus curriculum and teaching methods were successfully transplanted by Moholy-Nagy in the same year, when he established the New Bauhaus in Chicago. Reorganized in 1939 as the School of Design and again in 1944 as the Institute of Design, it is now a department of the Illinois Institute of Technology.

14. Gropius, *Scope of Total Architecture,* p. 3.

15. *Ibid.,* pp. xvii ff.

16. Bayer, Gropius, and Gropius, *Bauhaus,* p. 11.

17. Quoted by Roger Banham, *Architectural Reviews* (London) CXXI (February, 1957), 85–88.

18. From the catalog for the exhibition, *Unbekannte Architekten veranstalten vom Arbeitsrat für Kunst* (Berlin, April 1919).

19. Sibyl Moholy-Nagy, *Moholy-Nagy: A Biography* (New York, Harper & Brothers, 1950), p. 31.

20. *Ibid.,* p. 19.

21. Bayer, Gropius, and Gropius, *Bauhaus,* p. 22.

22. Gropius, *Scope,* p. 15.

23. *Ibid.,* p. 91.

24. Letter to the author, July 22, 1960.

25. Gropius, *Scope,* p. 92.

26. *Ibid.,* p. 6.

27. Siegfried Giedion, *Walter Gropius: Work and Teamwork* (New York, Reinhold, 1954), p. 22.

28. Gropius, *Scope,* p. 93.

29. Giedion, *Gropius,* p. 63.

30. *Ibid.,* pp. 64–65.

31. Moholy-Nagy, *Moholy-Nagy,* p. 53.

32. Gropius, "The Curse of Conformity," *Saturday Evening Post* (Philadelphia, June 6, 1958), pp. 18–19 *et seq.*

33. Gropius, *Architecture and Design in the Age of Science* (New York, Spiral Press, 1952), n.p.

34. Gropius, *The New Architecture and the Bauhaus* (London, 1935), p. 67.

35. Bayer, Gropius, and Gropius, *Bauhaus,* p. 96.

36. *Ibid.,* p. 74.

37. Giedion, *Gropius,* p. 27.

Notes to 10: MIËS AND THE CLIMATE OF PLATO

1. According to Arthur Drexler, *Ludwig Miës van der Rohe* (New York, George Braziller, 1960), p. 115.

2. *Journal of the Architectural Association* (London), Vol. LXXV, No. 834 (July–August 1959), p. 27.

3. *Ibid.,* p. 29.

4. Drexler, *Ludwig Miës van der Rohe,* p. 117.

5. *Journal of the Architectural Association,* p. 31.

6. Personal interview, Chicago, April 1960.

7. *Journal of the Architectural Association,* p. 31.

8. *Ibid.,* p. 38.

9. *Ibid.*

10. Personal interview.

11. *Ibid.*

12. Typescript in Avery Library, Columbia University.

Notes to 11: AMERICAN PLEASURE GARDEN

1. Loraine Kuck, *The Art of Japanese Gardens* (New York, The Japan Society, 1941), p. 5.

2. William Chambers, *Dissertation on Oriental Gardening,* cited in Osvald Siren, *Gardens of China* (New York, Ronald Press, 1949), p. 17.

Notes to 13: AT PEACE WITH THE PAST:
THE UNFINISHED CHURCH

1. Henry Adams, *Mont-Saint-Michel and Chartres* (Boston, Houghton Mifflin Co., 1928), p. 33.

2. "St. John the Divine," *Scribner's Magazine,* XLI (April 1907), 385-401.

3. *American Architect,* XCI (May 18, 1907), 203–4.

4. *Architectural Record,* August 1907, p. 212.

5. Letter to author from Chester A. Brown, member of the firm of Cram and Ferguson, Architects, Boston, November 18, 1954.

6. Karl Schriftgiesser, New York *Times,* January 15, 1927.

7. "St. John the Divine," *Scribner's Magazine,* pp. 385 ff.

Notes to 14: IN DEFENSE OF THE CITY

1. See Louis Winnick ("Economic Functions of The City," in Thomas P. Peardon, ed., *Urban Problems,* Proceedings, Academy of Political Science, XXVII [April 29, 1960], 12 ff.) for an excellent treatment of the market function of the city.

2. *Report of the Lucius Clay Committee on National Highways.* Cited by Daniel P. Moynihan, *The Reporter,* April 14, 1960, pp. 13 *et seq.*

3. Personal letter to the author, May 5, 1960.

4. *Architectural Forum,* Vol. 108, No. 3 (March 1954), pp. 116–17.

Notes to 15: THE ENGINEER: FRIEND OR FOE?

1. *Architectural Record,* January–March, 1892.

2. Letter to the author, cited in *Architectural Forum,* March 1956, p. 109.

3. *Architectural Forum,* March 1956, p. 110.

4. *Ibid.*

Notes to 17: THE CRITIC'S SHIFTING VIEW

1. Lewis Mumford, *Sticks and Stones, A Study of American Architecture and Civilization* (New York, Dover Publications, 1955).

2. Henry-Russell Hitchcock, *Modern Architecture: Romanticism and Reintegration (1750–1929)* (New York, Payson and Clarke, 1929).

3. *Ibid.,* p. 88.

4. In Europe, however, the term had already been employed by Gropius (*Internationale Architektur,* Bauhausbucher No. 1), by Ludwig Hilberseimer (*Internationale Neu Baukunst,* Stuttgart, 1928), and by Marcel Chappey (*Architecture Internationale,* Paris [1929?]).

5. Lewis Mumford, "Housing: The Need for a New Domestic Environment" in *Modern Architecture* (New York, Museum of Modern Art, 1932), p. 179.

6. Sheldon and Martha Cheney, *Art and the Machine* (New York, Whittlesey House, 1936), p. 299.

7. Henry-Russell Hitchcock and Philip Johnson, *The International Style* (New York, W. W. Norton, 1932), p. 68.

8. *Ibid.*, p. 75.

9. Hitchcock, *Modern Architecture*, pp. 13–14.

10. Cheney, *Art and the Machine*, pp. 14–15.

11. Hitchcock and Johnson, *International Style*, p. 36.

12. Mumford, "Housing . . . ," p. 189.

13. Aline Saarinen, "Four Architects," *Vogue*, CXXVI (August 1, 1955), 118 ff.

14. *House and Garden*, February 1952, p. 46.

15. Arthur Drexler, *Miës van der Rohe* (New York, George Braziller, 1960), p. 32.

16. James M. Fitch, "The Enrico Fermi Competition," *Architectural Forum*, June 1957, pp. 150 *et seq.*

17. Wayne Andrews, *Architecture, Ambition and Americans* (New York, Harper and Brothers, 1955), pp. xv-xvii.

18. Russell Lynes, *The Tastemakers* (New York, Harper and Brothers, 1954), p. 3.

19. Henry Hope Reed, *The Golden City* (New York, Doubleday and Company, 1959), p. 9.

20. *Ibid.*, p. 63.

21. *Ibid.*, p. 60.

22. *Ibid.*, p. 56.

23. *Ibid.*, p. 142.

24. *Ibid.*, p. 79 *et seq.*

25. *Ibid.*

Notes to 18: THE ESTHETICS OF PLENTY

1. Milton W. Brown, "The Tastemongers," *Challenge*, Vol. VI, No. 5 (February 1958), p. 18.

2. J. M. Keynes, "Essays in Persuasion." Cited by Norman O. Brown in *Life Against Death* (Middletown, Conn., Wesleyan University Press, 1959), pp. 35–36.

3. Brown, *Life Against Death*, p. 19.

INDEX

295

Index

302

Index